S0-BMY-069

8/17

THE

COURT OF

DATE DUE

THE COURT OF LAST RESORT

ERLE STANLEY GARDNER

OPEN ROAD
INTEGRATED MEDIA
NEW YORK

Copyright © 1952, 1954 by Erle Stanley Gardner

Cover design by Jason Gabbert

ISBN: 978-1-5040-4439-4

This edition published in 2017 by Open Road Integrated Media, Inc.
180 Maiden Lane
New York, NY 10038
www.openroadmedia.com

DEDICATION

As will be seen by those who read this book, turning the idea of the Court of Last Resort into an actuality called for a co-ordinated effort of considerable magnitude.

I want to take this opportunity to express my appreciation to my associates for their loyalty, and to make public acknowledgment to Harry Steeger, owner of *Argosy* Magazine.

It is all too easy for a magazine publisher to agree to a course of conduct in the white heat of enthusiasm, but to continue on an even course, month after month, year after year, when that course involves a considerable financial sacrifice, is an entirely different matter.

When we first started this work Steeger said to me, "Erle, you are going to be out on the firing line. There will be times when you'll have to make up your mind as to what should be done without having any opportunity to get in touch with my office. I want you to know that when such situations arise, you are to use your best judgment, and I'll back you to the limit. You have the power to determine the policy of the magazine in all matters relating to the Court of Last Resort."

Fortunately such occasions have been few in number, but there have been two or three times when it became necessary to reach and announce almost instantaneous decisions. These were in moments of stress when any hesitation would have been a sign of weakness. We had to announce that if certain things were done the magazine would fight to the finish. At such times it was a great satisfaction to know that Steeger had meant exactly what he said, and that he'd go on fighting with us to the last ditch and the last dollar.

During the six and a half years the Court of Last Resort has been functioning, Harry Steeger has never wavered, has never tried to pull back. He has done exactly what he told us he would do at the start of the organization.

I have known Steeger for some twenty-five years, during which time there has been a close, friendly association which I value as one of my most cherished relationships. We have been on numerous adventures together. I have learned to know, to respect and to admire his bulldog tenacity and his fighting stamina.

And now, on behalf of my associates and myself, I want to make public thanks to him for the steadfastness of purpose which made *The Court of Last Resort* possible.

So I dedicate this book to my friend:

HARRY STEEGER

Erle Stanley Gardner

The original edition of this book was published in 1952. Since that time the Court of Last Resort has been functioning even more vigorously and with a greatly increased sphere of activities. For this new edition, Mr. Gardner has considerably re-edited the original book and has added a great deal of new material.

1954

THE
COURT OF
LAST
RESORT

1

Man in general doesn't appreciate what he has until he is deprived of it. Then he starts to miss it. He takes good health for granted until sickness comes along. He takes three meals a day for granted until some unusual circumstance makes him go hungry. Liberty is only a term until he is deprived of it, and then he begins to realize what it means to have freedom of motion and freedom of choice.

Strange as it may seem, a diametrically opposite situation led to the origin of the Court of Last Resort.

I learned to value liberty not by having it taken away but by having such a marvelous demonstration of the advantages of freedom that I began to think what it must mean to be deprived of freedom.

In order to understand this somewhat paradoxical situation it is going to be necessary to touch on a most unusual murder case and give a bit of personal history.

The murder case is that of William Marvin Lindley, described in newspapers and magazines as "The Red-Headed Killer"; the personal history relates to a biographical sketch written by the late Alva Johnston which ran several installments in *The Saturday Evening Post*. This biographical sketch was entitled "The Case of Erle Stanley Gardner," and included some of the spectacular and unorthodox methods which I used in connection with the trial of cases when I was a practicing attorney.

I have always claimed that an attorney is not necessarily bound to confine his cross-examination of a hostile witness to questions and answers on the witness stand. If a witness is certain of an identification, he should be absolutely certain of it. He may testify under oath with all the positive sincerity in the world that the defendant is the man he saw running away from the scene of the crime two years ago, but if an attorney can get him to point to one of the assistant prosecutors by making the witness feel that the man at whom he is pointing is actually the defendant in the case, the witness's actions speak louder than words.

Of course, courts resent attempts to mislead a witness, so an attorney may well find himself in a position where the procedure, by which he might demonstrate that a witness is mistaken on a matter of identification, may be frowned upon by the court.

Therefore the problem of getting a witness to belie his words by actions, without violating the ethics of the profession or the rules of court is, at times, a rather tricky business.

During the days when I first engaged in the practice of law, legal ethics were not as sharply defined nor as rigidly enforced as they now are, and, with the singular optimism of youth, I was more confident of my own interpretation of what was proper.

I mention these matters because the early portion of my legal career, during which I was trying to build up a law practice in a city where I was virtually without friends or friendly contacts, was punctuated with spectacular incidents which made colorful copy for a biographer. As I expressed it at the time in a letter to my father, "I have built up a law practice in which I am dealing with large numbers of clients of all classes—except the upper and middle class."

Eventually my courtroom tactics attracted sufficient attention so that my practice became confined exclusively to clients of the upper and middle class, but Alva Johnston found the earlier chapters of my legal escapades much more interesting and therefore emphasized them in considerable detail.

Johnston also emphasized a quixotic streak which has always been part of my nature: to champion the cause of the underdog, particularly if he is without friends, without money, and his cause seems to be utterly hopeless.

By the time Johnston had finished stringing colorful incidents into his biographical sketch, his audience might well have received the impression that I made a habit of entering the lists on behalf of penniless defendants who were in hopeless predicaments, and by legal legerdemain could cause the doors of prison to swing wide open. The result was that just about every hopeless case in the United States was dumped in my lap in a deluge of fan mail.

Among these cases was that of William Marvin Lindley. This case was sent to me by Al Matthews, Jr., a Los Angeles attorney at law who has since become affiliated with the Public Defender's Office, but who, at that time, was a free lance. He had interested himself on behalf of Lindley after Lindley's conviction.

Lindley was at the time in the condemned row at San Quentin awaiting execution. He had been convicted of a brutal sex murder. The evidence against him was so overwhelming that until Al Matthews came along no one had extended the slightest sympathy or had bothered to give the case very much detailed study.

Al Matthews wrote me that he felt absolutely convinced Lindley was innocent, that he had been the victim of a bizarre combination of circumstances, and begged me to study the case.

At the time it seemed to me that every mail was bringing in a dozen similar pleas, but there was something about Al Matthews' letter, a certain sincerity that attracted my attention. I studied the outline Matthews sent down.

The murder had occurred during the aftermath of the great depression, and the characters who were involved in the crime were, for the most part, people who lived in more or less temporary camps along the banks of the Yuba River in California. One gathered the impression that these were persons of limited funds, limited education, and, in some instances, limited intelligence.

Some young girls, around the age of adolescence, had gone in swimming in the Yuba River. As a bathing suit, the victim of the crime wore simply a cotton dress.

William Marvin Lindley, a redhead, was at the time operating a boathouse on the banks of the river.

The victim of the crime had finished her swimming, changed her clothes, gone into the house where her folks were living, made some remarks to her father, then had gone out again.

Some twenty minutes or half an hour later she was found in a dying condition. She had evidently been attacked after putting up a terrific struggle. She was able to sob out to her father the statement that it was "that old red-headed liar in the boathouse, the old red-headed liar." Some time later, and without ever clarifying this statement, she died.

A sheepherder, a young boy whose intelligence was not keen, to say the least, was herding sheep on the other side of the Yuba River, a distance of some two hundred yards. This sheepherder had sat under a tree, watching the girls while they were swimming. They left the water and entered the boathouse. Later on he noticed one of the girls go toward home and another girl went down to the water to wash her feet.

Prior to this time, a man, whom the sheepherder identified as Lindley, had been standing in the willows. He, also, was watching the girls swimming. After the victim had started back toward the levee, the sheepherder stated he had seen her struggling with "Red," the man who had been standing in the bushes watching her. They "went down behind the willows."

The sheepherder identified the man as "Red" Lindley, the defendant. He based his identification in part upon the color of clothes that Lindley was wearing that afternoon.

At the time of the trial (and it should be noted that Lindley was not represented at this trial by Al Matthews, who didn't enter the case until after conviction) Lindley tried to produce an alibi. It was a nice alibi except that it broke down for the very period when the crime was being committed.

Apparently none of the persons connected with the case carried a watch, and it was necessary to work out time by depending upon the best estimates of the witnesses, starting from an event which had been pretty well established in the day's schedule.

All in all, Lindley's case seemed hopeless, merely another drab sex crime in which the culprit had become so inflamed at the sight of the adolescent girls bathing in the river that he lost all self-control, and despite the fact that there were witnesses who watched him and who could identify him, proceeded to go completely mad with lust.

Al Matthews had taken over, conducted an investigation and had filed a writ of *habeas corpus* in the State Supreme Court, also an application for a writ of error *Coram Nobis*, and a writ of *Coram Vobis*. Inasmuch as the Supreme Court had already considered the case on appeal and affirmed the conviction and sentence of death, it was necessary for the attorneys to resort to these last named, little used, hardly understood writs in order to have even a leg to stand on.

Enough of a showing had been made so that the Supreme Court had appointed a referee to take testimony, and then peculiar things began to develop. For one thing it turned out that the sheepherder was color-blind; and while he had stated that he had recognized the defendant by the tan-colored khaki clothes he had been wearing, it appeared by the time of the *habeas corpus* hearing that this witness was prone to describe virtually every color as tan. Not only was he color-blind but it developed that he had barely enough intelligence to enable him to testify. At one time he had told the referee that he did not know what it meant to testify under oath. He had identified a brown and white dress, worn by one of the women who was attending the referee's hearing, as black. He had then been asked to identify colored cards at a distance approximately equal to that at which he had seen the murderer, and he had identified a yellow card as being white, a gold one as being brown, an orange one as red, and a gray one as blue. At another time he had said that green was blue, gold was white, light brown was white, and pink was red.

The Supreme Court carefully reviewed the facts in the case as brought out in the hearing before the referee, co-ordinated those facts with the evidence in the case, and decided that Lindley had been properly convicted and must go to the gas chamber.

The date of execution was finally set. (There had been one or two reprieves while the various legal matters were pending, but now the date had been set, and Governor Earl Warren, who had been forced to leave the state temporarily on business, had pointed out to the lieutenant governor who would be in charge during Governor Warren's absence that he wanted no further reprieves in the Lindley case. The execution was to go ahead as scheduled.)

That execution date was but a short distance away. As I remember it, a matter of a week or ten days.

In any event, I telephoned Al Matthews, told him I would study the case, and he sent his wife down to see me, bringing with her the trial transcript and a few facts which would enable me to understand something of the nature of the case.

It was a long and involved transcript, and I labored through it, trying to become familiar with the case from the testimony of the witnesses and the study of the records.

There was one significant thing which Al Matthews had uncovered. There had been *another* red-headed hop picker in the vicinity on the day of the crime. That hop picker had not been working on the day of the murder. He had shown up later with marks on his face which could well have been made by a girl's fingernails. He had reportedly, in a drunken brawl that night, stated that he had been the one who had committed the murder, and he had mysteriously disappeared the next morning without even calling for his pay check. Some of those facts could be verified positively.

That was the case in a nutshell, and William Marvin Lindley was to die.

I carefully studied the evidence submitted by Lindley in support of his defense, and there was no question but what his alibi broke down at the very time the crime was being committed. The attorneys for the prosecution had made the most of that.

So then, having completed a study of the transcript, I decided to tackle the case from another angle.

Strange as it may seem, apparently it had never occurred to anyone to examine Lindley's alibi with reference to the movements of the murderer, whoever that murderer might have been, on the day in question.

I decided to do this and so found it necessary to work out a diagram of the scene of the crime according to distances, and to start co-ordinating the activities of the various people in relation to their contact with other people, forming a species of time schedule that was dependent entirely upon events rather than upon guesswork as to the hour, or the position of clock hands.

Once that was done, a very startling fact became manifest.

At the exact time witnesses had seen the murderer standing in the willows, watching the girls swimming, the defendant, William Marvin Lindley, had been riding in an automobile with the father of the murdered girl.

Again and again I went over this schedule and there simply couldn't be any other possible answer. The evidence given by the father himself, the evidence given by other witnesses, showed that this must be true. There wasn't any escape from it.

At that time there was no opportunity to do anything by strictly legal methods. Lindley's execution was almost a matter of hours. There was no time to make a formal appearance, no time to set in motion any type of legal proceedings even if it had been possible to conceive of any type of legal proceedings which had not been previously tried. The defendant had had the benefit of all the writs that the most adroit and ingenious attorney could possibly have conjured up.

There was only one thing to do.

I sent a letter to each justice of the State Supreme Court; I sent copies of those letters to the State's attorney general; I sent letters to the office of the Governor, pointing out page by page in the transcript the manner in which this synthetic schedule had been built up, making all due allowances for the greatest margin of time-elapse possible. Under this schedule there was no question that at the very moment several witnesses had seen this mysterious man standing in the willows, the man who was positively identified as being the murderer of the victim, the defendant, William Marvin Lindley, had been riding in the automobile with the girl's father some miles from the scene of the crime.

Afterward, and entirely off the record, I learned something of the scene of hectic activity which followed the receipt of these various letters. Still off the record, as I understand it, members of the California Supreme Court unanimously requested Lieutenant Governor Fred Howser, who was in charge at the time, not to permit the execution to take place until there could be a further investigation, and another stay of execution was granted.

The case began to attract quite a bit of attention. The press picked up the fact that I had written a letter in connection with it and set forth some of my contentions.

It will be noted that I am commenting in detail on the Lindley case because of its repercussions. The Lindley case standing by itself, however, is well worth serious study by anyone who is at all interested in the administration of criminal law.

Simply consider the facts of the case at the time Al Matthews, Jr., had taken an interest in it:

The girl had been found in a dying condition. She had made a statement which certainly pointed to the defendant Lindley as the perpetrator of the crime. The police had investigated and found an eyewitness who positively identified Lindley as the man who had been waiting in the bushes, watching the girls swimming, who had subsequently grabbed one of the girls, and, after a terrific struggle, had dropped down out of sight behind the bushes.

Lindley had claimed an alibi, trying to prove that he wasn't there at the time of the commission of the crime. That attempted alibi seemed to have broken down for the exact period that the crime was taking place. Lindley was without funds. An attorney had been appointed by the court to defend him, and the jury, evidently considering Lindley a murderer and a liar, had promptly brought in a verdict finding him guilty of first-degree murder, with no recommendation, thereby automatically making it mandatory that a death sentence be imposed.

I will never know what peculiar hunch attracted Matthews to the case, because a cursory study of the evidence would certainly indicate that the defendant was guilty, but when Matthews began to dig he uncovered new evidence showing that the eyewitness, who had identified Lindley largely because of the color of his clothes, was color-blind; and that another red-headed man, who had been in the vicinity of the crime, had scratch marks on his face, and, in a drunken condition the very night of the crime, had admitted that he was the perpetrator of the offense.

When I interceded on behalf of the defendant the wire services sent out "copy" which was published in various newspapers throughout the country.

At that time, my friend Raymond Schindler, the famous private detective (of whom we will hear more later on in this book) was an advisory editor of a factual detective magazine, working in connection with Horace Bailey Brown, who was editor in chief. Brown, himself a veteran article writer, with considerable editorial experience, was eagerly looking for new angles on crime stories so that he could get away from the usual hackneyed approach and turn out a magazine that would attract the interests of the reading public.

When Schindler and Brown read the notice in the press stating that I had entered the Lindley case, they wired asking me if I would care to write something about it for the magazine in question.

Nothing could have suited me better.

I was for the moment at an impasse. There was certainly no legal remedy left to the defendant. The lieutenant governor had granted a temporary stay of execution, but Governor Warren's attitude in the matter was quite well known, and now that Governor Warren had returned to the state there was no further authority left in the hands of the lieutenant governor to act in the matter.

So, feeling that nothing remained to be done from a legal standpoint, I decided it would be interesting to see what would happen if the people generally were given some firsthand knowledge of the peculiar situation disclosed by the transcript in the Lindley case.

So I wrote an open letter to Governor Warren, which I sent to the magazine and which was published.

I have been told that the Governor's office received a deluge of mail as a result of this letter. Governor Warren, despite any previous statements he may have made, did the right thing and he did it in a decent manner. He promptly commuted the sentence of the defendant to life imprisonment so that there would be an opportunity for a further investigation.

Lindley—never a robust man emotionally—had been living in the shadow of death for months. He had been figuratively dragged into the death chamber and then hauled out again, only to be once more dragged in and then jerked out. As a result, his mind had become unsettled. The man was, in the opinion of many, hopelessly insane. In fact I understand that some of the members of the Supreme Court had made definite recommendations that because of this insanity alone the execution should not be permitted.

In any event, Lindley, was declared insane, and his sentence commuted to life imprisonment. There the case stands to this day.

There is very persuasive evidence that another red-headed man may have committed the crime. An extensive search was made for this mysterious red-headed hop picker who had what may have been fingernail scratches on his face, who had certainly been in a state of extreme nervousness, and who had vanished so mysteriously on the day following the murder of the girl. That search was made far too late. It was made by private parties who did not have the facilities available to the police. The search was fruitless. The man has never been found.

The Lindley case is perhaps as good an example as we can conjure up at the moment of the necessity of making a scientific, careful investigation of all of the facts in a case while those facts are still available.

Because of the identification made by the dying girl (an identification which was, of course, not as definite as should have been the case if Lindley had actually committed the crime), the so-called eyewitness identification by the young sheepherder, the police became convinced that Lindley was the murderer. They diligently searched for any evidence that would enable the prosecutor to build up a good case against Lindley in court, and they brushed aside any evidence which might have pointed to developments that would have been in Lindley's favor.

As a result, this other red-headed suspect, who certainly should have been apprehended and interrogated, was permitted to leave the community without any attempt made to find him or question him. The itinerant witnesses vanished to the four winds, and Lindley was left with a sentence of life imprisonment.

The Lindley case, however, was destined to have far-reaching developments.

Harry Steeger, head of Popular Publications Inc., which publishes *Argosy* Magazine, and for many years a warm personal friend, had been corresponding with me about undertaking an adventure of sorts.

The year before I had taken an expedition down the entire length of the peninsula of Baja California, starting at Tijuana, and, after several weeks of wild adventure over twelve hundred miles of mountain and desert, reaching the very southern tip of the peninsula at Cape San Lucas.

I had written a book about that trip, and since, despite months of careful planning, the whole trip had almost been abandoned because of developments in the Lindley case, I had mentioned briefly the fact that only the commutation of sentence in this case had left us free to make the trip. The point was important in the book because the Lindley matter so materially shortened the time available for preparation that we had no alternative but to throw things into the car helter-skelter, and try to unscramble them on the road.

This book, *The Land of Shorter Shadows*, had fascinated both Harry Steeger and his wife, Shirley, a member of the New York Botanical Gardens, and a tireless and enthusiastic worker.

The upshot of it was that Harry and Shirley Steeger, two of my secretaries, Sam Hicks of Wyoming, and I started once more down the long twelve-hundred-mile route. We had plenty of shorthand notebooks, quantities of film, a veritable battery of cameras, and this time were determined to see that the peninsula was fully covered.

Even with the very best in the line of modern equipment, including jeeps and a "power wagon" equipped with power winches, four-wheel drive, oversized tires, etc., this trip down the peninsula of Baja California is a long, hard, and at times a dangerous grind. There are days when forty miles is a full day's journey, and several times we went for two days in succession without meeting a single car on the road.

Since this expedition started late in February, the days were short and the nights were long. It was necessary to make camp during the last of the daylight hours, and then after supper, when the dishes were done, the sleeping bags spread on the ground, air mattresses inflated, there would be an hour or two for just sitting around the campfire.

The peninsula of Baja California is distinctly and individually different. The elephant trees are almost exclusively indigenous to that terrain, and, as I understand it, the *cirio* trees are not found in any other spot on earth. The nights were nearly always cool and cloudless. The days were, for the most part, hot with the dry heat of the desert. The air was a tonic and a benediction rolled into one. At night the steady, unwinking stars marched tirelessly across the heavens.

All about us was the immensity of a wild country. The firelight was the only reassuring memento of man's ability to master his environment. It would throw a fitful circle of illumination for some thirty or forty feet and reflect back in a rosy glow from the weird *cardon* trees pushing their cactus-like limbs high into the air. Lower down, on the floor of the desert the flames would illuminate prickly pear, *cholla* cactus, ladyfinger cactus, and, perhaps in the background, a sweet *pitahaya* or organ-pipe cactus.

Beyond the circle of campfire, darkness filled an unknown terrain with a mystery which the human mind instinctively translated into terms of danger. . . . A sudden screaming howl from the encircling darkness caused us to give an involuntary start before we recognized the familiar voice of the coyote, and grinned sheepishly. And just outside of the lighted circle the coyote was probably grinning, too. They are the most daring, saucy, impudent, lovable rascals in the world (unless a man has sheep or chickens, in which event the coyote is a fiend incarnate).

So it was natural that during these long evenings, while we exhausted most of the subjects of conversation, we should find ourselves dwelling on the predicament of men who had been wrongfully imprisoned.

Freedom is, after all, only relative. No man has absolute freedom. We are bound by economic chains, by ties of personal dependency. We have telephones, taxicabs and taxes; work, worry and war.

Down there in Baja California life and living became unbelievably simplified. We ate, we slept, and we traveled. We had nothing else to do. There was no schedule, no telephones, no illumination at night save the light of the gasoline lantern which was used sparingly when supper was late.

Against this environment of extreme freedom from care and restraint, the life of a man condemned to live behind barred doors, within gray walls, became a persistent nightmare which colored even our waking hours.

The problem of getting firewood helped determine the length of our sleep at night. We would conscientiously save out enough wood for a breakfast fire, and burn the rest at night. When the evening campfire began to die down to coals we would move closer, until, at length, the last of the flames flickered out. Then we would watch the bed of coals until even the coals began to dull. By that time we would be ready for our sleeping bags.

Many times during those silent watches of the night I lay awake for half or three-quarters of an hour thinking about the problems inherent in the wise administration of justice. And the more I came to revel in my own liberty to go where I wanted to, whenever I wanted to, the more I found myself thinking of innocent men cooped up in cells. It was a nagging worry which I could and sometimes did push into the back of my mind—but not very far back, and it wouldn't stay there.

So one day I mentioned how I felt to Harry Steeger, and I discovered he had been experiencing the same reaction. Every time he wakened at night he found himself speculating on the problem, wondering what he as a publisher could do about it.

On one occasion when we discussed the situation, Harry reached a decision.

"Erle," he said, "if you ever find any other case where you think the man has been wrongfully convicted, *Argosy* will donate enough space to see that the case is given ample publicity, and we'll see what the public reaction is.

"You know what I'm trying to do with *Argosy*. When we purchased it from the Munsey Company it was an old-time adventure magazine printed on wood pulp paper. We've turned it into an illustrated magazine for men, and people are beginning to notice it. Of all the magazines we publish I think *Argosy* would be the most available vehicle for this sort of thing."

In the nights which followed that talk we began to carry this thought to its logical conclusion and to explore possibilities.

Some months previous to this we had discussed the peculiar fact that there was no popular magazine devoted to justice, and yet all of our vaunted American way of life was founded upon our concept of justice.

So, down there in Baja California, we began to speculate on the idea of welding those two thoughts together—testing the reaction of the American people to find out if they were really interested in the cause of justice and at the same time using space to correct some specific instance of an injustice.

Night after night, we planned just how a case could be presented to the American people, what their reactions would be and what the effect of those reactions would be upon the governmental agencies who had the final say in the matter.

We realized early in the game that it would never do for a magazine with a national circulation to come out and say in effect, "This man claims he's innocent. He's been convicted of murder. Erle Stanley Gardner thinks there may be something in the man's contentions, therefore we want the governor to grant a pardon."

We knew that we'd need facts, and these facts would have to be presented to the reading public in a form that would incite interest. No matter how much space *Argosy* donated to some worthy case, no good would be done unless people read what was printed in that space. And, even then, merely reading about the case wouldn't help unless people became sufficiently aroused to *do* something about it.

Public opinion must be molded, but it must be an enlightened public opinion based on facts, otherwise we would be charged, and justly charged, with the tactics of the rabble rousers.

It is customary in legal circles to refer to the highest tribunal in any jurisdiction as "the court of last resort." Out there in the wide open spaces of Baja California, we came to the conclusion that in a country such as ours no officially organized tribunal ever could be the *real* court of last resort. The real court of last resort, we felt, was the people themselves. It was a new and daring concept, yet it was essentially sound. Under our theory of law the people are superior to any department of the government, legislative, executive or judicial. They must, of course, exercise their wishes in accordance with the methods prescribed in the Constitution, but once those methods have been complied with, the will of the people is the supreme law of this land.

That didn't mean that in order to decide whether John Doe had been wrongfully convicted we needed to have the people pass an initiative measure, or, if we decided that John Doe had been wrongfully convicted that we needed to present a Constitutional amendment to get him liberated.

The constitutions of the various states provide that the governors have the power of pardon. The governors, on the other hand, are responsible to the people. Every four years they come up for re-election. They have to stand on their record. If any material thinking segment of a state's population should decide that John Doe had been wrongfully convicted and that the governor's pardoning prerogative was being unjustly withheld, that governor would be faced with a political liability at election time. Governors are not prone to assume political liabilities unless there is a corresponding political credit to be entered on the other side of the ledger.

But how could anyone present a case to the people without following the tactics of the rabble rousers? In the case of John Doe, how could we get the facts, how could we properly marshal those facts, how could we get the public to take a sufficient interest in those facts? How could we persuade a substantial segment of population to take a real interest in John Doe? It was a problem we discussed at length. We felt that we were on the right track if we could once find the proper approach; but the proper approach required that the public should understand the facts, should correlate them, and should then want to take action.

We knew that most magazine readers like detective stories. How about letting the readers study the case of John Doe, fact by fact, until they reached an intelligent opinion?

That would mean investigators in whom the readers would have confidence, and who could unearth those facts. It would mean that reader interest must be kept alive.

Was there any method by which all of this could be accomplished?

Gradually the idea of *Argosy's* board of investigators came into existence.

The basic idea was to get men who were specialists in their line, men who had enough national reputation so readers could have confidence in their judgment, men who would be public-spirited enough to donate their services to the cause of justice (because any question of financial reward would immediately taint the whole proceedings with what might be considered a selfish motivation). We also needed men who had achieved such financial success in their chosen professions that they were in no particular need of personal publicity. Moreover, the aggregate combination must be such that it would be virtually impossible for any prisoner to deceive these men as to the true issues in a case.

It was, of course, a pretty large order.

We thought at once of Dr. LeMoyne Snyder.

Dr. LeMoyne Snyder is one of the outstanding authorities on homicide investigation in the country. He is not only a doctor of medicine but he is an attorney at law, and he has for some years specialized in the field of legal medicine. His book *Homicide Investigation* is one of the most authoritative technical books on the subject in the country, and is at once a guide for peace officers as well as a treatise for those who are interested in the more highly technical aspects of the subject.

We decided to put the whole idea up to Dr. Snyder. Next, we needed some outstanding detective. So we thought of Raymond Schindler.

Raymond Schindler is perhaps the best-known private detective in the country. I had first met him when we were both in the Bahamas. He was then working on the famous case of Alfred de

Marigny, who had been accused of murdering his wealthy father-in-law, Sir Harry Oakes. I was covering the case for the New York *Journal-American* and some of its allied newspapers.

Raymond Schindler's career as a private detective dates back to 1906 when he first started work in San Francisco. Later on, it was through the efforts of Raymond Schindler that the corruption which existed in San Francisco under Abe Rueff and "Big Jim" Gallagher was cleaned up.

Many of Schindler's exploits have found their way from time to time into print, and a year or so ago Rupert Hughes, in a volume entitled *The Complete Detective*, gave a biographical summary of Schindler's life which has, of course, been exceedingly colorful.

So much for the detective end. If Schindler would work with us, we felt he'd be ideal for the job.

It also occurred to us that we'd want to have absolutely accurate information for our own guidance. We had to know whether the men we were talking with were telling the truth. That brought up a consideration of Leonarde Keeler's work with the lie detector. Keeler had not only done a great deal to develop the polygraph but was probably the outstanding polygraph operator in the country. (Before we were able to avail ourselves of Keeler's services to any great extent, he became ill and passed away. His place was taken by Alex Gregory, a man who has an excellent background as an investigator, a careful, conscientious worker, a former member of the Detroit police force, a keen student of psychology.)

There is, of course, some question as to the efficacy of the "lie detector."

To my mind the question of, "How accurate is a lie detector?" is equivalent to asking, "How good is a camera?"

The answer is, of course, the camera doesn't take the pictures. The photographer takes the pictures. Some photographers using a medium-priced camera can take pictures that win national awards. Some merely take mediocre pictures; others forget to turn the film and so get double exposures, or forget to pull the slide from the plateholder and so get nothing.

I think the same holds true with the polygraph. The polygraph is a scientific instrument. It determines certain specific reactions on the part of the subject. The problem of coordinating the graph of these reactions so as to know whether the subject is or is not telling the truth depends upon numerous factors—the questions which are asked, the manner in which they are asked, the manner in which the subject is prepared for the test, and the skill on the part of the operator.

It is quite possible that Alex Gregory, for instance, won't always be able to tell whether a man is guilty or innocent. But I feel that Alex Gregory would never say that an innocent man was guilty. He might say he didn't know. But if he said a man was definitely guilty, I wouldn't want to run against his judgment. And similarly if Alex Gregory assures us that a man who says he is innocent is telling us the truth, I for one am all in favor of going ahead and launching an investigation which may run into hundreds of hours of time spent.

So much for the polygraph angle.

So far as the legal appraisal was concerned, I promised Steeger I would study the transcripts of testimony in the various cases, and bring to bear such knowledge as I had acquired in twenty-five years of trial work.

Later on this investigating committee was to receive very substantial reinforcements in the persons of Tom Smith and Bob Rhay.

Tom Smith was at the time the warden of the Washington State Penitentiary at Walla Walla. Bob Rhay was working under him, and as presently will be seen, our first case brought us into intimate contact with both of these men. Later on they were destined to become exceedingly interested in the social significance of the program we had undertaken, and, when suitable opportunity arose, to affiliate themselves with it.

However, that page in our adventures in justice had not then been written. We were primarily concerned with the problem of getting together a board of investigators who would have enough prestige to influence public opinion, who would have a sufficient love of justice to be willing to donate a large portion of their time, and who had the proper technical qualifications to strip aside all fabrications and arrive at the right answer.

So we worked our way down the peninsula of Baja California, talking around every campfire of plans for our Court of Last Resort, wondering what, if anything, it could accomplish, but each day becoming more and more determined that we would find out by actual experiment just what it could accomplish.

2

The Court of Last Resort didn't have long to wait for its first case.

Within a matter of weeks after Steeger and I returned from Baja California I had occasion to consider the case of Clarence. Boggie, prisoner #16587, confined in the Washington State Penitentiary at Walla Walla, serving a life sentence for murder.

Boggie had written a letter enclosing copies of documents compiled by the Reverend Arvid Ohrnell, Protestant chaplain of the Washington State Reformatory at Monroe. This letter had been acknowledged, but was buried in a pile of similar appeals from prisoners sent in from all over the country.

Then I received a communication from the Reverend W. A. Gilbert, a part-time voluntary chaplain at Walla Walla, asking me for an appointment at my ranch.

Gilbert was the rector of St. Paul's Episcopal Church at Walla Walla. He also did a great deal of voluntary prison chaplain work purely as an extracurricular activity, donating his time furnishing spiritual guidance to prison inmates.

Bill Gilbert was attending a church convention in Santa Barbara. He drove the two hundred odd miles down to my ranch through Sunday traffic in order to confer with me about the Boggie case and then drove back that afternoon—nearly five hundred miles of Sunday driving in order to try and enlist my aid in the cause of a penniless unfortunate who had then been incarcerated in the Walla Walla prison for some thirteen years, and who was scheduled to remain there the rest of his life.

Bill Gilbert's devotion to a philanthropic cause seemed an unusual sacrifice of time and energy to me then. Now I have seen enough of the work done by prison chaplains to know that it is merely an ordinary incident in their lives.

A book could—and should—be written about the activities of these men. They sacrifice their own time, their own funds, pile up mileage on their automobiles, trying to do what they can to assist in the spiritual and material welfare of prisoners, many of whom shamelessly take advantage of this unselfish devotion to a self-imposed duty.

The best of prison chaplains never worry about what a man has done. They are only interested in trying to see how they can help the man prepare for the future. They know that for the most part they are carving in rotten wood, but they keep carving nevertheless, hoping that when they have stripped away the layers of mental and moral disease they will come to a basic foundation which can take and hold a permanent impression.

In a surprising number of instances they are successful.

At that time I personally had no realization of the extent to which prison inmates are isolated behind a curtain of steel and concrete. I had no realization that their correspondence was limited in many instances as to quantity, and in nearly every instance to a chosen list of approved correspondents.

As a practicing attorney any letters I cared to write to prisoners had been delivered and answered. That, as it turned out, is because an exception is made in the case of attorneys. Prisoners are permitted to correspond freely with attorneys. On the other hand, as a general rule, prisoners are not permitted to correspond at all with representatives of the press, and their personal correspondence is very, very limited.

Since I had left the active practice of law my correspondence with prison inmates had been somewhat limited, and in most of the instances my status as attorney had resolved the doubt in my favor and the correspondence had gone through, but once when I tried to find out something about the facts in a case I had been curtly refused permission to correspond with the inmate.

These instances had served to arouse my ire and I had determined that if we started investigating a case with *Argosy* Magazine behind us, we were going to engage in a verbal slugging match if we weren't permitted to interview the prisoner.

So I explained to Bill Gilbert that I would fly up to Walla Walla to interview Boggie. I told Gilbert to explain this to the warden of the penitentiary and to tell him that I didn't want to have a lot of red tape thrown at me when I arrived.

I remember that I explained to Bill Gilbert that heretofore we had been trying to catch our flies with molasses. I was tired of that, and had decided it might be more effective to catch them with a fly swatter.

Gilbert told me that he felt quite certain I would have no trouble in interviewing Clarence Boggie, but he would sound out the warden in the matter.

Bill Gilbert returned to Walla Walla and wired me that I would have no difficulty.

That was a masterpiece of understatement.

Tom Smith, as has been previously mentioned, was the warden. He was more than ready to meet us halfway.

"Now look," he said finally, "you're not going to meet any red-tape opposition up here. If Clarence Boggie is innocent we want to find it out just as much as you do. Bill Gilbert has told me about your organization. I know something about the reputation of these men who are associated with you in the work you're doing. If you're going to make an impartial investigation of the Boggie case, and if it isn't going to cost the State anything, I'll do everything in my power to facilitate the investigation. I also think you'll find the State officials here will have a similar attitude. Anything I can do to help promote such an attitude I'll be glad to do. Now, then, you take over from there."

In short, I found Tom Smith to be entirely different from the type of warden I had expected to find.

In the intimate association with him which was to come later I learned to know the man's big heart, his almost naïve idealism, and his passionate desire for justice.

At the time, I was surprised to find a warden who had absolutely no resemblance to the type of warden fiction writers are too prone to create. There was nothing of the sadistic disciplinarian about him. He was intensely human, eager to learn everything he could about prison administration, to apply what he had learned, and to see that every man had complete justice.

Later on that day I met the incredible Clarence Boggie.

I refer to him as "incredible" because everything about the man was completely and utterly incredible. Virtually every time I talked with him I discovered some new facet of the man, some new twist of his background, some episode which seemed to be absolutely incredible, yet which later turned out to be the truth.

For instance, Boggie, a penniless prisoner serving a life sentence, with two previous convictions behind him, maintained stoutly that he had never been guilty of any crime.

That, of course, seemed absurd.

Yet subsequent investigations indicated the man's story might well be true. In each instance of a prior conviction he had received a pardon apparently predicated upon the fact that an investigation showed he had been wrongfully convicted.

The man, of course, had some sort of a prison neurosis. He also had a very strong love for his mother which made him place her on a pedestal. He was emotionally unstable, given to sudden spells of crying, particularly if someone would mention his mother. He had been incarcerated long enough so that he had the mental outlook that is sometimes referred to as being "stir simple."

Yet here was this penniless man who would, at a later date, casually mention to us that he was the owner of a copper mine worth several million dollars.

I don't know when he first made that statement. We took it as a complete fairy tale, something that had been conjured up in his dreams during the long period of his confinement.

The story of the copper mine was very interesting. The mine, he explained, had been given to him by a woman whom he had never seen, but she wanted to get rid of her earthly property so she had deeded Boggie the mine. The deed had been lost.

You listen to a story like that from a two-time loser serving a life term in a penitentiary for murder, and it is enough to make you want to forget the whole thing. The guy is not only a crook but a liar. You kick yourself for having traveled twelve or fifteen hundred miles to act the part of a gullible sucker.

Yet essentially this story was true.

It wasn't until we happened to stumble onto certain facts that we learned the background of the story, and I mention it at this time because it is so completely typical of Clarence Boggie.

As mentioned above, Boggie worshiped the ground his mother walked on, and any woman more than twenty years his senior would promptly arouse in him a like feeling of worship.

During the great depression, Boggie, a lumberjack, was out of work, walking the streets of Portland, Oregon, when he saw a frail, white-haired woman being, as Boggie expressed it, "abused" by the police.

It seemed that a police officer had stopped in front of the woman's house and was pointing out to her that the roots of a tree which was growing at the curb had broken up the cement sidewalk.

The woman apparently either was short of cash or else didn't know how to go about having the repairs made, because she was trying to get an extension of time from the officer, but the officer, according to Clarence Boggie, was "pushing her around."

Boggie said he hung around for a minute or two, listening to the conversation. The woman, he explained, was "a little sweetheart, just a dear little white-haired woman, frail and helpless, but just as sweet as she could be, and the officer was abusive."

So Boggie, big strapping lumberjack that he was, entered into the argument. As he explained it, he "chased the officer."

Apparently what he did was to tell the officer that he, Boggie, would see that the matter was straightened out, to quit annoying the woman and go on about his business. She'd been given a warning and that was all there was to it. The officer had no further business there. The sidewalk would be fixed that afternoon. How did Boggie know? Hell, Boggie was going to fix it himself.

Boggie marched up town, where he went into one of the pool halls, rounded up a squad of lumberjacks who were out of work and weren't doing anything anyway, got some sledge hammers, a crowbar and an ax, and went back to the house of the "white-haired sweetheart."

Those lumberjacks put on a job of work that was rarely seen within the city limits. They smashed up the sidewalk, cut the offending roots of the tree, smoothed down the ground, poured cement, erected barriers, kept the cement properly moistened, and within a little more than twenty-four hours had a perfectly brand-new sidewalk, smooth and level.

The "white-haired sweetheart" was, of course, grateful, but Boggie refused to take a cent. Despite the fact that the lumberjacks were all broke and "on their uppers," none of them would take a dime. They wouldn't even let her pay for the cement, which had been procured "here and there."

Boggie, of course, was the ringleader and probably the spokesman, but undoubtedly the men all felt very much the same way.

However, the woman did get Boggie's name and address.

It turned out that this woman in turn had a friend in the East who was wealthy and quite elderly. This friend had come to the conclusion that before she died it would be much better for her to strip herself of her property, feeling that worldly wealth and spiritual solace were incompatible.

Looking around for worthy objects of benefaction, she remembered the letter which had been received from her friend in Portland, Oregon. She looked up this letter, and, sure enough, there was the name and address of Clarence Boggie, the man who had made such a chivalrous restoration of the sidewalk.

So the woman promptly made out a deed to Clarence Boggie, giving him title to a piece of ground on which copper had been discovered.

The deed was sent to Boggie at that address. Boggie at that time, however, was in prison. Someone attempted to record the deed and it was lost in transit. Boggie didn't hear about it until some time later. By that time the woman who had made the deed was dead, relatives were in possession of the property, the copper mine had been developed into one of the big copper mines in the country, and Boggie apparently "didn't have a leg to stand on." He couldn't even produce the deed, or even testify that he himself had actually seen it.

However, such investigation as we were able to make indicated that he was absolutely truthful in his statement of the facts of the case. The deed actually had been executed and mailed to him, and then, by someone who was trying to record it, had been misaddressed and lost.

Boggie, moreover, told us great stories of his prowess as a logger. These stories made him sound like a reincarnated Paul Bunyan. They were, of course, digested with a tolerant smile. Boggie had been in prison for a long time and doubtless as he thought back over his exploits he kept gilding the lily and painting the rose.

Boggie told us that he could take a crew of men and move more logs in less time, with less expense and greater efficiency, than the average expert.

It is an ironical twist that everyone thought Boggie, because of his emotional instability, his background and his mannerisms, was simply drawing on his imagination in everything that he told us about his background, for a man who is "stir simple" frequently tries to impress people with tales of his former prowess.

Eventually we learned a lot more about Boggie's abilities, but that is, of course, an entirely different story. What I am trying to convey at this time is a picture of Clarence Boggie as we first saw him, a man with a prison neurosis, a mother fixation, and a well-defined emotional instability.

We found it exceedingly hard to believe his story. However, we had determined to make an investigation of the case, and it was, after all, the case rather than the man that we were primarily interested in.

It was at the time of this first meeting that Boggie turned over to me what, for want of a better name, I have come to refer to as an inmate's "heartbreak file."

Just as a girl will keep a hope chest, so does an inmate frequently keep a file which contains the records of his attempts to gain freedom. It is really a heartbreak file.

Here are held the notations on when he is to come before the state parole board, documents setting forth facts in the prisoner's favor, carbon copies of correspondence hopefully sent out. Then the heartbreak. Parole application decision deferred for another year— letters unanswered.

In Boggie's case the heartbreak file was about the most voluminous and the most pathetic I have ever seen.

It is not a simple matter for a prison inmate to write a letter to an official who he thinks may be interested in his case. In the first place there are as a rule only a few typewriters within the walls, and the men who know how to use them are a favored class. A prisoner who wants to have a letter typed must make certain concessions by way of trade.

Money, of course, is contraband within prison. Too many things can be accomplished with money. So the prisoner must make his purchases through the limited credit allowances which can be made by transferring money from his prison account, except, of course, in the case of business transactions which then must have the approval of the warden.

The average prisoner, in order to get a letter written, must turn over his cigarette allowance, or go without some little prison luxury.

For thirteen years Boggie had been forgoing his prison luxuries, getting people to type letters for him. Only by the wildest stretch of imagination could a prisoner have felt that these letters would do any good. They were letters to senators and representatives, even an occasional letter to the President. They had all been neatly typed and had been mailed hopefully whenever Boggie could arrange for the typing and get enough to cover postage. Whenever a new official was elected to office, he could count on receiving a letter from Clarence Boggie.

It was the replies that were heartbreaking. Letters obviously typed by a secretary and signed without reading. Letters that were signed with rubber stamp signatures. Letters that were from secretaries advising Boggie that the matter was being placed in an important file and would be called to Mr. Bigboy's attention at the earliest possible moment, that Mr. Bigboy, it must be remembered, was swamped with problems incident to his election and a national crisis, but Boggie could rest assured his letter would receive Mr. Bigboy's attention just as soon as the matter could be investigated.

In most of the modern penitentiaries a prisoner would not have been permitted to mail the letters that Boggie sent out, but because these were appeals to public officials, to attorneys, and because they were based on Boggie's assertions of complete innocence, the wardens had permitted these letters to be mailed, and the replies to be received.

In one way it was a pathetic heartbreak. In another way it had given Boggie the encouragement necessary to carry on. There was always the hope that one of these days, now that Mr. Bigboy had got caught up with the problems incident to assuming his new office, he would remember his promise and turn his attention to the case of Clarence Boggie. . . . So Boggie carried on and waited. Why not? Didn't Boggie have letters over Mr. Bigboy's signature assuring that such would be the case?

Then there was Boggie's transcript.

The State of Washington insisted that furnishing a transcript of testimony for use on appeal was a private matter, and as such, entirely up to the defendant.

Without the transcript there could be no appeal. Without money there could be no transcript.

Boggie had no money. It appeared that the transcript was going to cost some seven hundred and fifty dollars.

Boggie, inside the prison, pulled every wire he could think of trying to get money enough to defray the cost of a transcript. His parents were in no position to help. They were elderly and having a hard time to make ends meet. Boggie was penniless—and who was going to help a convicted murderer to the extent of seven hundred and fifty dollars? No one.

Then, after a lapse of some ten years, a peculiar thing happened.

A man who had some few thousand dollars was convicted of crime and sent to the penitentiary. The crime of which this man was convicted is a violation of the moral law and of the statutes. By all man-made standards of conduct this individual is reprehensible.

Yet within the prison this man has done much to help out here and there. Quietly, unostentatiously, he has done the best he could to alleviate the lot of a good many of the inmates. He heard about Clarence Boggie's problem. He heard Clarence Boggie's protestations of innocence. He put up the seven hundred and fifty dollars which enabled Boggie for the first time since his conviction to get a transcript of the testimony taken at the trial. So, when I called on Boggie, he was able to hand me this transcript.

The study of that transcript testimony was a long, uphill job, but reading it, I began to get a picture of the Boggie case.

The case itself was fully as incredible as any of the other things connected with Clarence Boggie.

On June 26, 1933, Moritz Peterson, an elderly recluse seventy-eight years old, was rooming at a private boarding house in Spokane, Washington. He owned a little shack some distance away at the rear of a deep lot on East 20th Avenue in Spokane. There was an occupied dwelling house on the front of this lot, and also one on the adjoining lot.

Peterson was in the habit of leaving his boarding house in the morning, taking a street car to the little shack, and there spending the day puttering around in the garden, taking care of his chickens, pulling weeds, etc. In the evening he'd go back to the place where he boarded. Most of his clothes were kept in the little shack house.

Peterson, in common with most of the world, was in rather straitened circumstances at the time. He had a diamond ring which he believed to be worth five hundred dollars, but he had been trying in vain to sell it for one hundred dollars. (This was at the time when the country was in the depths of a depression and ready money was a very tight commodity.)

The man's financial circumstances are mentioned because it would be almost out of the question to think that anyone who actually knew Moritz Peterson would contemplate trying to rob him.

On the other hand there is the distinct possibility that someone who didn't really know him might have thought this eccentric old man, living an ordered life, could well have laid by a little ready cash which he could have kept concealed in his shack or on his person.

Sometime on Saturday night, June 24, 1933, someone broke into Moritz Peterson's shack during the night and made a most thorough job of ransacking the place. Towels having been pinned over the windows so that people in the nearby houses would not notice any light, the intruder proceeded to search every nook and cranny, opening boxes, scattering canceled checks and documents all over the floor.

If one could judge from external appearances the intruder must have been searching for a particular document of some sort. Canceled checks would ordinarily be kept in neat bundles, and it is hardly possible that an intruder would have opened these bundles of checks and strewn the papers over the floor in a search for money, yet that could have been the case. The burglar could well have reasoned that the money might have been secreted in the most unlikely places.

Sunday morning, when Peterson arrived at the shack, he was confronted with the wreckage and complete disorder. He was, of course, very much upset, but he refused to allow the police to be notified. He even went so far as to state that he knew the identity of the intruder and didn't want anything done about it.

Peterson put in Sunday straightening up the place. By afternoon he told the neighbors that the only things which had been taken were a pair of coveralls and a pair of black shoes.

If anyone had wanted to hold up or assault Moritz Peterson the worst day that could possibly have been selected would have been Monday, the conventional washday.

Yet apparently someone was concealed in the Peterson house on Monday, the 26th day of June, 1933, waiting for him to arrive.

The neighbors of course didn't see this person enter, but they did hear the sound of a terrific struggle emanating from the little shack. The time was probably between ten and twenty-five minutes after ten in the morning.

The sounds of that struggle attracted a great deal of attention. Housewives and children ran from their houses. They were in time to see a stocky, heavy-set, bushy-haired individual, who ran with a peculiar "sideways gait," running from the house. They chased this individual for some two or three blocks. Then the man disappeared in a wooded area. No one had been able to get a look at his face.

While one of the housewives and some children were chasing the individual who ran away from Moritz Peterson's shack, one of the other women had looked in at his door, found Peterson lying, moaning, with his head virtually beaten in. She dashed to her house and telephoned the police.

What happened after that was what might be called a tragedy of errors.

The little party who were running after the fugitive, trying to keep him in sight, followed him until he entered a thicket of underbrush, whereupon they turned back.

The first officer to arrive on the scene was a motorcycle officer, who came tearing up with siren screaming, and came to a stop before the house at the front of the lot.

The excited audience explained to the motorcycle officer what had happened. The motorcycle officer promptly decided that his duties were along other lines and in other fields. He dashed away from there, fast.

Police officers from the central station tore through the streets with sirens screaming, to come to the Peterson shack.

Apparently it was at this time that the officers found Moritz Peterson lying on the floor, his head so terribly smashed that one of the eye sockets had been completely broken. A homemade weapon was on the floor beside the dying man.

The officers were told by the boys that the assailant had jumped into the brush a couple of blocks up the street, so the officers valiantly permitted themselves to be guided to the spot where the murderer had disappeared, at which time they suddenly discovered they had "forgotten their guns." So they returned to their automobile, and, with siren screaming, went tearing back to get their guns.

In the meantime an ambulance had been summoned and the ambulance, also accompanied by the sound of sirens, went to the scene of the crime to pick up Moritz Peterson and transport him to a hospital. The officers, by this time having fully armed themselves, came dashing back to the scene of the crime.

A description of all this confusion and particularly the noise of the sirens is important for reasons which will presently become apparent.

After Peterson had been removed to the hospital, the police made a rather cursory examination of the premises and took into their possession the weapon with which the crime had been committed. It was a homemade bludgeon which had been fashioned with considerable skill and ingenuity, and consisted of a round, water-washed rock wrapped in burlap. This burlap had been tightly twisted and stitched so that the long twisted burlap made a semi-flexible handle. The whole thing was a most potent, deadly weapon, which could strike terrific blows. The assailant had repeatedly struck Moritz Peterson on the head with this weapon.

Strangely enough, however, despite the fact that Peterson had received these fatal injuries, he still remained conscious. The dying man apparently experienced a sensation of great pressure on his brain and thought there was a weight-still on his head, but by the time he reached the hospital he was able to talk. He kept complaining of this terrible weight that was crushing his head.

Sometime after reaching the hospital Moritz Peterson's daughter was summoned, and at the bedside of her dying father asked him in the presence of witnesses if he knew who had done this thing to him.

Peterson admitted that he did but didn't want to mention the man's name. The daughter kept insisting, and finally Peterson stated that if she would take the terrific weight off of his head he would tell her; and then, after further questioning, mentioned a name, a name which was heard very distinctly by the daughter.

This name was not the name of Clarence Boggie, nor could that name at any time ever be connected in any way with him. At the time there was nothing to connect Clarence Boggie with Moritz Peterson or with the burglary of the Peterson shack.

The police, in the course of their investigation, were reported to have arrested a suspect who was positively identified by the witnesses who had seen the man running away from the Peterson shack, but after a while the police announced that this man had a perfect alibi and he was released.

This fact, mentioned casually in the local press, was subsequently to assume a very great significance, but at the time it appeared as one of the various diversions, and was snowed under by the conjectures and surmises and press releases given out by the police in order to show that they were diligently working on the case.

Then gradually the case petered out. The police ran down clues, gave the usual optimistic statements to newspaper reporters, and wound up by getting nowhere.

Moritz Peterson died shortly after being admitted to the hospital, and had lost consciousness a very short time after making the statement to his daughter in which he had named his assailant.

At this time, Clarence Boggie was on the streets of Portland, Oregon.

The time, it will be remembered, was during the depression. People who didn't have cash had virtually no way of getting any. People who did have cash didn't know what to do with it. Banks were failing. People were being laid off. Jobs were scarce.

Boggie had no job, and he did have a criminal record.

He had been convicted of a bank robbery in Oregon.

Boggie's story of how he happened to be convicted of that bank robbery is as completely incredible as any of the other Boggie stories. We have never even investigated to find out whether this story was true because apparently the Oregon authorities had made such an investigation and had granted him a pardon—not a parole but a full pardon.

Boggie's story was that he had been camped in the "jungles" under a bridge across a little creek bed, that a car dashed by at wild speed above the bridge, and someone threw a coat over the bridge. The car went hurtling down the road, and after the car, the sound of screaming sirens indicated pursuing police.

Boggie thought somebody was being pinched for speeding.

He went over and picked up the coat. It was a good fit, and Boggie was badly in need of a coat.

About the time Boggie had nicely adjusted himself to the coat, the creek bed began to swarm with officers. They grabbed Boggie and searched him on suspicion, and in the pockets of the coat they found a lot of currency which had been taken in a bank robbery.

Boggie was convicted. Months passed. Boggie kept protesting his innocence and asking for an investigation. Evidently such an investigation was finally made. He was pardoned, but only after he had spent some years in the Oregon penitentiary.

Now, at about this time, there enters the picture a very interesting character whom we shall refer to as Convict X. This man is, so far as I know, still serving a term in a penitentiary. He is a shrewd, ingenious operator, a clever opportunist, and he may be possessed of a quiet sense of humor. I don't know. I do know that when I was trying to interview him he was completely hostile. He didn't want to talk with me. He didn't want to answer questions.

One of my associates said to him, "Don't you know who this man is? This is Erle Stanley Gardner. He'll give you a square deal. Haven't you ever read any of his books?"

Convict X twisted his lip in a sneer. "Bah!" he said. "Escape fiction."

This convict came across Boggie on the streets of Oregon at a time when the convict was looking for accomplices. Boggie's story as to why the man wanted them is a story in itself.

In a little town in the state of Idaho the ex-chief of police knew that, because of the instability of the banks, certain relatively affluent citizens were keeping money in large quantities concealed in their houses. Boggie insisted this ex-officer had conceived the idea that if stick-up men should rob one of these houses and should take in a good haul of ready cash, it would be a bad thing for the victim, but it might be turned into a good thing for the ex-chief of police.

The former officer is supposed to have known that a certain individual had thirty thousand dollars concealed in his house. This citizen kept his house carefully locked at all times and had resorted to elaborate safeguards against robbery.

According to Boggie, word went out through the underworld that this ex-chief of police would like to have a sociable talk with some thoroughly competent men who could pull a smooth job. The word trickled through the devious channels of organized crime and reached the ears of Convict X, who promptly got in touch with the former officer. A deal was made.

And this is one place where Boggie's story to us may have been somewhat colored. There is evidence indicating that at the start Boggie may have been the one who passed the story of the ex-chief of police on to Convict X. The history of what happened and what Boggie claimed happened have some variations which are probably significant.

In any event, Convict X and the ex-chief made a deal.

The ex-chief agreed to call on the man who distrusted banks. He would very conveniently leave his car, with its tank filled with gas, on the outside, and the ignition keys would be in the car.

The former official also agreed that when he entered the house he would manage to turn back the spring lock and snap the catch which would hold it back, so that anyone could enter the door by simply turning the knob and pushing.

It was that simple.

Convict X and an accomplice were making the haul, but they wanted someone to sit outside as a watchman. They wanted someone who was so simple that he would follow instructions, so dumb that he could be used as a fall guy in the event anything went wrong.

At this point, stir-simple Clarence Boggie with his mother-complex enters the picture. Boggie was made to order.

According to Boggie's story, the men were to take a trip to Idaho. Boggie was to go along. Some time later he got cold feet. He tried to back out, then he tried to escape. The men wouldn't let him go, but Boggie finally did get away from them.

He started hitchhiking. He was picked up by a man who gave him a ride in return for Boggie's promise to do some of the driving.

So he rode along with this gentleman until it became dark. Then it turned out the man's lights wouldn't work. Boggie decided there was a shorted wire somewhere. He stopped at a sort of service station and general merchandise store and went to work. He had located a short in the wire and was making repairs with tape when another car pulled in and pilloried Boggie in the white lights.

This was the car driven by Convict X; the identical car from which Boggie had made his escape.

There was a short, quiet talk. Convict X quite apparently had associated with Boggie long enough in the Oregon prison to know Boggie's weakness. If Boggie didn't come along and do exactly as they said, Convict X assured him they were going to hunt up "Mummy" and kill her.

Even after a lapse of some fifteen years, Boggie couldn't tell about this without becoming hysterical. Up to this point he could control himself, but when he reached this phase of the story tears streamed down his cheeks and he completely lost his self-control.

There was never any question in the mind of anyone who talked with Boggie that his fear that these men would have killed his dear "Mummy" was an actual, tangible force. So far as Boggie was concerned, he accepted it as a basic fact that these men would do exactly what they threatened, and the only way he could save "Mummy's" life was to go along in absolute docility no matter what happened. From that time on Boggie was their man.

Boggie, Convict X and another accomplice, went to the little town in Idaho which had been picked for the robbery. At the appointed time the ex-chief of police drove up and parked his car. He explained to the owner of the house that he wanted to listen to his radio set for a while.

He was duly admitted and, according to plan, as he stepped inside he turned the spring lock on the door so that anyone could walk right in. Then he carefully closed the door.

Boggie was to be the lookout man. He was to signal the others if anything started to go wrong.

Convict X and his accomplice glided quietly up to the door and tried the knob to make certain that the officer had been able to manipulate the lock. Finding that he had done so, they suddenly pushed the door open and jumped into the room with drawn guns.

THE COURT OF LAST RESORT   39

It was part of the plan that the former chief, despite the menace of the guns, was to put up a valiant battle.

Convict X told me about all this, a little at a time. For the most part, getting information out of him was pretty much of a job. He was inclined to answer questions in monosyllables or not answer them at all, but when he came to the point where he described the battle with the former chief of police he needed no urging. His eyes lit with enthusiasm. That was one part of the job that he thoroughly enjoyed and he loved to tell about it.

It seemed the two criminals really did a job on the former officer. He had asked to be beaten up, and these boys carried out that part of their assignment with an enthusiastic zeal that gave the man everything he had asked for—and more. He had wanted to be marked up enough so that it would be perfectly apparent he had struggled valiantly against overpowering odds.

"Boy, oh, boy," Convict X said ecstatically in telling me about it, "we hung a couple of beautiful shiners on that so-and-so."

The ex-officer, having been overpowered, was immunized by one of the convicts who held a gun pointed at the man's stomach, while the other intruder went to work on the householder and his wife, trying to find out the place where the thirty thousand dollars were secreted.

Now the story develops a touch of grim humor.

The victim explained to the holdup men that they were acting on a wrong tip, that he didn't have any money in the house. He was supposed to have money concealed but he was too smart for that trap. He preferred to take a chance on a bank despite the fact that there was some chance the bank might fail.

He pulled a checkbook out of his pocket. He showed check stubs to the robbers. And he was so absolutely convincing that he talked them out of it.

Imagine the feelings of the ex-chief of police, standing there with his hands in the air, his face badly banged up, his eyes swelling shut, listening to what was going on, hearing the man who he knew full well had thirty thousand dollars concealed on the premises talking the bandits into believing he had nothing. How he must have wanted to enter the discussion by shouting to the bandits, "You poor fools. Don't let him talk you out of it. I told you he had thirty thousand dollars here and I wouldn't have told you that unless I'd known. Get busy and find that money, you poor bungling amateurs!"

But the ex-chief, forced to act out the part of a valiant officer, who had been overpowered, beaten up, slugged, and was now facing the gun of a trigger-happy desperado, could only stand there and listen.

The householder, apparently very much frightened, was perfectly willing to surrender "all the money he had on the premises," a few hundred dollars. He was so frightened that if he had had any more he would unquestionably have given it up. He put on quite an act. Convict X believed him. So did the other man. They took the money that was available and made a dash out of the front door, piled helter-skelter into the waiting car and took off.

The man who had been held up was nobody's fool. Certain things about the holdup caused him to become suspicious. It had been a little too opportune.

The bandits were apprehended, the whole story came out, and Convict X and Clarence Boggie found themselves facing a long prison term in Idaho.

Boggie made a statement. He wanted to turn State's evidence.

Convict X told him grimly, "You rat on us and we'll frame something a lot worse than this on you." (Later on a deputy sheriff, who had overheard this and other remarks, was to make an affidavit that from what he had overheard he had every reason to believe Convict X had framed Boggie for the Peterson murder—and the authorities were to brush that affidavit aside.)

Boggie, Convict X and the accomplice were all sentenced to terms in the Idaho State Penitentiary.

It appeared that on his way north to pull this job Convict X had stopped for a short time in Spokane. Boggie had some people he wanted to see and Convict X wanted to make preparations for a job he was to do.

This was but a short time after Moritz Peterson had been murdered.

Through a fortuitous chain of circumstances Convict X had an absolutely perfect alibi for the Peterson murder. He had been serving a term in a Canadian prison and had been released from that prison on the day *following* the death of Moritz Peterson. Therefore, so far as that crime was concerned, Convict X was in the clear and knew it.

On the other hand, Convict X, who had an adroit, ingenious mind, studied the local newspapers while he was stopping over in Spokane and gave a lot of thought to the Peterson murder, reading about the various clues the police were "running down." He noticed the police were going in circles while issuing the usual optimistic reports that they were confident the culprit would be in custody within a short time, etc. So Convict X decided that the Peterson murder might come in very handy in case of necessity.

Just how handy will presently become apparent.

Convict X needed funds and he was a very desperate man. As he explained the matter to me later in a burst of indignation, the Canadian prison had turned him loose with a prison suit of clothes and a Canadian ten-dollar bill in his pocket. "Why, that wasn't enough," he charged bitterly, "for operating capital."

I asked him what he meant by "operating capital."

"Not enough to buy a 'rod' with," he retorted, still angry at this evidence of Canadian lack of hospitality.

So Convict X was in urgent need of "operating capital." By the time he reached Spokane he had remedied the defect as far as the "rod" was concerned, but he was still short of money.

Spokane officers believed he had participated in a robbery and kidnaping while in Spokane, and under the so-called "Lindbergh Laws" which were being passed by the various states in a wave of indignation over kidnapings, Convict X could have been extradited from Idaho to Washington, and sentenced to death.

The Washington authorities went up to Idaho with the idea of extraditing Convict X to Washington, trying him and demanding the death penalty.

This, it is to be remembered, was after Convict X had been arrested in Idaho but before he had been convicted there. If Idaho was willing to release him to Washington, Washington could prosecute him, and, if convicted, could execute him.

Convict X didn't like that prospect.

At this point it becomes necessary to put two and two together and rely upon a certain amount of surmise and circumstantial evidence. But the indications are quite plain and there is considerable evidence that Convict X said to the officers, "If you boys will let me stay up here in Idaho and take the rap on this robbery charge without extraditing me back to Washington, I'll do you a favor; I'll solve the Peterson murder for you."

In any event, and regardless of what actually did happen, the fact remains that the Washington authorities after a talk with Convict X did not extradite him. They let him remain and take the rap in Idaho, and they *did* claim that they now knew the identity of the real murderer of Moritz Peterson. There is reason to believe they returned with a pair of coveralls and a pair of black shoes, which Convict X assured them had been given him by Boggie, and which Boggie had told him were the property of "the old man."

Perhaps there was no trade. Perhaps it was all merely coincidental.

The fact remained that the crestfallen officers found that they didn't have a case, because the coveralls did not belong to Moritz Peterson, and the shoes were not the right size.

Rumor has it that on careful investigation the police found a laundry mark in the coveralls, and that this laundry mark established an entirely different chain of ownership.

It is, therefore, apparent that Convict X had formulated some pretty definite plans in his shrewdly ingenious mind. From his viewpoint the Peterson murder case represented an ideal opportunity to buy his way out of any jam in the state of Washington.

The Spokane police were anxious to solve the murder. People were indignant over the idea of a harmless, inoffensive, well-liked citizen being bludgeoned to death by a murderer who had only a relatively short start on the police and who was never apprehended. Spokane police wanted very much to solve that murder case.

Convict X had an unshakable alibi.

Therefore if Convict X could offer the Spokane police a "solution" of the Peterson murder, he would be in a marvelous trading position. For a man of Convict X's temperament, personality and occupation, being in a good trading position with the police was well worth the investment in a couple of stage props—a pair of secondhand coveralls and some old shoes.

Of course, Convict X needed just a little more than that. He needed a fall guy, and a man looking for a fall guy couldn't have found anyone more made to order than Clarence Boggie.

So, putting two and two together, it would seem that Clarence Boggie had served several purposes on that fateful trip north from Portland.

And the story that Convict X is known to have told the officers is weird in the extreme. Boggie, he said, had boasted of killing Peterson, had taken Convict X to a place where he had buried the "loot," had there dug up a small coffee can, had taken off the cover and extracted a worn, empty billfold which he had offered to Convict X and which Convict X had taken.

Thus a pattern of double-crossing chicanery emerged—the dog-eat-dog attitude of factual occurrences in everyday life as opposed to the version that is handed out to the public.

Of course, the Spokane police didn't give up that easily.

They looked up Boggie from all conceivable angles, but all that they had to connect Boggie with the crime was the word of Convict X, and Convict X, of course, with his long criminal record, his extremely personal interest in the matter, would hardly make a witness on whom a district attorney would like to depend.

There must have been a shrewd suspicion in the minds of the officers that they had been taken for a ride by a quick-thinking, fast-talking convict, but if that was the case the officers couldn't do anything about it without publicizing their own gullibility, and Convict X kept assuring them of his complete good faith. Clarence Boggie, he insisted, was the man who committed the crime, even if Boggie had lied about the coveralls and the shoes, and the officers could rest assured that Convict X was giving them the real low-down. If there had been any prevarication about the coveralls and the shoes, it had been Boggie's lie and not that of Convict X, etc.

The Moritz Peterson case went into the unsolved file. The officers busied themselves about other matters; but, always in the back of their minds was the feeling that Clarence Boggie had perhaps outsmarted them in some way and had juggled the evidence. They felt that he was the man who had committed the murder.

Not only did Convict X say that Boggie had confessed to him, but later another Idaho convict claimed Boggie had confessed to him while in the Idaho penitentiary—had, in effect, walked right up to him, and without preliminary conversation said, "I killed Moritz Peterson," and then turned and walked away. It was that simple.

In this way, Convict X was able to assure the Washington officers of his entire good faith in the matter. He was never returned to Washington and tried on the kidnap case.

Then, many months later and "on a tip," the officers went to a place near a small Oregon town where Boggie had stayed for a while, and there they found an overcoat. There was some evidence that Boggie had worn this overcoat to the house when he arrived. The overcoat had been left there. It had received rather hard usage and was in a dilapidated state.

However, that overcoat was identified by the daughter of Moritz Peterson as having been an overcoat worn by her father during his lifetime.

That did it. The officers came down on Boggie like a thousand ton of bricks.

The murderer of Moritz Peterson had been identified as a person having wild-looking bushy black hair. Clarence Boggie, apparently from the time when he was brought under suspicion, started slicking his hair smoothly down with quantities of hair oil.

This didn't stop the officers. They would bring him in, ruffle his hair up, ask witnesses to identify him, and then take Boggie's picture. Naturally, some of these pictures of Boggie with his thickly greased long hair, pulled up high above his head, resembled the pictures in Frye's geography of a Dyak of Borneo. These pictures were given to the press.

Boggie's story about how he came by the overcoat was incredible.

He had, he said, been in a secondhand clothing store in Portland, Oregon. A man came in with an overcoat, a pretty good-looking overcoat, with a pair of slippers in the pocket. He offered to sell this coat to the proprietor of the store. He wanted a dollar for it. The proprietor hadn't liked the looks of the man and had refused to buy the overcoat.

Boggie spoke up. "*I'll* give you a dollar for it."

It made the proprietor angry. He didn't think Boggie had any right to interfere in that way. If he had been dickering in the hope the seller would make a lower offer, Boggie's interference would have lost him a good purchase.

The man who was offering the overcoat for sale promptly and eagerly accepted Boggie's dollar. So Boggie bought himself a one-way ticket to a life sentence in the. Washington State Penitentiary at Walla Walla.

Little things, which may or may not have been significant so far as the jury were concerned, indicated the background of the Boggie trial. The prosecution, for instance, was permitted to show by witnesses that Boggie had been in a car, with a revolver, and that Boggie's statement explaining the ownership and possession of the revolver was that the authorities had given it to him so he could protect himself.

This, of course, was greeted with the equivalent of hoots of derision.

Later on, the defense tried to prove the actual ownership of the revolver and the reason it was in the car with Boggie by no less person than Fred C. May, the deputy sheriff of Shoshone County, Idaho. The court refused to permit such testimony to go in, on the ground that it was irrelevant.

In vain did counsel protest. The court stated that questions concerning the revolver had been completely irrelevant, and charged the attorneys for the defense that if they permitted irrelevant matter to be brought in by the prosecution they could not thereby make an issue of it. Such are the technicalities of law.

It is to be remembered that the running murderer had a peculiar, "sideways gait." Boggie did not have any such gait, but he did have ₐ very slight limp. No one of the witnesses had seen the murderer's face, but witnesses were called upon to identify Boggie as "looking like" the man who had been seen running away from the scene of the murder two years earlier.

It is to be noted that the witnesses who had seen the murderer running away from the scene of the crime were not given an opportunity to look at Boggie when the police had first had reason to suspect him of the murder. It was not until a lapse of some two years (after the overcoat had been located) that the witnesses were called on to make an identification, and then there was no line-up or anything of that sort. The witnesses were simply brought in to see Boggie and asked if that was the man. There is, in fact, considerable evidence in the record itself that the identification, made in this way, could not have been made if the defendant had been in a line-up.

A junk dealer stated that he had seen Boggie visiting Peterson on the Friday before the murder. Another witness, who had one of the houses in the front of the lot, insisted that she had seen a man whom she thought was Boggie visiting there on a Friday, but on cross-examination, when the witnesses had been separated, it appeared that each was testifying to a different Friday.

It is to be noted that the man who was seen running away from the scene of the murder that twenty-sixth day of June, was not carrying an overcoat, nor, in the heat of a Spokane summer, was he wearing any overcoat. Virtually the entire case against Boggie hinged on the identification of an overcoat, and that identification was made some two years after the crime had been committed.

The murderer, running away from Moritz Peterson's shack that June day, had been followed by one of the housewives who had been doing her washing, and some of the children. The other housewife had been telephoning the police. No one had seen the murderer's face, but one woman had been close enough to see a part of his cheek, the color of his skin, and had observed the running figure closely.

At the time of the trial the prosecution had called her as a witness and the examination had been rather peculiar. For one thing, the prosecution did not ask her to identify Clarence Boggie as the man whom she had seen running away from the house; and when the attorney for the defense cross-examined her, he, probably fearing a trap, was careful not to give her any opportunity to make a positive identification. So this woman was in effect asked a few general questions about hearing the struggle in the shack, seeing the man run away, following him for a couple of blocks, and then she was excused.

One of the other witnesses was much more positive in her identification of Boggie, but there were certain circumstances which tended to weaken the identification. Among other things was the intimation that she had previously identified another person, only to retract that identification when she found out that she must have been mistaken.

There were, of course, other angles to the case. A couple of days after the murder Boggie had been bumming a ride in Pendleton, Oregon. He had spoken in enthusiastic terms of the hunting near a certain place in Oregon, a place where he lived at the time. The driver of the car had expressed a wish to go hunting with Boggie, and Boggie had thoughtfully given him his name and address.

Later on, reading in the newspapers that Boggie was wanted for murder, the driver of the car got in touch with the police.

The prosecution contended that Boggie had made a headlong "flight" from the scene of the murder. (A strange flight by a man who makes it a point to impress his personality upon the individual with whom he is riding, and gives his name and address.)

However, when Boggie tried to explain away the situation and tell his story, he was asked an impeaching question. Wasn't it true that he had twice been convicted of a felony?

Boggie was forced to admit that such was the case; and that was all there was to it.

Boggie was convicted, and, fortunately for him, escaped the gallows. He was sentenced to life imprisonment. . . .

In summarizing the facts in this case it seems remarkable that even with the urging of the chaplain we would have wasted time investigating the Boggie case. His story was incredible. The case against him, while not particularly sturdy, was, nevertheless, a pretty good case. The penitentiaries are filled with people against whom the prosecution didn't have as good cases as they had against Clarence Boggie. And, on the other hand, there was virtually nothing to establish Boggie's innocence except his word that he wasn't guilty.

The prosecution was able to show that Boggie, with a long criminal record, had the dead man's property in his possession, and had confessed to Convict X, and to another convict in Idaho, that he had killed Moritz Peterson. Witnesses who had seen the murderer running away from the scene of the crime had identified Boggie as being the man.

Despite this positive evidence each link in the chain of evidence had certain weaknesses. Convict X had a definite interest in the matter, or could well have had, if he had made a trade with the Spokane police. The overcoat had not been picked up until two years after the murder. It had been hanging in a barn, and was a fairly worn-out garment by the time it was shown to the daughter of the murdered man for identification. Boggie had not been identified in a line-up, but had simply been exhibited to witnesses who were asked if this was the man they had seen running away from the house at the time of the murder.

Identification evidence is a most tricky subject. The subconscious mind frequently plays tricks upon witnesses who are acting in the greatest good faith, and in the Boggie case witnesses were not called upon to identify him until two years after the date of the crime.

However, as I have said, we can go to any penitentiary in the country and find hundreds of cases where the evidence on which the man was convicted is no more solid than the evidence on which Boggie was convicted.

There was one factor in Boggie's favor. Boggie had made an application for *habeas corpus* and a hearing duly came up in a Federal court. Hon. Lloyd L. Black, the Federal judge before whom that hearing was held, is a patient, a kindly individual who is prone to try to get at the facts of a case and not rush through these numerous *habeas corpus* applications in order to "clear his calendar."

He became very much interested in the case when the daughter of Moritz Peterson, the same woman who had been present at the time the dying man had made a statement that he would name the person who had killed him, stated very definitely and positively that she did not believe Clarence Boggie had killed her father or knew anything about the murder, that she simply didn't believe Boggie was known to her father.

Judge Black found no reason to grant the writ of *habeas corpus* but he was very much impressed by the sincerity of the daughter and by her declaration. He at least intimated in open court that he would like to see some further investigation made in the case.

And so those were the facts which confronted me when I arrived in Walla Walla, talked with Tom Smith, met Clarence Boggie, talked with him, went over his heartbreak file and then studied the evidence in the case.

I decided that considerable investigative work was going to be needed and got on the long-distance telephone to Raymond Schindler in New York. I found that he was at the moment in Los Angeles, and was on the point of taking a plane back to New York. I persuaded him he had better fly up to join me, so he took a night plane and arrived in Walla Walla, where I had a chartered plane ready. We flew to Spokane.

Obviously one of the highlights of the case from a legal standpoint was the manner in which the prosecution had interrogated the housewife who had seen the murderer running away from the Peterson shack, yet who wasn't specifically asked to point out Boggie.

My courtroom experience indicated that there must have been a very definite reason for the peculiar type of questions which had been asked this woman on the witness stand. The prosecution had asked all of the usual questions, had got her right up to the point in her testimony where the next logical question would have been to ask her to point out the murderer, and then veered off into a detour from which the attorneys had never returned to the main highway of ordinary procedure.

Frequently those things happen when a prosecutor lays a trap for the defense attorney. Knowing that he has a very positive witness whose testimony would be damning, the prosecutor pretends to fumble around and leaves a beautiful "opening" for the cross-examiner. The cross-examiner sticks his head through that opening and promptly has it chopped off.

But somehow as Schindler and I read and discussed this woman's testimony, we didn't feel that it had been a trap. We felt that there was something in the background, some reason that the prosecution had pretended to fumble the ball.

Of course, many years had elapsed since the trial, but we felt that if it was still possible to find this woman, we wanted to talk with her.

We found her, and when we did we uncovered a shocking story.

This witness and her young son had seen the murderer emerge from the Peterson shack. They had followed as he ran down the street, not trying to overtake him but trying to keep him in sight. They had never seen his face. (None of the witnesses had ever seen the face of the fleeing man.) But this woman had been in a position to see the side of his cheek and had noticed the color of his skin.

A considerable time after the murder, and apparently at a time when Boggie was under arrest, this woman had seen a man prowling around the vicinity of the Peterson shack. (It is to be noted in passing that long after the time of the murder several other home-made lethal weapons had been found in the bushes nearby, the over-all characteristics being somewhat similar to the murder weapon in the Peterson case.)

This woman felt absolutely certain in her own mind that the man she saw was the same man she had seen running away from the scene of the murder. She went to the telephone and called the police, telling them excitedly that the man who killed Moritz Peterson was outside and to come and pick him up.

The police told her to forget it, that the man who had killed Moritz Peterson was Clarence Boggie, that Boggie had been arrested and was safe in jail awaiting trial.

The woman insisted that this man was the murderer, that in any event he was a prowler who had no business there, and she wanted the police to come out and arrest him.

The police hung up.

After a while the prowler went away.

Nor was this all. The day before Clarence Boggie was to be tried, the deputy prosecutor had gone to the school where this woman's twelve-year-old son was in attendance.

According to this woman the deputy prosecutor painted a very glittering picture. The boy was told he was to be a very important witness. He was to be excused from classes the next day. A big police car with a driver was to come to school and get him. The boy was to go to court. He was to stand up and be sworn as a witness, and for this he would receive witness fees which would be entirely his own money, which he could spend any way he wanted to.

The deputy prosecutor, however, wanted him to be sure and identify Boggie, who would be sitting right there in the courtroom. He wanted the boy to mention that he had seen the face of the murderer who was running away from the Peterson shack, and that this man was Boggie.

But the boy protested he *hadn't* seen the murderer's face.

According to this woman's story the deputy prosecutor had then said, "But I want you to say that you saw the man's face. You know that I am a public official. I wouldn't ask you to do anything that was wrong. That's the thing I want you to do, to say that you saw the man's face."

The perplexed, bewildered boy shook his head. He couldn't say he had seen the man's face because he hadn't.

In the end the deputy prosecutor warned the boy against saying anything to his mother about the conversation. So the boy went home from school, a very troubled, worried young man who couldn't eat any supper.

The mother questioned him, trying to find out what was wrong, but, mindful of the warning he had received not to talk to his mother about the conversation, he didn't want to tell her. By this time, very much alarmed and sensing that something was radically wrong, she kept after him until finally he broke down and tearfully told her the story.

This mother was a good, straightforward American woman. She took the boy by the hand and walked up to the prosecutor's office, where lights shining through the windows indicated that last-minute preparations for the courtroom battle the next day were going on.

"What," she indignantly demanded, "are you trying to do to my son?"

No wonder the prosecution had handled her with gloves. No wonder they hadn't asked her to identify Clarence Boggie. Had they asked her she would have said that she didn't think Clarence Boggie was the man, that she didn't think he had the same build, that she didn't think he had the same complexion, that she thought the real murderer was the man whom she had seen prowling around the premises at a time when Clarence Boggie was in jail and at a time when the police refused even to come out to investigate.

It is to be remembered that more than fifteen years had passed from the time of the Peterson murder to the date of our investigation. We couldn't talk with the boy because he had grown up to be a young man, had gone to war and had given his life for his country.

On the other hand, the deputy prosecutor had cut one corner too many, had been himself convicted of crime and sent to prison.

So there we had a story on our hands that we couldn't verify. The mother, of course, hadn't heard the conversation with the deputy prosecutor. She only knew what the boy had told her, but the mother had confronted the deputy prosecutor with her boy, and so to that extent was a witness who could testify in any court to that much of the story. . . . And what a sordid story it was. A deputy prosecutor trying to suborn perjury, trying to get a young boy just at the threshold of life to do something that he knew was wrong, trying to send a man to the gallows by assuring a twelve-year-old boy, "I'm a public official. I wouldn't ask you to do something that was wrong, would I?"

Such was our introduction to the investigation of the Boggie case, the first intimation we had that the Court of Last Resort might be a lot more important than we had at first realized and might find some very tightly closed doors leading into some dark and dingy rooms.

When Steeger and I had discussed the manner in which *Argosy* would donate its space to the activities of the investigating committee for the Court of Last Resort, it was agreed that we wouldn't try to carry the investigation through to completion and then publish what we had found out.

We felt that if we were going to do the job we wanted to do it would be necessary to take the reader right along with us. We wanted to get readers interested in the cause of justice. We wanted to get them interested in a case, and in order to get them interested we wanted them to participate in the investigation.

It was decided we'd make only the most cursory preliminary investigation, that we would then start working on the case, not knowing whether the defendant was guilty or innocent, simply knowing that it was a good case for investigative work, and that the readers of *Argosy* could look over our shoulders while we were making it.

In fact, it is to be continually borne in mind that the Court of Last Resort was not the magazine and was not the investigators, but was the public, the readers of the magazine themselves. The board of investigators was nothing more nor less than an investigative board.

For that reason I carried a portable typewriter along with me when I flew to Washington, and each day I made a summary of what our work had disclosed. Each night we carefully studied the transcript in the Boggie case and made an analysis of the evidence. Since there were several volumes of this transcript the schedule which we set ourselves was a hard one. By day we talked with witnesses. At night we studied transcripts, and put together an analysis and the condensation of the evidence. In the small hours of the morning I would whip out copy to send to the magazine, and when enough copy had been sent in for the first installment of the Boggie case, Schindler flew back to New York and I left for my ranch in California, taking the transcript back with me.

A peculiar situation developed. The authorities in Washington suddenly realized that a case which had taken place in their state was being publicized, and the authorities didn't even know what the case was all about, and didn't have anyway of finding out.

The attorney general of Washington called me and wanted to

know if I would mail the transcript to his office. I told him I didn't feel I could do that, but that I would be very glad to let anyone whom he might designate study it at my ranch.

So Ed Lehan, a special deputy attorney general, flew down from Washington and spent several days going over the transcript.

At the end of that time Lehan concluded that the evidence had not been such as to warrant a conviction.

Ed Lehan returned to Washington to carry on an investigation for the attorney general.

Raymond Schindler and I flew back to Washington and were joined by Harry Steeger. Here we made a supplemental investigation and learned that the proprietor of the secondhand store, where Boggie claimed he had bought the overcoat, was still in business in Portland, Oregon.

We flew down to Portland, located the man and asked him if he remembered the occasion of the overcoat being purchased while he was contemplating whether or not he would buy it.

The proprietor remembered the occasion perfectly. He was still indignant at the manner in which Boggie had stepped into the picture. According to his understanding, Boggie was a customer. His only excuse for being in the store was to buy something that was on display or to offer to sell something. Aside from that he should keep out of any business transactions.

He remembered the man coming in with the overcoat, with the slippers in his pocket, and he didn't like his looks. The overcoat looked "hot" to him. He couldn't tell us why he felt that way, but it was simply the reaction of a man who had done business with a lot of people, many of whom were crooks. He thought this man was a crook and didn't want to do business with him. He didn't know whether he would have changed his mind if the price on the overcoat had been lowered or not. But while he was debating the matter with himself, Boggie had stepped in, offered a dollar and taken the coat.

This man had been a witness at the time of Boggie's trial and he felt that a deliberate attempt had been made to intimidate him.

For the most part the proprietor of a secondhand store can't do business unless he has the friendship of the police. It was at least intimated to this man, or he thought it was intimated to him, that it would be exceedingly unwise for him to be a witness on behalf of Boggie. However, he took the stand and told what he knew.

The prosecutor had sought to discredit this testimony by showing that two years after the date of the transaction the witness *couldn't identify the overcoat.*

Of course he couldn't.

If he had, it would have been a most suspicious circumstance.

All that this man remembered was his natural feeling of exasperation when Boggie stepped in to buy the overcoat in question.

Steeger, Schindler and I went back to Washington. We had quite a conference with Smith Troy, the attorney general.

I think Smith Troy is one of the most fair-minded attorneys general I have ever met. He puts his cards face up on the table and he calls the turns as he sees them. As a district attorney he was a remarkably able prosecutor. As an attorney general he is popular, well liked and efficient, and as attorney general he decided that if Clarence Boggie had been improperly convicted it was up to his office to take the responsibility of conducting an investigation, and this was done with vigor and absolute fairness.

When Smith Troy was ready to make a report to Governor Monrad C. Wallgren, Raymond Schindler, Harry Steeger, Tom Smith as warden of the penitentiary, and I went to call on the Governor. He invited us to his executive mansion for cocktails and later on for a supper. We spent the entire evening with him.

Ed Lehan was supposed to join us there earlier, but his plane from Spokane was delayed on account of bad weather, and he didn't arrive until later in the evening. He and Smith Troy gave the Governor the facts in the Boggie case as they understood them and stated they were willing to make a definite recommendation.

Governor Wallgren was very much impressed. He said he certainly didn't want an innocent man in prison, but he did want the report from Ed Lehan and Smith Troy to be in writing.

Ed Lehan agreed to put his report in writing, and Smith Troy agreed to take Lehan's report and supplement it with a report and recommendation from his office as attorney general of the State of Washington.

We felt that the case had been completed, and after shaking hands all around started back to our respective domiciles.

Thereafter, however, things began to drag. There were intimations that someone with considerable political influence in the State of Washington wasn't particularly enthusiastic about having Clarence Boggie pardoned.

And then came a peculiar development.

The Seattle *Times* had in its employ a very alert, able reporter named Don Magnuson. Magnuson had, at one time, talked with Clarence Boggie when he was on a trip to the prison at Walla Walla, and may even have read or glanced through the Boggie transcript.

Nothing had been done about it so far as his paper was concerned.

However, when the articles began to appear in *Argosy* publicizing a case which was, so to speak, in the back yard of the Seattle newspapers, Don Magnuson got busy and proceeded to write a series of articles which very nearly duplicated the legal analysis of the testimony in the case which we had left with the various officials in the state of Washington.

At the time we didn't pay a great deal of attention to these articles. We felt that the Governor had given us his word in the Boggie case; that the attorney general had made an investigation which indicated Boggie had been improperly convicted, and that the Governor was going to grant Boggie a pardon; that if the Seattle *Times* wanted to publish an analysis of the Boggie case based upon work that had been done by *Argosy* investigators they were quite free to do so.

But we couldn't understand the peculiar delay, and it bothered us.

When we had originally set up the Court of Last Resort it had been planned that we would take one case and present it to the readers, letting them look over our shoulders as we made the investigation, and then get their reaction. We had assumed that we could take a case and carry it through in a complete presentation to the reader and have the case closed within two or three installments.

We didn't count on the public reaction, and we didn't count upon the series of interminable delays in the Boggie case. We thought that since we had analyzed the evidence in the case, secured new evidence, made a presentation to the attorney general, secured the Governor's promise that if the attorney general's report was favorable Boggie would be released—that was all there was to it.

But the minute *Argosy* began publishing "The Court of Last Resort," letters began coming in, and as they continued coming in we found that readers wanted to know more about the developments in the Boggie case. They wanted to have us bring the case to a satisfactory conclusion one way or the other.

By this time, we began to realize only too well that a magazine of general circulation simply can't "donate" space to a cause. A magazine is in a highly competitive market. People who pay twenty-five cents for a magazine want to get twenty-five cents' worth of recreation, entertainment, amusement and interesting information. If any substantial part of the magazine is filled with something they don't like, the reading public feels that it has to that extent been deprived of its money's worth and is going to turn to some other magazine.

The letters from readers of "The Court of Last Resort" made it clear that we would either have to discontinue the feature or put it on a permanent basis. Either course presented very grave problems, particularly in view of the fact that things had come to a standstill in the Boggie case.

So I flew up to Olympia, the state capital of Washington, to find out what was happening.

At first I couldn't seem to get anywhere. Then Smith Troy, the attorney general, asked me if our group would be willing to cooperate with the Seattle *Times*. I told him, sure, we'd be glad to cooperate with anyone, but personally I didn't see why the Governor didn't go ahead and grant Boggie a pardon.

Troy told me that there had been new developments in the case which he wasn't in a position to disclose, but felt that if I talked with Henry MacLeod, the city editor, and Don Magnuson, I might receive some startling information. Smith Troy said he felt that these gentlemen would talk with me if we'd promise to co-operate.

I told Troy I'd be only too glad to talk with them, and telephoned New York to ask Steeger if he would be willing to co-operate with the Seattle *Times*. Steeger said, "Certainly," to go right ahead. We'd co-operate with any newspaper that was trying to get at the facts in any case.

So then MacLeod, Magnuson and I sat down for a talk and I learned that when the first article had appeared in print an individual had telephoned the paper and said in effect, "Why, I know all about the murder of Moritz Peterson. I know who did it. I told the Spokane police about it at the time. I didn't know that anyone had ever been convicted. I know this man Boggie never did have a thing to do with it. It was another person."

Naturally the *Times* had rushed Don Magnuson out to see this witness.

The witness had been a businessman in Spokane. A certain peculiar character, whom we will refer to as John Doe, came into the store of this witness on several occasions, and, on one occasion shortly before the murder, had in his possession a weapon which had been made by putting a round, water-worn rock in a piece of burlap, wrapping the burlap around and around, so that the various thicknesses of cloth formed a substantial handle, and stitching the burlap tightly around this handle with the end result of a perfect weapon.

As soon as this witness saw a picture of the weapon that had been used to kill Moritz Peterson he recognized it as being the same weapon which had been in the possession of John Doe a short time earlier. He had promptly notified the Spokane police.

So the police had picked up John Doe. They found that John Doe had been in the neighborhood of the Peterson cabin on the morning that the murder was committed.

But had he been at the scene of the murder *when* it was committed? There was the question.

In investigating this case the police found a witness who had seen John Doe some little distance (as I remember it, it was nearly a mile) from the scene of the murder at "*the time that the sirens went by.*"

What sirens?

The police assumed that the statement of the witness related to the time the sirens had signaled the passing of police cars on their way to answer the frantic telephone calls from Peterson's neighbors.

But had that been the time?

In the first place, the police had no way of knowing exactly what time that was. In the second place, the proceedings had certainly been beautifully mixed up. Just recall the procession of police sirens.

The police knew when the call had been received at the police station. It will be remembered, however, that the first man on the job was the speed cop on his motorcycle. He had listened to the excited story poured in his ears by the witnesses who insisted that the murderer had "gone thataway," and had vanished in the wooded lot only a few seconds before.

The officer shook his head. Chasing murderers wasn't part of his duty. He jumped on his motorcycle and tore away.

Then came the police. The police heard the story and the children eagerly escorted the police up to the place where the murderer had gone into the brush. The police, you will recall, had forgotten their guns, and they wouldn't go into the brush without them.

So back they went to the police station to get armed.

Some time along in there, and at a time on which police records are silent, an ambulance came and took Moritz Peterson to the hospital.

All in all, there must have been a whole procession of sirens going back and forth, and the fact that some witness had seen John Doe at a certain place *"when the sirens went by"* was hardly the type of evidence which could be used as an alibi. It hardly seems possible that police could have considered *"the time the sirens went by"* as being any sort of an alibi. It simply didn't prove anything.

What sirens? When?

But the police had turned John Doe loose, and, by the time the Seattle *Times* had dug up this witness, were singularly unenthusiastic about reopening the case.

This was, of course, a very interesting development. MacLeod, Magnuson and I talked it over in detail, and it was decided that the first thing to do was to try and locate John Doe.

John Doe had been an itinerant, a man who was, according to the Spokane witness, eccentric to the point of being peculiar. He had vanished and left no trail.

So I moved down to Spokane with Magnuson and an assistant reporter from the Seattle *Times*. Raymond Schindler and Shelby Williams, the manager of his New York office, flew out to Spokane.

Schindler, Williams and the two reporters started running down clues, trying to uncover some lead which would disclose the present whereabouts of John Doe.

The trail was fifteen years old and, of course, as so frequently happens in a case of that kind, ninety-nine per cent of the leads that were investigated turned out to be blind alleys.

They found that John Doe had gone to Arizona, then he had disappeared for a while. They found that he had been in prison, and to add to the long chain of coincidences found that he had actually served a term in the Washington state penitentiary at Walla Walla at the same time Boggie was there serving his life sentence.

Naturally, as a writer, the dramatic possibilities appealed to me. Suppose it should appear that the man who actually murdered Moritz Peterson had rubbed elbows in prison with the man who had been erroneously convicted of that murder. What were his feelings? What would he do? Would he hunt Boggie up and try to form a friendship with him to see how Boggie was taking it, or would he avoid him? Or would he be sufficiently callous to go about the even tenor of his ways, completely ignoring Boggie?

I decided that later on I would make an investigation of this and perhaps confront John Doe with Boggie, but in the meantime, since we were working under cover, we dared not breathe a word of any of this to Boggie or even intimate that we were trying to close in on John Doe.

Finally the investigating team struck pay dirt, and after a long and arduous investigation uncovered a clue which they felt would enable them to put their hands on John Doe within thirty days. In other words, they found where John Doe was going to be thirty days from that date and there was every assurance that he would be there.

So Schindler, Shelby and I went home. The newspapermen stayed on the job, and at the end of thirty days did uncover John Doe and had the Spokane police pick him up for questioning.

They got precisely no place.

At that time Henry MacLeod rang us up and wanted to have Leonarde Keeler come out with a polygraph to give John Doe a lie detector test.

It turned out, however, that this wasn't going to be a simple matter. From telephone descriptions of John Doe's character, Keeler felt that there was a possibility John Doe might not be a "good subject." There was also the very strong chance that by the time Keeler got out there John Doe would refuse to take a lie detector test. Nor did Keeler want to fly out on a matter of that importance and make an immediate test. He wanted to take some time to investigate the man with whom he was dealing and familiarize himself with all details of the case.

By that time *Argosy* had spent many thousands of dollars on the Boggie case, and the outlook didn't seem at all promising. The magazine feature, "The Court of Last Resort," had proven terribly expensive, and no one knew for certain whether the readers of the magazine cared a hoot if innocent men were imprisoned or freed, or whether they simply wanted an end to a "story."

The investigators were all donating their time, but the traveling and incidental expenses had been enormous. We had put in literally months of work. The long-distance and telegraph bills alone were fantastic.

So, while John Doe was being detained, *Argosy* in New York held telephone conversations with Leonarde Keeler in Chicago, and I kept the wires buzzing to Seattle.

Looking back on it, it is incredible to think that we could so have misjudged the American reading public.

Later on it appeared that readers everywhere had been following the Boggie case; that the reading public cared very much indeed whether innocent men who had been wrongfully convicted were held in prison.

At the time we weren't aware of this. We were feeling our way. The avalanche of public approval that was to dispel all our doubts was just beginning to form. We had no means of knowing what a terrific power it was to become.

In the meantime the Spokane police stated that they wanted to see whether the witness uncovered by the Seattle *Times* could make an identification of the murder weapon which, it is to be remembered, had then been in their hands for sixteen years. The witness had seen that weapon sixteen years earlier and hadn't seen it since.

The Seattle *Times* agreed to have their witness go to Spokane and make an identification of the weapon.

When the witness arrived the Spokane police tossed out a collection of weapons, all as nearly identical as they could make them, and asked the witness to pick out the one he had seen.

It seemed that the Spokane police had been busily engaged in duplicating the murder weapon.

Here again we have another incredible fact in the Boggie case. The witness sat down and carefully examined each of the weapons, and then *picked out the exact weapon which had been used to murder Moritz Peterson sixteen years earlier.*

"This is the one," he said.

And he was right.

Nor was that identification merely a matter of chance. It happened that this witness was one of those unusually keen observers, who possessed a remarkable ability to recall what he had seen. Moreover, there was one peculiarity about the murder weapon *which had escaped the notice of the Spokane police but which had clung to the memory of the witness.*

I know that it wasn't merely an afterthought or a coincidence because the witness himself had told me about this peculiarity when Don Magnuson had arranged for me to meet him, a meeting which had taken place some weeks before the interview with the police in Spokane.

Then came another development.

Ed Lehan, the deputy attorney general, whom Smith Troy had delegated to fly down to my ranch and inspect the transcript in the Boggie case, had been very much interested in subsequent developments. He had worked carefully on the case, had made a report to Smith Troy, who, in turn, had made a report to the Governor.

Digging into police records in Spokane, Lehan found that during the time John Doe had first been arrested by the Spokane police, and prior to the time he had been released because he had an alibi for the time that *"the sirens went by,"* every one of the witnesses who had seen the murderer running from the cabin of Moritz Peterson on that fateful Monday morning had positively identified John Doe as being the man they had seen.

The witness who had at the time of Boggie's trial glibly identified him as the man she had seen, had actually, nearly two years before, when the occasion was fresh in her mind, identified John Doe as being the man who had run away from that cabin and had been so positive, according to police records, that she had made the definite statement, "I'll stake my life on it."

It will be remembered that when we examined the transcript in the Boggie case there was indication that this witness had previously made an identification of another man, and that there had been a retraction of the identification when it appeared that the other man had a perfect alibi and couldn't possibly have been connected with the crime.

That man was John Doe and the alibi was merely a statement that he had been seen at a certain place some distance from the scene of the crime *"when the sirens went by."*

As Smith Troy, the attorney general, succinctly stated, "The State now has a better case against John Doe than it ever had against Clarence Boggie."

But who was going to prosecute John Doe?

Certainly not the authorities in Spokane.

Clarence Boggie had been convicted by the authorities in Spokane. It would have been a bitter pill to have to swallow, after all these years, to admit a mistake and seek to convict John Doe.

John Doe seemed to sense that if he "sat tight" he would come out all right.

He sat tight.

After a while John Doe was quietly released.

Those, generally, are the facts of the Boggie case and the murder of Moritz Peterson. There are certain other facts which I could disclose, but I don't think they would do any particular good at this time.

With the Seattle *Times* and *Argosy* Magazine hammering away at the Boggie case, Governor Wallgren finally granted Boggie a conditional pardon in December, 1948.

Don Magnuson received an award for his outstanding reporting, and the Seattle *Times* was showered with congratulations in the press. No one saw fit to mention that *Argosy* Magazine had been investigating the case for months, and even had a virtual commitment from Governor Wallgren long before the Seattle *Times* had even published a word. Bill Gilbert and some of the others who had known of our work started writing indignant letters.

However, I for one am frank to admit that political pressure might well have prevented any action from ever having been taken if it hadn't been for the work of the Seattle *Times* in uncovering the witness, who, apparently, had never read any of the articles in *Argosy*, but who did read that first article in the *Times*.

As I expressed it at one time, I think perhaps *Argosy* was ninety per cent responsible for proving that Boggie had been improperly convicted, whereas the Seattle *Times* was ninety per cent responsible for proving that a case much stronger than the case against Clarence Boggie could have been made against someone else.

Even at this late date the attorney general's office at Washington is looking for further evidence against John Doe in connection with the murder of Moritz Peterson. It has some hope that it may be forthcoming.

I know that I personally welcomed the assistance of the Seattle *Times* at the time we joined forces, and I welcome it now.

Henry MacLeod, Don Magnuson, and Magnuson's assistant, a newspaper reporter who, by the way, took a violent personal dislike to me, were first-class newspapermen. It was a revelation to see the way these men, with their knowledge of local conditions and the power of a local newspaper behind them, dug into the facts of the case. Their work in the Boggie case is one of the best illustrations I know of why we should have a free press, and why readers and advertisers should support powerful local newspapers. An advertiser who buys space in his local newspaper gets value received in terms of a dollars-and-cents return on his investment. In addition to all this he is making a tax-exempt investment in liberty and in freedom of the press. Without our local newspapers citizens would find themselves in a very sorry plight.

The truth of this is so apparent it seems a waste of time to mention it. Yet, strange as it may seem, this is an angle that many local businessmen and newspaper readers overlook.

I know that in my own case I didn't fully realize what a powerful factor a newspaper could be in safeguarding liberties until I saw the way these men from the Seattle *Times* with their knowledge of local conditions could get information that would have been unavailable to us.

From that time on we realized that whenever possible it would pay to have some local newspaper take an interest in our cases.

So far as the Court of Last Resort was concerned, the Boggie case demonstrated certain problems which, incidentally, we have never been able to solve.

In order to secure a committee the personnel of which would command confidence on the part of the public, would carry sufficient prestige to impress state officials, and at the same time be composed of men who were well established financially so that there was no need of personal publicity, it was necessary to get men who had active business interests. If a man is successful he has numerous demands on his time. If he isn't successful people aren't inclined to accept his opinion.

Dr. LeMoyne Snyder's services are in constant demand. Leonarde Keeler was tremendously busy during his lifetime, and Alex Gregory at the present time is working on a crowded schedule. Raymond Schindler has the job of co-ordinating the investigation in countless cases. He is constantly flying back and forth from New York to Los Angeles, up to San Francisco, down to Florida, and occasionally over to Europe.

Harry Steeger, in addition to the responsibilities of supervising the destinies of *Argosy* Magazine, has some three dozen magazines in his publishing string. For my part I am always metering minutes, trying to be in two places at once, and do two things at the same time.

The result was that when we would fly to Walla Walla, Olympia or Spokane, and start an investigation, the long-distance telephone would be hammering out a constant succession of calls concerning some "emergency" which had developed in our various businesses while we were away.

We could only get away a few days at a time; then we would have to go dashing back and face the discouraging prospect of a desk piled high with mail which had accumulated in our absence.

The members of the investigating committee had agreed to donate their time, the magazine had agreed to defray traveling expenses. But when, for instance, a man has to fly from New York to the Pacific Coast to work a few days on a case, then dash back to his office, expenses pile up.

When three or four such individuals get together for a conference, the bill runs into big money.

Those of us who felt that we could afford to do so stopped sending in vouchers and donated all our expenses as well as our time. But some of us simply weren't in a position to do this; contributing the time alone had been a very great sacrifice.

Such factors made the Court of Last Resort terribly costly, and made it debatable as a cold-blooded business proposition. Despite the fact that the reading public was indicating its approval it was, of course, quite clear that if the money spent on the Court of Last Resort should be used to increase promotional allotments and editorial rates, the expenditures would be far more profitable.

But, offsetting this tremendous expense was the knowledge that the work is a badly needed activity in connection with our whole scheme of justice.

Harry Steeger wanted *Argosy* to stand for something. He wanted the magazine not only to entertain, but to be a constructive force, and he overruled his editors when they pointed out how much more desirable it would be to use the money spent on the Court of Last Resort for promotional purposes.

Harry Steeger has a certain bulldog tenacity, and having started the Court of Last Resort he "stayed put."

Had we known what we now know about investigating the cases, the investigation of the Boggie case could have been greatly simplified. We learned a lot from that case.

Before finally leaving it, I think it is only fair to mention certain obvious truths which should be given careful consideration.

The police may not have forced the identification of Clarence Boggie in the manner in which a good card magician forces the man from the audience to pick out one particular card from the deck, but there can be no question that the tactics used by the police were such as to greatly influence the witnesses in making an identification.

One of the witnesses who had "identified" Boggie as "looking like" the man seen running from the scene of the murder, was asked if she could have made her identification had she been called upon to pick Boggie out of a line-up.

She admitted, at the time the question was first asked, that this would have been most difficult. Later on she said that she hadn't understood the question.

It is also evident that the jurors were out of sympathy with Clarence Boggie, and paid undue attention to his previous record of convictions. A certain amount of persuasive evidence was marshaled against Boggie, but it is difficult to understand how anyone could have felt that this evidence proved him guilty beyond all reasonable doubt.

Identification evidence, even when asserted with vehemence, should always be considered in the light of surrounding circumstances.

Some persons who are inclined to be positive and opinionated will get on a witness stand and swear with every ounce of sincerity at their command that the defendant in the case is the man they saw at such-and-such a time, at such-and-such a place.

Unfortunately the man who should be the most doubtful is, nine times out of ten, the man who is the most positive.

The fair man, whose testimony is apt to be accurate, is more likely to say, "Well, I can't be absolutely positive, but I *think* that this is the man. Of course, it's been some time ago, but I think this is the man."

Defense attorneys are inclined to pounce upon such a witness and by showing that he isn't positive and only "thinks" the defendant is the man, sneeringly subject the witness to ridicule.

In many instances, such tactics are unfair.

Jurors should not readily condone a fair witness being torn to pieces by a jeering, sarcastic defense attorney who is crucifying the witness upon the cross of his own fairness.

On the other hand, juries should not be too much impressed by the testimony of the man who, after seeing some individual for a few seconds during the excitement attending the commission of a crime, swears positively that the man seated in the courtroom is the criminal. Jurors should consider all the facts.

Carefully conducted experiments show that it is rather difficult to make a positive identification, particularly where the individual was seen casually.

I remember at one time when I was attending one of Captain Frances G. Lee's seminars on homicide investigation at the Harvard Medical School, Dr. Robert Brittain, a brilliant Scotsman, one of the shrewdest medicolegal brains in the profession (at present Lecturer in Forensic Medicine at Leeds University in England) was lecturing to a class of some fifteen state police officers, men who had been chosen for the course because of aptitude and ability.

Dr. Brittain was commenting on description and identification. Abruptly he ceased his lecture, turned to the assembled group and said, "By the way, how tall am I? Will someone speak up, please?"

Someone said, "Five foot eight."

Dr. Brittain was like an auctioneer. "Anyone here who thinks I'm taller than five foot eight?" he asked.

There was something in his voice that made it appear the estimate might have been on the short side, so someone promptly said, "Five foot eight and a half," and then someone went to five foot nine.

After a while Dr. Brittain said, "Well, who thinks I'm *shorter* than five foot eight?"

That immediately drew a customer.

Then Dr. Brittain went on to the question of his weight and his age. Before he got done he had a series of descriptions which were simply meaningless. Between the extreme estimates there was a margin of difference that represented some fifteen years in age, some twenty pounds in weight and some four inches in height, and it is to be remembered that these descriptions were furnished not by men who were excited because they were being held up, or by men who were getting a fleeting glimpse of an individual in a dim light—they were sitting there looking directly at Dr. Brittain, whose figure was only partially obscured by a table, and they were trained observers, men who made it their business to classify and describe.

But what of Clarence Boggie? What of the man himself?

Boggie, it is to be remembered, had been convicted and sent to prison in Idaho for the robbery which had been perpetrated by Convict X.

Boggie had served considerable time in Idaho, always protesting his innocence, and finally, because of various factors in the case, including an affidavit by a sheriff who had overheard conversations which made him believe Boggie might have been forced into the crime, the authorities had launched an investigation.

An investigator had actually found the place where Boggie had been repairing the lights which had short-circuited on the car of the man who had given him a ride. The attendant of that service station remembered that another car had drawn up and Boggie had been forced to get into it. Then the car had driven away.

The Governor of Idaho granted Boggie a pardon, but Boggie never had an opportunity to enjoy even five minutes of liberty under that pardon. The Washington authorities had grabbed him at the moment the pardon was delivered and had whisked him away to try him for the murder of Moritz Peterson, to convict him of that murder and to send him to prison for life.

Boggie at the time of his release found himself in a world that was all but strange to him. He had been in prison for nearly twenty years, and the outside world had made a good many strides during that time.

It was also difficult for him to make an emotional adjustment to freedom.

Moreover Boggie had received quantities of fan mail.

We had relied on publicity to get justice done in his case and the publicity had swelled into a tide which threatened to sweep Boggie off his feet.

Lawyers inspired him with the idea that he could sue the State of Washington for a huge sum of money for false imprisonment. People wrote to Boggie wishing him luck. Some of these fan letters were from women.

Boggie, who had spent some twenty years of his life entirely removed from the company and companionship of women, had placed his mother upon a pedestal and idolized her.

It was no time at all until Boggie was engaged to be married.

The power of the press had brought about Boggie's liberation, and from the moment of Boggie's release he became "good copy." Practically everything he did, every floundering mistake made in attempting to adjust himself to his newfound liberty, was publicized in the newspapers.

Then he found himself. He married a childhood sweetheart. He settled down, and finally found someone who had enough confidence in him to put him in charge of a logging crew.

Boggie's previous statements to us that he was one of the best aerial loggers in the country had been taken with a grain of salt and a barrel of pepper. His similar statements to prospective employers had apparently been dismissed as not even worthy of serious consideration.

Now Boggie had a chance to show what he could do.

That was the last unbelievable thing about the unbelievable Boggie. He was just as good as he said he was.

Boggie started breaking all records for handling logs. He tore into the work with a fervor and an efficiency that amazed everyone.

And then just when Boggie had adjusted himself to life on the outside, when he had married and established a home, when he had demonstrated his ability to handle a responsible job of putting out logs, the problem of physical adjustment proved too much for him.

Boggie had one triumphant day in which he broke all previous records for an output of logs.

His heart, which had been weakened by twenty years of confinement within walls, twenty years of routine prison diet, couldn't stand the strain that was thrown on it. Boggie came home. He told his wife that he had broken every previous existing record at the camp for moving logs.

Smiling his tired, twisted smile; Boggie went to the bathroom to wash his hands and fell over dead.

3

Probably the lowest ebb in the affairs of the Court of Last Resort occurred at about the time when Steeger was trying to decide whether he should send Leonarde Keeler to Spokane, Washington, on the more or less nebulous chance that John Doe would not only betray himself on the polygraph but could be led to the point of making a confession.

It is to be remembered that the polygraph has no standing in court. Even if Keeler's findings had been that John Doe was guilty, those findings would have been of no value in solving the Boggie case unless John Doe were to implement them with a confession. We already knew Boggie was innocent. At that stage of the case we didn't need a polygraph to give *us* the answer. What we needed was something to prove definitely that John Doe had murdered Moritz Peterson.

John Doe wasn't the type who was likely to make a confession. He'd been in and out of prison. He knew how to handle himself in an examination. As Keeler pointed out over the telephone, the chances that he would confess were mighty slim.

I think it is generally conceded that Keeler was one of the greatest polygraph experts who ever lived, but much of his reputation was founded upon his uncanny ability to understand the mind of the man he was examining, and at just the proper time to say just the right thing that would prompt the man to pour forth his soul in a confession.

Keeler didn't do this by any third-degree or by any persistent, continued pounding of questions. Neither did he do it by the type of trickery which is often utilized by police officers in getting a confession from a suspect. He did it by knowing the type of man with whom he was dealing and by having a good idea of how the crime had actually been committed. That last, of course, from reading the subject's record on the polygraph.

One interesting illustration of his work comes to mind which I think is worthy of inclusion at this point.

Some time ago, Raymond Schindler, Dr. LeMoyne Snyder and Leonarde Keeler were due to join me at my ranch shortly after lunch.

They didn't show up until the small hours. (This was before my ranch had a telephone and it was impossible to get any word through to me.)

It seemed that the three had dropped in to pay their respects to an investigator of the metropolitan police force. They sat around for a while, talking shop. Just before they were ready to start for my ranch the investigator started telling them about a case that had baffled the police there for some time.

A man, it seemed, had reported that his wife had gone back East to visit relatives. Neighbors became suspicious. The police were called in.

On the surface it was just another one of those things. A man who had murdered his wife and then announced that she had gone away to visit relatives.

But the police couldn't find the wife's body, and they couldn't trap the man into any admission. They simply couldn't get a scintilla of evidence. They asked if he would be willing to take a polygraph test. He readily agreed.

So the police gave him one, and when they had completed it, they knew no more than they did before.

The man was genial, friendly, co-operative, but all he could say was that his wife had told him she was going to visit relatives. He was terribly sorry that it was causing all this trouble. Probably she had some other man that she liked better and had-gone away with him. It was a regrettable situation all the way around but there was nothing he could do about it.

And there was nothing the police could do about it. They couldn't even establish a *corpus delicti.*

The man was released from custody.

So Dr. Snyder suggested, "If he's so co-operative, ask him if he'd object to having another polygraph test. Tell him that Keeler's out here and that it's advisable to clear the matter up."

So the police got in touch with the individual, who assented.

That test was a remarkable demonstration of Keeler's powers. Aided, of course, by the graph shown on the sensitive machine, it wasn't long until Keeler knew definitely just about all there was to know about this man's temperament and reactions.

Questions, it will be remembered, are so phrased that the subject is expected to answer them by either a straight "yes" or "no." Qualifications or explanations, if any, are to come after the test is concluded.

So, after Keeler felt he knew what had actually happened, he suddenly swung into a new line of questioning.

"Did you burn your wife's body?" he asked.

"No."

"Did you submerge your wife's body in water?"

"No."

"Did you bury your wife's body?"

"No."

It was a cold, rainy day. Wind was whipping sheeted rain against the windows of the office where the test was being conducted.

Keeler went on quietly, "Did you bury your wife's body near the house?"

"No."

"Did you bury your wife's body far away from the house?"

"No."

"Did you bury your wife's body in the basement of the house?"

"No."

"Did you bury your wife's body in a shallow grave?"

"No."

"Did you bury your wife's body in a deep grave?"

"No."

By this time the very nature of Keeler's questions indicated to the suspect that Keeler knew, as he did know, that the wife's body had been buried. The subject became somewhat apprehensive. Gradually the self-control which had enabled him to pass other polygraph tests without betraying himself began to break.

Abruptly Keeler pushed the machine away from him, looked at the man sympathetically, and said, "Your wife must be awful cold and lonely out there in that shallow grave in the flower garden. Why don't we go dig her up and get it over with?"

The subject ripped off the apparatus, jumped to his feet and said, "Come on, let's do it."

So the police, the subject, Dr. Snyder, Raymond Schindler and Leonarde Keeler went out to the flower garden.

Standing there in the cold, driving rain, the man indicated the spot they should dig. They dug down and uncovered the wife's body.

I think that is a typical illustration of the manner in which Keeler worked. A less skillful man could well have been baffled, but Keeler knew what to say, when to say it and how to say it.

At the time of the Boggie case, we who had so readily agreed to donate our time to the investigative work, had but little idea of what this was to mean. Everyone looked on us with suspicion and distrust, looking for the ax they felt we must have to grind. All of our first cases meant months of careful investigation, and after that had been completed we could usually count on some political pressure being brought to bear to see that we got precisely nowhere.

Taken by and large, prosecutors didn't like the idea of our Court of Last Resort.

And I think there was a period when everyone lost sight of the fact that the Court of Last Resort is the people, the readers of the magazine, men and women who are willing to become interested in the cause of justice and who will take up the cudgels and fight.

We had had a good many letters while the Boggie case was under investigation, but as it turned out we had no indication of the hundreds of thousands of readers who were anxiously following that case and waiting only for it to come to a conclusion to tell us how they felt.

Suddenly we were deluged by an avalanche of mail. Everywhere we heard about the work of the Court of Last Resort.

It seemed that we could no more stop our work with the completion of the Boggie case than we could turn back Niagara in the middle of the falls.

Steeger asked the group if it would be willing to keep on for a while, and signified his willingness to go the limit. His question was unanimously answered in the affirmative.

In the meantime, of course, each individual was also being deluged with letters from people who wanted our investigating committee to take up their case or the case of some loved one who had been "wrongfully" convicted.

On the face of things many of these letters represented the typical, so-called "bum beef." Some of them were challenging. Many of them were implemented with facts. But there were enough of them to keep an army of investigators busy. We could barely find time to read, classify and reply to the mail, let alone investigate the hundreds of cases that were pouring in.

However, we decided to carry on and do the best we could.

4

To the north of Palm Springs lies an elevated plateau country, interspersed with long ridges of granite mountain; the valleys between are dotted with Joshua trees, the weird-looking vegetation which is so symbolic of the southwestern desert regions.

Into the wild arid stretches of this country a few hardy people had made their way.

These were, for the most part, a dehydrated group of leather-skinned individuals, with muscles of rawhide, faded blue eyes which had been bleached by sunlight and which were accustomed to look out over the long open reaches of the desert. Frequently these steady eyes had been called upon to line up the sights along a gun barrel.

These men were self-reliant. They had to be. There were no roads worthy of mention. For the most part, in the back country, supplies were carried in on burros or pack horses. Water was scarce; hardships were plentiful. The grim desert lay waiting, wrapped in perpetual silence, ready to levy a deadly toll for any careless slip.

There was gold in the country. Several very rich mines had been developed, some likely prospects were being worked.

Here, also, were ghost towns, places which bore silent witness to the fact that Dame Fortune is a creature of coquettish vagaries. She smiles today, and frowns tomorrow.

Here are almost perpendicular granite walls, rising one, two or three hundred feet high; abrupt dikes jutting up out of the desert, stretching long granite fingers into sandy coves, reaching up into the black-blue of the desert sky. In between these dikes, or ridges, are valleys which are well covered with desert foliage—particularly the Joshua tree, growing to a height of thirty or forty feet, looking like some surrealist's idea of a cubist tree afflicted with arthritis. There are also many cacti, and the other more conventional forms of desert plant life.

This particular section of the desert is now a national monument. When I first knew it and when I first met Bill Keys it was simply one more stretch of desert, one more trackless expanse, where a man might find gold in abundance if he should be lucky, and death from thirst if he should prove to be careless or unfortunate.

Bill Keys first entered this section of desert more than forty years ago. At that time there were no roads and it was necessary to pack supplies in on horseback. Naturally, with all of the desert to choose from, Keys picked a choice location for a house.

There is a legend that at one time the rock-enclosed valley Keys picked was used by cattle rustlers as a secret watering hole where stolen horses and cattle could be kept without anyone being the wiser.

Of course, in these days of airplane reconnaissance these mysterious hidden valleys no longer have any great significance, but back a generation ago this country, with its labyrinth of valleys, bordered by towering granite ledges, was a maze of confusion.

In 1927 I owned a camp wagon, a miniature cottage mounted on a half-ton truck which had a compound transmission and oversize tires. This was before the days of "house trailers."

I always look back on those days with nostalgia. My camp wagon carried fifteen gallons of drinking water. There was also a thirty-gallon water tank placed around the muffler so that driving the automobile heated this water to boiling point. The little portable house had an icebox, a gasoline cooking stove, a full-sized bed, and a rigid desk where I could set up a typewriter and pound out stories.

I would concentrate on the practice of law until I became fed up with routine, until there was a break in the schedule of cases I had to try. Then, after working until ten or eleven o'clock at night, I'd walk across to the garage, get in the camp wagon, which I always kept fully provisioned with canned goods and staples, and start out for the desert. Around two or three o'clock in the morning I'd pull off to the side of the road, get three or four hours' sleep, and then by ten or eleven the next morning find myself far out in the desert, away from human habitation and free from all interruptions. There I could pull out my typewriter and go to work.

When I became tired of writing, I'd take a bow and arrow and wander out into the desert, shooting at jack rabbits, return to the camp wagon, cook up a simple meal, wash the few dishes, roll into bed, and promptly drop off into the deep sleep of complete oblivion. Such cares and responsibilities as I had were left far behind.

Naturally I came to know a good many of the little winding side roads in the desert. My half-ton truck, with the big tires and the compound transmission, enabled me to grind my way along some pretty atrocious roads.

Judged by the standards of present-day house trailers, living quarters were very cramped, and these modern houses on wheels have many of the conveniences that I didn't have, but all in all I was quite happy out in the desert, alone with space, stars, and silence.

It was in that way that I came to know Bill Keys. By that time a road of sorts had been put in to his place. Bill used the road and so did others. Bill also had acquired a neighbor, a man who lived some three and a half miles away.

Keys claimed this man had "jumped" one of his claims. The man claimed that Keys was a "retired outlaw." There was not the best of neighborly feeling between them.

Even as late as 1927 newcomers were not particularly welcome in that country. Visitors were looked upon with suspicion. The people who lived there had been alone for a long time and, for the most part, they wanted to be left alone.

I made the initial mistake of becoming friendly with Bill Keys' neighbor, the one he said was a claim jumper. Keys therefore was inclined to view me with suspicion bordering on hostility, but, from time to time, when I was in the desert I would go up and call on him, and gradually this hostility softened. Finally I achieved the goal of being friendly both with Bill Keys and his neighbor and being welcome up in this remote section of the desert whenever I wanted to come rolling in.

Keys has a very remarkable wife, a woman who invariably captivates those who meet her. A soft-spoken, white-haired, quiet little woman, who has learned to adapt herself to the desert, who has raised a family out where she was far removed from medical attention and supplies. She learned to cope with emergencies and combat the elements, yet she has, through it all, retained a degree of feminine charm, a soft melodious voice, and a quiet philosophy of life.

Bill Keys, on the other hand, is one of the restless, ambitious individuals who is constantly plugging away at something. He is always feverishly developing some mine he has just discovered, or is prospecting, looking for another mine. And because Bill had picked one of the choice spots in the entire desert he was able to construct a little impounding dam where he could hold rain water and so build up quite a lake.

The man always reminded me of a busy beaver, working without the aid of machinery, using, for the most part, his two hands and such mechanical devices as he could rig up with the aid of leverage and block and tackle. Watching him work I used to think, "Good heavens, the man's never going to be able to accomplish anything. Just one man plugging away with his bare hands against the whole desert. He can't even dent the desert in a lifetime of that sort of work."

But, surprisingly enough, Keys did accomplish things, lots of things. Every time I'd be away for a few months and then go back to visit him I'd hardly know the place. And that's still true today. What he has done is a very good example of what can happen if a man simply keeps everlastingly at it, doing a quota of work each day, just steadily plugging along.

Bill raised a fine family out there. Sons and daughters who were sturdy, self-reliant, well-trained children of a bygone era.

They could follow trail by the time they were six; knew all of the vagaries of the desert by the time they were ten; and from the time they were able to toddle about on their two legs, were completely self-reliant. Bill trained them that way and the environment helped.

Then came the gasoline sales tax and paved roads, machinery for putting down blacktop, improved automobiles, and, above all, the exploitation of Palm Springs.

With the discovery that during the cold of winter the desert offered perpetual sunshine, warmth and fresh air that was like a tonic, the great influx started. Hollywood moved right into Palm Springs. Real estate agents grabbed up everything within fifty miles, subdividing like mad, and citing statistics of the growth of Palm Springs to dazzle buyers into putting out money for house lots in the middle of the desert.

Then came the greatest surprise of all. These subdivisions started to grow and prosper. People bought lots and built houses on the lots. Little communities grew up. Civilization invaded the desert.

Bill Keys' place is probably not over thirty miles in an airline from Palm Springs, fifty miles by road.

By that time people had found out the marvelous beauty of the country which surrounded Bill Keys' homestead. Before one could say "government priority" the whole thing had been turned into a national monument, and Bill Keys found himself living in the midst of uniformed rangers, surrounded by red tape and regulations, watching the rising clouds of desert dust as tourists went pouring through the monument, most of them on their way to see the famous "Keys' View."

Keys' View is one of the most interesting sights the desert has to offer. The Joshua Tree National Monument lies on a plateau and the road past Keys' place runs up a long, steady incline until, at an elevation of around a mile or so above sea level, one comes to the edge of the plateau and suddenly the whole country falls away beneath, dropping abruptly down into the Imperial Valley and Salton Sea, which is *below* sea level.

All in all, it is an awe-inspiring view, and Keys used to take his friends up to show them the sight.

Gradually people heard about it and it became listed on the automobile road maps as "Keys' View." Then, with the advent of better roads, Keys' View became famous and appeared on virtually all of the desert maps.

Naturally the new Joshua Tree National Monument took in Keys' View as one of its main attractions, and, while the name was preserved (for a while), the title was very firmly vested in the United States Government and neatly lettered signs directed the increasing numbers of tourists. There were lots of tourists. Bill Keys saw the steady influx of cars, and naturally didn't take too kindly to the encroachments of civilization.

Bill had fixed up his ranch so that it was capable of supporting a few head of cattle, and since he had homesteaded and received patented title to some of the choice real estate right in the middle of the national monument, there were those who envied Keys his position, his holdings and his complete independence.

Offers were made Bill Keys and he turned them all down. His place wasn't for sale.

The offers gradually increased until Bill was offered a large price for his place. He refused to consider any offer. That was his home. It had been his home for a long time. He wanted to stay there. He wanted to be left alone.

Cattlemen had secured grazing privileges in the surrounding country, and some of them coveted Bill Keys' place. It was in a strategic location and would be ideal for their cattle to water, hole up and rest.

There began to be friction and hard feelings. Then there was a gun fight.

I don't really know the facts in connection with this shooting. I only know generally that it was an old-fashioned Western gun fight.

Bill Keys says the fellow was gunning for him and that he shot the revolver out of his hand.

Bill insists, with that quiet assurance of his, that there really was nothing to it, nothing at all. He could have shot the fellow full of holes had he been so minded; but he didn't want to hurt him. He simply didn't want the man to kill him, so he shot him in the gun arm.

In any event, the jury believed Bill Keys' story. He was tried and acquitted.

The whole thing, however, was significant as a guide to Bill Keys' character and his background. If his story is true, Bill Keys, facing a man who was armed with a six-shooter, casually shot the man in the gun arm, just as the cowboys do in the comic strips and in the movies.

If he is telling the truth and he had missed that first shot, he could have been riddled with bullets. Regardless of who might or might not have been the aggressor, once Bill Keys fired that first shot he had opened the season on himself. The other man could have killed Bill Keys as dead as a mackerel, and Bill would have been blamed. His killer would have gone free. There was time for only one shot, and Bill either chose the relatively small target of a man's gun arm, or else his bullet happened to hit that target and Bill went on to claim, "I planned it that way." It had to be one way or the other.

The point is that Bill Keys shoots when he is under pressure with the calm of an ordinary man shooting at a target. That much at least is indicative of Bill's character.

I personally have never seen him shoot, but I have heard many stories of his prowess with a gun. I have talked with people who have told me they have seen Bill Keys shoot the tail off a running ground squirrel. Not once, but on several occasions.

In any event, Bill Keys can make a shooting iron really talk. He is one of the coolest characters I have ever met, and he considers a weapon almost as much a part of his wearing apparel as his hat. Ammunition is expensive and hard to get. Bill didn't have any money to throw away. So, over the years, he developed a habit of making certain that the bullets from his gun went where he wanted them to go. That was all there was to it.

By this time it should be readily apparent that some of the sunburned tenderfeet who invaded the Joshua Tree National Monument for the purpose of inspecting Keys' View began to look on Bill Keys with open-mouthed awe and perhaps a little fear. Stories grew into legends, legends grew into wild tales.

And it is to be remembered that inevitably there were certain interests that wanted Bill Keys out of there.

So the scene was set for the arrival of Worth Bagley.

There is some little mystery about the manner in which Worth Bagley came to the desert. In the light of after-acquired knowledge there could well be a certain sinister aspect in his motivation, or it could have all been the result of fortuitous circumstances.

Worth Bagley was a former deputy sheriff who had made something of a fetish of developing skill with a six-gun. He was not only an expert shot but he was a fast shot; a man who was quick on the draw, highly proficient in the use of a six-gun, and who spent day after day at the police target range, hammering away until he was able to make records that placed him in the classification of the most expert of marksmen.

By that time Bagley had acquired certain definite tastes in guns. He had filed and honed the trigger mechanism on his favorite gun until it had a pull that was only half of standard. The action was smooth as glass and a mere touch of the finger would send a regulation police bullet crashing toward the bull's-eye.

Then a sinister and significant change began to take place in Worth Bagley. Having developed his skill he began to develop a killing complex, probably due to a brain lesion.

This wasn't found out until after the Court of Last Resort started its investigations, so that perhaps it should be reserved until later.

All that the desert dwellers knew was that Worth Bagley had become mentally ill, which incapacitated him for further service with the sheriff's office. Then, for some reason which is not entirely clear, everything seems to have been expedited so that Worth Bagley came to live on the desert as a neighbor of Bill Keys.

Keys, of course, felt that his enemies were behind this move. There is no proof either one way or the other, although it was perhaps rather a peculiar thing that this particular man should have abruptly left the ramparts of civilization and almost overnight become ensconced as a neighbor of Bill Keys. On the other hand, Bagley had to go somewhere and become a neighbor of someone. Be that as it may, Bagley didn't intend to take any nonsense from

Bill Keys. He lost no time letting Bill know that. He had been told Bill was fast with a gun, and he wanted Bill to know that he, Worth Bagley, was just as fast, or perhaps a little faster, and could shoot just as straight, or perhaps a little straighter.

Sometime after Worth Bagley came to the desert, he and his wife had domestic difficulties, and Mrs. Bagley, seeking to be divorced from her husband, filed a sworn allegation in court stating that her husband intended to kill Bill Keys, that he had carefully laid plans to enable him to do so, and unless stopped in some way would carry out those plans.

Strangely enough no one paid any particular attention to this statement.

It must be remembered that Bill Keys was distinctly *persona non grata* with the district attorney. The district attorney had prosecuted Bill over that other shooting, and the jury had decided that he had the wrong side of the case. The district attorney hadn't liked that, and naturally he hadn't liked Bill Keys. Therefore from the standpoint of the law enforcement officers Keys was a gunman who was on the wrong side of the law.

Bill began to have serious trouble with his new neighbor. He complained to the law enforcement officers that Worth Bagley was threatening to kill him and trying to start trouble.

The amused skepticism with which these statements were received indicated that the officials simply weren't taking the verdict of that jury in the earlier case as having determined the true merits of the controversy. The idea of someone persecuting Bill Keys brought smiles to the faces of the officials to whom he took his troubles. They may have been right, they could have been wrong, but that was their attitude.

That left Bill Keys pretty much on his own.

For instance, Bill had a Spanish jack which he prized very highly. It may or may not have possessed great commercial value, but Bill liked the animal. One day he found the jack dead. Looking the carcass over pretty carefully Bill found a hole which had evidently been made by a small caliber bullet. Cutting into the jack, Keys was able to recover the bullet itself. So Bill cut out the piece of hide that contained the hole, and took it and the bullet to the district attorney's office.

Bill tried to act the part of a law-abiding citizen. He complained again that Worth Bagley had threatened his life, that he was killing his stock, that he felt certain Bagley had watched for an opportunity and had killed this jack. He wanted the bullet turned over to a ballistics expert to be tested under a microscope with the landmarks in the barrel of Worth Bagley's .22 rifle. If the bullet had been fired from his gun he wanted Bagley prosecuted.

The manner in which Keys' complaint was investigated was indicative of the official attitude in the case, one which unfortunately still prevails as far as Bill Keys is concerned.

A deputy sheriff was instructed to go and make a checkup. So the sheriff went to Worth Bagley's house, told Bagley that Bill Keys had accused him of shooting the jack, and asked Bagley if he had any objection to letting the deputy sheriff take Bagley's rifle to the courthouse for testing.

"Why, not at all," Bagley said. "I'll be only too glad to cooperate."

So Bagley got up and walked back into the other room, and, according to an affidavit which was made by Mrs. Bagley sometime later, Bagley brought back not his own gun but her .22 rifle.

"Here," Bagley said, "take it. Make all the tests you want."

The wife, who swore in the affidavit that she was in fear of her life, sat there and said nothing.

The deputy sheriff made no attempt to find out whether this was or was not Bagley's rifle, or whether there was more than one .22 rifle in the house. He took the gun, went back to the county seat, made tests, and then brought the gun back to Worth Bagley saying, "Just as I thought. Another one of Keys' wild ideas. There's absolutely nothing to it." According to the story we received, *he then turned the bullet and the piece of skin that Keys had cut from the jack over to Worth Bagley!*

It is indicative of what prejudice can do. It shows how much chance Bill Keys stood of getting any relief from a law enforcement officer.

According to affidavits now in our possession it looks very much as though Bagley actually had fired the bullet from his rifle into the

Spanish jack. Bill Keys had painstakingly secured this evidence which should have been sufficient to bring the crime home to Bagley, and which might very well have resulted in having the court put Bagley on probation and thereby stopping the feud before it went any further.

But the officers tested the wrong gun, made no attempt to find out if they had the right gun, other than to take Bagley's word for it, told Bagley what they wanted and why they wanted it, and then came back, returned Bagley's gun to him, and, incredible as it may seem, gave Bagley the evidence in the case.

A man who had less iron in his disposition than Bill Keys might well have pulled up stakes and left. He might have sold out for whatever price he could get and decided that in view of the attitude of the authorities he was licked.

Instead Bill shrugged his shoulders and went about his business. If that was the way the law wanted it, that was the way it would be. He had asked the authorities to straighten out the situation. In place of putting Worth Bagley under bond, the authorities indicated they thought Bill Keys had been trying to frame something on Bagley.

So Bill went about the even tenor of his ways, but he took darned good care that he didn't walk into any ambush.

It wouldn't be an easy job to ambush Bill Keys. He has keen eyes, steady nerves, cool judgment, and he's wise in the ways of the desert.

Bill habitually used a road which crossed the Bagley property. The road had been used by Bill and his predecessors in interest for dozens of years. Under the law of California it was a private roadway, and those who had used it could continue to do so.

Bagley warned Bill to keep off the road.

Bill asked the park authorities whether it was a road or whether it wasn't. The rangers told him it was, so Bill went ahead and used it.

So on May 11, 1943, Bill crossed the Bagley property on the road, went down to a well which was operated by a gasoline pump, and prepared to start pumping water for his cattle which were in that locality.

Keys had a lot of trouble getting the motor started. He decided the magneto was too weak, so he removed the part, put it in his automobile and started to go home.

Just as he was approaching the Bagley property he saw a sign in the road and the trunk of a Joshua tree which had been rolled squarely across the rutted tracks.

Keys stopped his automobile, got out and read the sign.

This sign was rudely lettered on a piece of cardboard similar in size to that which is furnished by some laundries in returning a laundered shirt. Keys claims the sign had been written by Bagley and there was never any attempt on the part of the prosecution to show that the sign was not in Bagley's writing, or rather, printing.

The sign said:

"KEYS THIS IS MY LAST WARNING STAY OFF MY
PROPERTY."

There was a little rise just ahead of the car and Keys decided he had better reconnoiter. He walked slowly up to where he could look on the other side of this rise and, as he did so, Keys testified that he saw the trunk of another Joshua tree rolled across the road, and in the act of coming over that Joshua tree was Worth Bagley. Keys insists that Bagley was in a crouched position and had a gun in his hand. He swore that Bagley, watching the road, apparently didn't see him at this time.

Keys' rifle was back in his automobile. He testified that the engine was running and he thinks the door was open.

Keys turned, and as he did so, the crest of the hill gave him a second's respite. He ran back to the automobile and jerked the gun out. Just about the time he was getting the gun in his hand, Worth Bagley, according to Keys' testimony, appeared at the top of the rise, saw Keys standing there by the automobile and immediately raised the revolver and fired at Keys.

Keys' rifle was an automatic, and Keys swore that he fired a shot at Bagley's gun arm.

Immediately after firing that one shot at him, Keys testified, Bagley began using "tactics." Keys used this expression several times, and, when called on to clarify it, stated that Bagley was jumping and running in zigzag jumps, holding his revolver and trying to get another shot, or, as Keys said, "Jumping as though he was keeping from trying to. . . . what we call a gunman's tactics, dodging bullets." Keys further said Bagley was running sideways and still had the gun in his hand.

Perhaps at this time it would be well to quote from Keys' testimony:

"As soon as I could catch up with him with my gun, holding it like this [illustrating], without taking sight, as there was no time to sight, as soon as I caught up with him I shot again and he turned, and I shot immediately afterwards and he fell over."

Now comes the part which I think perhaps did more to alienate the sympathy of the jury than anything else.

Keys didn't go near the place where he had seen Bagley fall. He got in his car and went home. He had lunch, he changed the magneto, he returned to the well (all this time using a roundabout road so he would not have to cross Bagley's property), started the motor, and ran about five hundred gallons of water into the tank.

Bill Keys sees nothing particularly unusual about this. He knew he was going to be out of circulation for quite a while. He knew that out there in the desert country water was absolutely essential, and that if his cattle didn't have water they would die. The tank was dry so Bill Keys decided he'd pump the tank full of water before he went in and surrendered himself to the authorities.

I think the jurors felt that this was a cold, calculating attitude. If any one of the jurors had been in a gun battle he would have been shaking and sweating. He'd have dashed to the authorities, babbling out an all but incoherent story.

Bill Keys took the whole thing in his stride. He'd had a gun battle. The man had been trying to kill him and had made the mistake of missing that first shot. Bill had known the thing was coming for a matter of years. Bill had tried to get the law to take a hand, and the law wouldn't interest itself, so it was a question of dog eat dog—Bill Keys on the one hand and Worth Bagley on the other. The thing had finally come to a showdown and Keys had shot it out with Bagley— but that didn't keep the cattle from getting thirsty.

The following question and answer is highly significant of Keys' entire attitude:

Q. Did you know at that time that Bagley had been killed?
A. Oh, yes, I thought so. We had had a gun battle.

There you have Bill Keys' attitude in a nutshell. Trained in the rough school of the desert, Bill Keys had learned to accept danger and emergencies in a matter-of-fact way. His cattle needed water, gun battle or no gun battle. So he fixed the engine, pumped water for his cattle and then went in to Twenty-nine Palms to surrender to the authorities.

The officers and posses all started streaming out into the desert, some of them getting lost; but the ones who took Bill Keys with them walked up to find the body of Worth Bagley lying on the ground. Bagley's favorite six-gun, drawn and fully cocked, was clasped by the stiff fingers of Bagley's dead hand, showing that when he was killed he had been ready for a second shot. (One shot had been fired.)

There were three wounds on the body. A wound where a bullet had creased the right arm, just burning it in passing; a wound in the left elbow and a wound in the side. It was the opinion of the doctors that in all probability the wound in the elbow and that in the side had been made by the same bullet.

The score, therefore, was (if Bill Keys was telling the truth) that he had first shot at the man's gun arm and had actually hit his target so that the bullet had seared the skin, but hadn't hit with sufficient impact to cause Bagley to drop the gun. The second shot had probably been a miss, and the third shot had gone through Bagley's elbow and into his left side.

But was Bill Keys telling the truth?

It was only natural that the officers, right from the start, assumed that Keys was not telling the truth; that Keys had in some way managed to kill Bagley from ambush, then had drawn Bagley's gun, fired one shell, cocked the revolver, put it in the dead man's hand, and then gone in to give himself up.

The officers, however, were never able to advance any explanation as to how Bill Keys could have walked up in the loose sandy soil of the desert and done all these things without leaving any tracks.

The soil showed very plainly where Bagley had been running at the time he was shot, where he had been apparently making those zigzag jumps which Bill Keys had described as "tactics." There were no other tracks anywhere near the body.

Some persons condemned Bill Keys for not going over to see whether the man had been killed or merely badly wounded and whether there was anything Keys could do for him. The point is that Keys knew exactly how the officers of the law felt toward him, and if Keys had ever gone over to that body he would have been convicted of first-degree murder. The officers would then have claimed that he had ambushed Bagley, had faked the evidence, fired Bagley's gun, fitted the weapon into Bagley's hand, and reported a purely synthetic gun battle to the authorities.

Even as it was, and without any tracks, the officers advanced this contention, and apparently the jury took it seriously; at least some members did.

Subsequent investigation showed that near the door of Bill Keys' automobile was a peculiar metallic streak. Scrapings were made of this metal. It was analyzed under a spectroscope and showed that this was indeed the path of a bullet which had been fired from Worth Bagley's gun and had glanced off Keys' machine, leaving a tiny streak of metal where it had struck.

It happened that the bullets found in Bagley's gun were of an unusual composition. So the spectroscopic analysis proved beyond any question that the metallic smudge on Bill Keys' car had been made by that one bullet fired from Bagley's gun. It apparently had missed Keys' head by not more than an inch.

That was the case.

The prosecution strove desperately to show that Keys had ambushed Worth Bagley and then had fixed up the evidence, managing in some mysterious way, because of his great knowledge of woodcraft and his skill in tracking, to confuse the issues so that the tracks all seemed to substantiate Bill Keys' story.

Short of complete magic no one was ever able to indicate how this could possibly have been done.

However, an expert for the prosecution testified that while he had never seen the body on the ground he had seen the bloodstains, and from the size and shape of the bloodstains on surrounding vegetation he had come to the conclusion that Worth Bagley had been shot, not while he was running, but while he was lying in a prone position on the ground.

That, of course, was a deadly blow at Keys' theory of the case.

Neither the expert nor anyone else ever advanced any theory as to what inducements Bill Keys made to Worth Bagley to get him to go out in the middle of the desert and lie down so that he could be shot while he was in a recumbent position.

The jury, however, didn't bring in a verdict of first-degree murder. They brought in a verdict of manslaughter. Obviously this was a compromise verdict. If Bill Keys had ambushed Bagley, he was guilty of first-degree murder. If there had been a gun fight as Bill had described, he had acted in self-defense.

It is to be noted in passing that apparently everyone failed to appreciate the significance of the "last warning" sign. If Bill had chosen that time to ambush Worth Bagley, he must not only have managed to catch Bagley off guard, but must have somehow persuaded Bagley to write a "last warning" just before the ambush. This would have not only taken unusual woodcraft, but hypnotic powers of persuasion.

Out in that section of Western country the words "last warning" have a certain deadly significance. If Worth Bagley backed up this "last warning" with a bullet, he must have done exactly what Bill Keys said he did. If he wrote out a "last warning" and then failed to back it up with a bullet, he showed an appalling ignorance of Western etiquette.

Be that as it may, Bill Keys was convicted of manslaughter.

Now comes a peculiar chapter in the case. Bill Keys appealed, and the Appellate Court decided the lower court had erred in certain technical matters of law. Ordinarily Bill would have been entitled to a new trial.

But there is a peculiar provision in the California law. It provides that when an Appellate Court finds there has been error in the trial of a case which has been appealed to it, it cannot grant a new trial unless it shall find, after an examination of the record, *including the evidence*, that the error had resulted in a miscarriage of justice.

So the Appellate Court "examined the evidence" and came forth with the startling statement that since Worth Bagley had been shot in the back while he was running away, Bill had no right to claim self-defense, and it therefore made no difference if error had been committed by the lower court–there wasn't any miscarriage of justice.

Apparently Bagley had been doing just what Bill Keys had said he was, jumping in zigzags at the time the fatal shot was fired. But by no wildest stretch of the imagination could it be said Bagley had been shot in the back. The bullet was just about as near the center of the man's side as it could be measured. One doctor thought it was just a shade back of the median line. Dr. Snyder says the photographs show the wound was in the exact middle of the side, as nearly as he could measure from the photographs.

If Bagley *had* been running away the bullet *would* have been in the back. However the point is that Bill missed a new trial because the court misunderstood the facts.

Bill Keys' wife appealed to the Court of Last Resort.

Once more we started an exhaustive investigation. There were twelve volumes of bound, typewritten testimony in the case which had to be carefully read through and digested. Then we had to go out and study the scene of the shooting.

In the Boggie case there had been no opportunity to call Dr. LeMoyne Snyder's technical knowledge into the case.

In the Keys case it was different.

There were photographs of the body. There were maps and diagrams, and there was the actual scene of the shooting carefully identified on the maps and illustrated with a series of photographs.

There was, moreover, a record of the testimony of the expert witness for the prosecution who had carefully preserved certain bits of dry sagebrush and desert weeds on which he had found "pear-shaped" blood spots, which, in his opinion, showed that the decedent had been lying on the ground and the blood had "spurted" in such a way as to cause the peculiar pear-shaped drops. (An unfailing indication of blood that is in motion when it strikes an object.)

To us it seemed far more logical to presume that Bill Keys was telling the simple truth and that the pear-shaped bloodstains had been due to the fact that Worth Bagley had been running in zigzags at top speed when the fatal bullet had crashed into his body. Bagley's body had therefore pitched forward on its face in such a manner that the drops of blood showed the pear-shaped characteristics of motion.

The expert, however, had stuck by his guns at the time of trial and had insisted that the evidence, in his opinion showed that Bagley had been shot while lying on the ground.

No one asked him to approximate a hypothesis which would account for what had happened after that. He had simply thrown in this testimony and then let it go. The jury had done the rest.

So we started publicizing the facts in the Keys case.

Vernon Kilpatrick, an assemblyman from the Los Angeles district, chairman of a legislative committee on jails, became interested in the case. He joined with us in our investigation.

Through his efforts we were able to get certain factual information which otherwise would have been exceedingly difficult to secure. We learned, for instance, that Bagley had consulted a psychiatrist because of his sudden killing complexes. Bagley, it seemed, had a dog to which he was very much attached. Yet one day when one of his strange fits possessed him he had killed the dog—for no apparent reason.

Dr. Snyder felt certain the facts indicated a definite brain lesion, but, of course, no one knew about all this at the time of the shooting, or at the time of the trial. It wasn't until Vernon Kilpatrick found the records that we knew of it.

Assemblyman Kilpatrick and Montivel A. Burke, his associate on the interim committee, put in untold hours of their time simply because they were satisfied there had been a miscarriage of justice in the Keys case.

Dr. LeMoyne Snyder came out and quietly started digging into the records, getting the things that would have significance only to a medicolegal expert, studying particularly the findings in connection with the post-mortem examination.

Then Dr. Snyder, studying the autopsy record, discovered a startling fact. The fatal bullet had severed the abdominal aorta. Dr.

Snyder pointed out that when this happened the man's blood pressure immediately reduced itself to zero. There could have been no more "spurting" of blood from such a wound than there could have been a stream of water thrown out by a fire hydrant after the water main had been cut.

If the blood couldn't have spurted, the testimony of the police expert as to the reason the blood stains were pear-shaped must have been in error, hence his conclusions as to ambush must have been fallacious.

Armed with this information, plus some interesting facts we had been able to discover from an analysis of the record, and the information which Vernon Kilpatrick had uncovered about Bagley's past history, we asked the California Adult Authority for a hearing.

The Adult Authority in California is similar to the Board of Sentences and Parole in other states.

The California Adult Authority is loaded, in fact one might say overloaded, with responsibilities. Their work covers all cases in the state of California where the offender is an adult. They have to determine when men may be paroled; determine the length of prison sentence; keep an eye on the institutional record of each man who is confined in the various state prisons so that they will know when that man is ready for transfer, parole, pardon or discharge; and as a governor's advisory board, pass on applications for pardon.

Clearly if the Adult Authority broke into their program to hear detailed applications on the part of individual prisoners, they would never have any opportunity to do their work. As it is, cases are thrown at them so rapidly that they can only devote a few minutes to the consideration of each case—a consideration which is, of course, preceded by a study of the facts in the matter and the reports of the various investigators.

However, the Adult Authority very courteously consented to make an exception in our case, and set aside a day for a complete investigation, permitting me to meet with them in the morning, and Vernon Kilpatrick in the afternoon.

I went to the meeting armed with facts and figures and didn't waste time with argument, but presented factual matters in rapid-fire order. I don't think there is any question that at the close of the first half-hour the board was fully convinced that Bill Keys had been wrongfully convicted.

However, a peculiar situation developed.

For certain technical reasons in regard to time, etc., and for reasons of expediency, the only relief that we felt it would be politic to ask for at the moment was in the nature of parole. The board members had made a pretty careful study of Bill Keys' institutional record and decided that Bill didn't have any particular business being in prison, and were quite willing to grant him parole simply as a matter of routine. Bill, however, scornfully rejected any suggestion that he would be paroled. That, he claimed, would be tantamount to acknowledging that he had been guilty of something in the first place. He'd stick there in San Quentin and serve his sentence out and be damned.

However, I was able to convince Bill that if the board would be willing to parole him because they had come to the conclusion that he was innocent, that would be another matter.

So I marshaled facts in front of the Adult Authority, and that afternoon Vernon Kilpatrick hit them with more facts. The result was that they offered Bill an immediate parole, and while they didn't say in so many words that it was because they had decided he had been wrongfully convicted, the background was such that Keys was willing to accept it on this basis.

So Bill Keys came home to his ranch in the desert after five years in prison.

There was something pathetic about that homecoming.

He is around seventy years old. Working there in the desert in a barehanded struggle against existence, he and his wife had gradually acquired their holdings of real estate, and built up a herd of cattle.

After Bill Keys' arrest, and in order to raise funds for an attorney, Bill had been forced to sell all of his cattle for what he could get for them, raising several thousand dollars which paid for his attorney but left Keys with nothing but the real property and a little house.

Now, at the age of seventy, Bill Keys had to begin all over again out there in the California desert. It was not an inviting prospect.

Raymond Schindler, however, had by this time been able to interest some of his friends in the problem of rehabilitation, and limited funds were available to help various people. Keys had an opportunity to do a little construction work if he had some capital, and Schindler was in a position to furnish that capital from his rehabilitation fund.

I was out to see Bill Keys a few months ago. I found this wiry fellow, dehydrated by the hot desert sun until his muscles were tough as rawhide, engaged in building a dam to impound flood waters which fall fitfully in the desert region, many times in the form of cloudbursts and flash floods.

Bill was pushing and prying away at big rocks with a crowbar and a block and tackle, working away at a pace that would have been too much for many a younger man, working all alone, asking no odds of anybody; slowly starting once more the long, uphill fight of improving his property, protecting his water supply, making a living for his family and hoping to save enough money to get once more into the cattle business.

And he was cheerful. He was too busy to be angry or bitter. He was filled with ambition, with plans for the future; and while he recognized the handicaps he hadn't the slightest doubt in his mind but what he'd surmount them all.

Of late there has been too much thought about "security." The only security Bill Keys has is his two hands. That's all he wants. Bill isn't accustomed to having people do things for him. He wants to do things for himself. And Bill is bubbling over with ambition and enthusiasm. His eyes sparkle when he speaks about how much water he is going to have available when the dam is completed and filled. He's just recently discovered a couple of new mines, or, rather, prospects that he thinks are going to develop into something, and eventually he's going to get back into the cattle business again.

In the meantime, Bill has to chop all the wood that lasts his family through the winter—and finding suitable wood in the desert is something of a problem. He has to do the chores, make a living, pay taxes, and set aside what little he can, building up another nest egg.

It's refreshing to meet with self-reliance like that. It's refreshing to meet with a man seventy years old who is vigorously planning for the future with all of the zest and enthusiasm of a newlywed.

Visiting with him evokes a picture of our early pioneers and the training that shaped their character. These men were self-reliant because they had to be. There was no one to whom they could appeal. They were engaged in a fight against their environment, carving success out of the conflict.

Those who couldn't beat their environment were subdued by it. Those who could developed a feeling of sturdy independence that became an integral part of the national character.

Bill Keys isn't fooling himself. He knows that he's seventy years old. He knows that his time is limited. That's why he's working so hard. He's fighting against the calendar. He's going to make it. There isn't the faintest question about that in his own mind. He simply doesn't contemplate the possibility of failure.

The only thing that worries Bill, the thing about which he is just a little bitter, is that the Park Service changed the name of the historic "Keys' View" to "Salton View."

He was there first. He discovered that part of the desert before the city people knew it existed. He placed his name on Keys' View and the cartographers placed that name on all of the maps. Now the Government has arbitrarily taken that away from him and called it "Salton View."

Bill doesn't like it.

But it isn't cramping his style any. He's going right ahead, as busy as a sparrow in a tree, hopping around getting things done. You can say what you like about Bill Keys, and, largely because of the official attitude, there are two schools of thought about him, but there's one thing everyone has to admit, and that is, that now Bill Keys is back there's a *man* on the place.

5

By this time cases were beginning to pour in thick and fast. The Court of Last Resort was getting a great deal of national attention.

I have said that the intention of the magazine was to get a group of professional men who had no need for *individual* publicity. From this it is not to be inferred that the *work* we were doing did not need publicity, did not get it, or that we did not seek it.

In fact, the entire idea back of this Court of Last Resort was that no public official, from governors on down, could be completely immune to the force of public opinion, and the only power that the magazine had was to arouse an intelligent public opinion and marshal it into a force that would get action. That in itself was the Court of Last Resort.

There is, of course, theoretically, a remedy for a person who has been improperly convicted; but, if he is penniless, once he has become buried in an institution that remedy is largely theoretical.

Who is going to take the trouble to determine whether he was improperly convicted?

Certainly not the governor.

Governors these days are busy state executives. They have a thousand and one problems that are taking up every minute of their time. They can't be bothered trying to determine whether some penniless unfortunate confined in prison was wrongfully convicted.

So those matters are largely delegated to various advisory boards. In some states the parole board automatically passes upon applications for pardon and makes a "recommendation" to the governor. In other states the same officials who constitute the Board of Sentence and Parole convene under another name as an advisory board and advise the governor in matters of pardon.

Human nature being what it is, there is an unfortunate tendency on the part of many such boards to feel that a prisoner who makes an application for pardon to the governor is trying to "go over their heads."

This feeling is by no means universal, but it is by no means non-existent. Quite frequently some member of a parole board, who is also on the governor's advisory board, will adopt the attitude, "If we thought this man was innocent we'd have released him long ago. If we thought he wouldn't be a menace to society we'd have put him out on parole. He's applied for parole and been turned down. Now he's trying to get a pardon. He's trying to go over our heads."

Under such circumstances there is a tendency to slap the man down and put him "back where he belongs."

But even where there isn't this tendency, boards of parole are overworked organizations. They don't have the time to reopen a case and listen to the evidence, and they don't have the inclination. They feel, perhaps with cause, that once they opened the door to re-adjudicate the facts they would be swamped with applications.

It must be remembered that a man who is in prison serving a sentence which has already been fixed has everything to gain and nothing to lose by trying any expedient which may cut short the term of his confinement. That's understandable.

Virtually every parole board is overworked. Prisons are bulging until they are parting at the seams. The construction costs of high security units are constantly increasing. It's economically impossible to build new prisons fast enough to keep up with the influx of new criminals.

Let's consider an average case, a man convicted by a jury after a five-day trial. The transcript of testimony consists of seven hundred pages. Who's going to read that transcript? Members of a parole board?

Don't be silly.

Even if someone did read that transcript and felt there had been an error, what is going to be done about it?

So, generally, boards of parole wash their hands of the responsibility by saying, "A man is presumed innocent until he is proven guilty. Once he has been proven guilty, he's presumed guilty until he proves himself innocent."

How is a man going to prove himself innocent?

Sometimes fortuitous circumstances intervene. Perhaps someone else confesses to the crime. Perhaps a man, who was the key witness against the defendant, finds himself dying and confesses that he committed perjury in order to send such-and-such an individual to the penitentiary. Such things *do* happen.

Then what?

In many cases the prosecutor will ignore the confession. To admit its validity would be to acknowledge that he had convicted the wrong man.

Of course, he rationalizes his position by claiming that it "would undermine public confidence in the processes of justice," and he really feels the confession is spurious. It pays him to feel that way. It's very easy for some prosecutors to convince themselves.

Of course, they're not all that way. Some of them are, some of them aren't. As will presently be seen, many prosecutors want real justice, no matter what it may do to their record of convictions.

But when one has a confession corroborated with a wealth of detail which can be verified (as we have had in a recent case), when the man who was convicted of the crime is shown to be innocent, and that innocence is corroborated by a wealth of detail, it is exasperating to encounter a prosecutor who is still sincere in his belief that he convicted the right man and that the confession is spurious.

So, for the average, penniless individual who has been wrongfully convicted, once the iron doors have clanged shut, he's lost hope of legal redress. He's in prison serving a sentence, and that's that.

There is a widespread popular belief that a convicted defendant can appeal to a higher court. This is perhaps the most fallacious of all the numerous erroneous popular beliefs about law.

A convicted defendant can appeal to a higher court asking it to review *questions of law*. However, with very few technical exceptions there can be no review of a *question of fact*.

Once a trial judge or a jury has determined, on conflicting evidence, a question of fact, that determination is final. It is binding upon the appellate courts. If there has been an error of law the defendant has a remedy by appeal. If there has been an erroneous finding of fact the defendant has no remedy. He is forever bound by the finding of the trial judge or of the jury.

Now it should be obvious that trial judges and juries aren't that good. They're right most of the time. They're probably right ninety per cent of the time—let's call it ninety-five per cent—but you can't allow them a much greater average than that.

Two men take the stand and tell stories that are diametrically opposed. One of them is perjuring himself. Perjury is a crime, but judges don't pay too much attention to it. It's too common. It takes place in almost every lawsuit. Of course, if corroborating facts enable perjury to be detected that may be different. On the whole, prosecutions in cases of perjury are far less than one-tenth of one per cent.

The judge or the jury tries to tell who is lying. Sometimes the honest man gets the decision. Sometimes a graceful, artistic liar gets the nod. A judge isn't infallible.

So our Court of Last Resort offered something new, an opportunity for the public to take a real interest in the cases of men who had been wrongfully convicted. The public is seldom interested in law, but it is always interested in justice.

Our reports to the readers of the magazine were by this time attracting widespread attention. Readers took a very real interest in what we were doing. Of course, the average magazine is read by more than one individual, even if it is purchased by a bachelor who has no family—the magazine is given away to some charitable organization or is passed on to a friend. Magazines aren't burnt up. They have quite a reading life, and, of course, where a magazine is purchased by someone who has a family, every member of the family will at least glance through the magazine.

So *Argosy's* increasing reader following began to make itself manifest in a good many ways.

Members of the Court of Last Resort's investigating committee were invited to appear on television, to address gatherings of people who were interested in the administration of justice. Bar associations became interested in what we were doing, so did clubs and literary gatherings. In fact, from all over the country there came a steady stream of invitations asking us to appear and explain the work we were doing.

The work itself was keeping us busy, and added to that was the necessity of making a living and keeping up with our own business commitments, so there wasn't a great deal of time for speaking. The various members had to cull the invitations carefully, accepting only those where it was felt the most good could be done. But there was such a sizable number of those invitations, and enough appearances on radio and television and before clubs to add materially to the large audience that was eagerly following everything we did.

That, of course, meant more and more applications for aid.

It was about this time that our attention was directed to the case of the Brite brothers.

Coke Brite and John Brite were serving a life sentence in Folsom penitentiary in California. There seemed to be absolutely no chance that they would ever receive any form of leniency. They had been convicted of the unpardonable crime of killing two peace officers who had been sent to arrest them, and killing one of the complaining witnesses in the bargain.

There had, however, been so much adverse public sentiment in the isolated mountain county where the killing had taken place that some of the state newspapers had wondered whether the Brites had received a fair trial. One of these newspapers, the Sacramento *Bee,* retained a young attorney, Arthur DeBeau Carr, to make an investigation. Carr had reached the conclusion that the Brite brothers were probably innocent, that they had undoubtedly acted in self-defense, and had been amply justified in doing what they had done.

However, his intervention was at first without avail. The Brite brothers, who had been convicted of first-degree murder, had been sentenced to death.

Actually they spent more than two years in Death Row waiting to be taken out and hanged by the neck until they were dead. (This was before the California law was changed, making the gas chamber the end of the "last mile.")

In the meantime, however, there was continuing agitation on the part of those who felt the men had not been guilty of murder. The investigation of the Sacramento *Bee* bore fruit, and finally the case virtually became a campaign issue during one of the gubernatorial campaigns.

Culbert L. Olson stated publicly that if elected he would commute the sentence of the Brite brothers to life imprisonment, and, I understand, gave semiofficial assurances that he would then make a further investigation to determine whether or not the Brites should receive an outright pardon.

Olson was elected and promptly commuted the sentence to life imprisonment. Nothing else was done, however.

There were those in Siskiyou County, California, the place where the killing had taken place, who were so bitter against the Brite brothers that it was freely predicted they would be lynched if the irate citizenry could ever get hold of them.

Siskiyou County is a rugged mountain terrain, peopled with men who are, for the most part, thoroughly familiar with the outdoors. Pick almost any man at random in Siskiyou County and the chances are that he could qualify himself as a fairly expert tracker. He'd probably know more or less about mining. Give him a .30-30, turn him loose in the hills, and he'd be back before sundown with a nice buck deer.

A short time previous to the Brite case, there had been another shooting in the county. Two men were hunted on the charge of killing officers in the discharge of their duties. One suspect was apprehended. He may well have been guilty. No one took the time to find out. The citizens got a rope and strung him up. That had established a precedent.

John Brite and his younger brother, Coke, had been cow-punchers in Arizona. They had drifted into Oregon and then down into Siskiyou County. They loved the out-of-doors. They didn't care much about working for wages. They loved to prospect and "live on the country." They had previously been "in trouble" in Arizona, and had served a year in the Arizona State Prison. The charge involved the theft of some blankets from a store. The Brite brothers stated it was due to a general misunderstanding, that they had understood they had been given permission to get the blankets. I have never investigated this original case. It is quite probable that had the facts been as they stated, a judge would have given them probation, or a jury would have acquitted them. Since this was not done they may well have been guilty of theft. The fact remains that they served a term in the Arizona State Prison and were thereafter classified as "felons."

Feeling the stigma which had been placed upon them, they decided to get out by themselves and make a living by prospecting.

This was during the depression when jobs were scarce as hen's teeth, and money was even more scarce. The Brite brothers, however, were ingenious, self-reliant men who speedily developed an uncanny sense of woodcraft, and learned so many tricks about hunting gold that they were able to find the precious metal in country which had been pretty thoroughly combed over by other prospectors.

In fact the Brite brothers supported themselves and their parents by going out in the hills, carrying only what they could pack on their backs, and returning with enough gold dust to buy provisions.

These provisions they left with their "old folks."

B. F. Decker had a ranch on Horse Creek, at the foot of the mountain trail which led up to the little homestead which the Brites had rented for their parents. He told me that almost as regularly as clockwork during the depression, when other people were having difficulty eating, the Brite boys would come in with a pack horse loaded with provisions, move on up the hill, and stock the larder of their parents.

Then the Brites would be off into the hills again, taking nothing with them, completely confident of their ability to support themselves from the country itself, grubbing out enough gold to enable them to come back with more provisions.

They did, of course, take some of the necessary stock provisions with them. A little flour, salt, coffee, tea and sugar. However, for the most part, they lived on the country.

Such a life, coupled with an economic depression when people who are willing and anxious to work are milling around in circles, wondering where their next meal is coming from, tends to make a man a little bitter toward "civilization." He wants to get out into the open where he can be by himself, and he becomes impatient of all forms of control.

A short distance below B. F. Decker lived a man by the name of Baker, apparently illiterate, who had many of the prejudices which go with leading an isolated existence in the mountains.

Baker had been using a small mountain homestead at little or no cost to himself because the owner was unable to secure a tenant. When the Brites moved down from Oregon they inquired about the possibility of getting the homestead for their parents. Their inquiries naturally led them to Baker, who immediately told them that he was leasing the homestead and intended to keep it leased.

However, the Brites learned that Baker had been unable to reach an agreement with the owner, so they got in touch with the owner, agreed upon a rental, and moved their father and mother into the little mountain cabin.

That started a feud with Baker, which Baker harbored to his dying day.

The Brites insisted that they tried to be "good neighbors," and there is some evidence to support them in this. However, it was inevitable that friction would develop. Baker testified that one of the Brites used profane language in the presence of his wife, so Baker got a club and clubbed him to his knees. The Brites state that Baker's assault was unprovoked, that no resistance was offered, that Coke Brite, who had been felled by the club, arose and said, "Baker, you are an older man and I don't fight old men," and had turned and walked off the property. This was corroborated by the one disinterested witness who saw the affair.

However the Brites may have felt about fighting older men, they were perfectly willing to take on younger men at the drop of a hat.

As they subsequently described these fights to me, they were "just Saturday night fights where you wouldn't use anything except your fists, and Monday morning you'd meet and shake hands and have no hard feelings."

Baker had a friend by the name of Seaborn, an officer either in the Merchant Marine or in the Navy, who visited Baker occasionally during deer season for the purpose of hunting deer. Baker naturally looked up to this individual and always tried to show him a good time.

On August 29, 1936, the Brite brothers were planning on another trip into the hills. They had driven up to the end of the road and were camping on Decker's property. They had a .30-30 carbine model rifle, and a .32 automatic pistol. They also had an improvised sleeping bag consisting of a light blanket and a tarp which had been folded over so they could have protection from the ground below and from any dew which might fall from above. It was a warm night and the brothers were men of few wants and simple tastes. An air mattress would have meant nothing to them. They simply threw the sleeping bag down on the ground, kicked off their shoes, crawled in and went to sleep. They wore blue shirts and overalls, and the idea of taking off more than shoes in order to go to bed would have impressed them as being effeminate.

They had, however, celebrated their return to civilization by getting a jug and a quart bottle of wine. Having made their simple camp, they drank enough wine to feel good, then rolled into bed and went to sleep.

In order to understand what happened it is well to have a picture of the country. B. F. Decker owned a place on Horse Creek. The road ran up along the stream and ended at Decker's place on the north.

A quarter of a mile downstream Baker had his place, and a branch of the road led to his ranch.

To the west was a steep mountain up which led a trail until, after about a mile, the ground leveled off at the Brites' mountain ranch.

On the night in question the Brites had rolled into their sleeping bag early. It was dusk, but not dark.

Baker and Seaborn came walking into the Brites' camp. There is considerable question as to what caused them to do this. Baker says he was looking for a horse and that Seaborn accompanied him just for the walk. On the other hand, there were those who claimed that Baker had deliberately manipulated an excuse so that he could get Seaborn into the Brites' camp, feeling that there would be trouble, and that Seaborn, because of his influence and position, would see that the Brites were adequately punished.

The Brites said they were awakened from sleep by hearing some stranger ask who was camping there, and hearing Baker say, "Those are the two sons of bitches I was telling you about, the fellows who live up on the hill."

Baker swore that he never said any such thing.

There seems to be no dispute that the Brites jumped up out of bed, pulled on their shoes, told the two to get the hell out of their camp and get out fast. A fight ensued. Just who struck whom, and what with, depends on which version of the story you want to believe.

Anyway, Baker admits he was looking for a club, but claimed that one of the Brites found a club first and hit him over the head.

Baker, accompanied by Seaborn, promptly went down to the office of the justice of the peace, and one of them swore to a complaint charging the Brites with assault with a deadly weapon. Baker insisted that the warrant be served immediately.

Yreka, the county seat, was some distance away, and it was difficult for the justice of the peace to get officers who could come up and serve the warrant. The justice of the peace thought it should be put off until a later date, but Baker was insistent that the warrant be served immediately. Baker claimed he was afraid. There is, of course, some possibility that he was trying to subject the Brites to a maximum amount of inconvenience. There is also the possibility that he actually was afraid.

The Brites, in the meantime, thought nothing of the fracas. It was just one more incident in their adventurous lives, and they promptly crawled back into bed. This time they didn't bother to remove their shoes—something which caused a lot of comment later on.

Shortly after midnight a couple of officers, Martin Lange and Joseph Clark, arrived at the office of the justice of the peace, a few miles from where the Brites were camping. The officers heard the story of Baker and Seaborn, were given the warrant, and forthwith set out to make the arrest.

There is no logical explanation for the things that happened next.

Why the officers should have taken both complaining witnesses with them has never been satisfactorily explained. These men were veteran officers. They knew the country. They knew where the Brites were camped. All they had to do was to drive their automobile up to the Brites' camp, hold the headlights on the bed, say, "Get up, boys. You're under arrest," and take them back to the justice of the peace.

What they did staggers the imagination. There must have been some factor in the situation which was never disclosed, some factor which caused the officers to depart from the logical pattern of procedure.

It is to be remembered that these men were old hands at the business. Martin Lange was a constable and Joseph Clark was a veteran deputy sheriff. Someone certainly must have told them something that caused them to decide the logical method of approach wouldn't work in this case.

It appears that the officers drove up the Horse Creek road to Baker's ranch in their automobile. Baker and Seaborn led the way in Baker's automobile. Arrived at the ranch, the officers waited while Baker and Seaborn went in and put the car away, and then waited for Baker and Seaborn, the hostile prosecuting witnesses, to accompany them up to where the Brites were camped. It is hard to conceive any recipe more certain to concoct trouble.

Baker admits that he told the officers the Brite brothers were killers, and that Seaborn also said so, and that the officers should take no chances.

At this date no one will ever know whether Seaborn and Baker armed themselves.

Baker said that Seaborn changed from a light shirt to a dark shirt. That statement is, in itself, quite significant. Baker stated that Seaborn had a few spots of blood on his light shirt and he didn't want to wear that up to the camp.

This sudden concern over his personal appearance is exceedingly interesting because he had had no compunctions about going down to the justice of the peace wearing the shirt that had blood on it, and it is significant that, as Baker described it, he changed from a light shirt to a dark shirt.

In any event, a terrific battle took place at the Brites' camp.

The first two witnesses who came on the scene after the shots had died away testified that Seaborn had a gun on him.

Did Baker have a weapon?

Baker swore that no such thought ever entered his head. He swore that he didn't even think of getting a gun. But, at another time, Baker, also under oath, stated that he had asked the officers for permission to arm himself.

There can't be any question about these two contradictory statements because they were both taken down in shorthand by an official court reporter.

Before the grand jury, Baker told the officers that he wanted to go in and get a rifle so he could go up there armed, and the officers told him that he didn't need any arms, that they were the law. Yet when Baker had previously told his story at the time of the coroner's inquest, he swore that he didn't ask permission to go in the house and get a gun, and that the thought had never even entered his mind.

In any event, instead of driving their official car up to the Brite brothers' bed and advising the men they were under arrest, the two officers, accompanied by Baker and Seaborn, proceeded to pussyfoot cautiously up the road until they had reached the very edge of the bed where the Brites were sleeping.

The Brites state that the first they knew was when they heard Baker's voice, right by the head of the bed, saying, "There they are. Pour it to those sons of bitches," and the next thing they knew assailants were swarming all over the bed, clubbing them on the head.

Baker swears that the two officers said, "Wake up, boys. We're the law. You're under arrest," or words to that effect, and then jumped upon the bed, jerked the blankets back far enough to uncover the heads of the sleeping men, and began to club the two Brites with their blackjacks.

Years afterward, Baker, in talking with Arthur DeBeau Carr, did admit, according to Carr, that he said, in effect, "There they are. Pour it to those sons of bitches."

However, what happened afterward cannot be explained in the light of reason.

When Baker first told his story to the district attorney, he claimed that the officers had announced that they were officers, that the Brites were under arrest, and then immediately had jumped on the bed and begun to hit them with blackjacks. Later on, when he retold his story, he insisted that before the officers started clubbing, the Brites had said, in effect, "No goddam officers are going to arrest us."

By the time Baker told his story in front of the trial jury, he had gone further and stated that one of the Brites was on his hands and knees, sort of clawing for something in the bed. (The intimation, of course, being that he was looking for a weapon.)

The details of Baker's story varied just about every time he told it. Each time he would make some excuse for having overlooked some significant fact in his previous version.

Regardless of what version of the affair is taken, it is definite that the two officers did jump on the sleeping bag, did club the Brites over the head with their blackjacks, that the Brites did eventually manage to get up, that the night was thereupon rent by a fusillade of gunfire, and when it was over the two officers and Seaborn were dead or dying, and Baker had run frantically up to Decker's house for help.

Decker, who lived a little over a hundred yards from the scene of the shooting, had heard the fusillade of gunfire and had gone to the window. He saw Baker running up out of the moonlight, wildly excited and swearing that the Brites were trying to kill him.

Decker, who knew the Brites, dressed and walked down to the Brites' camp. He was completely unarmed. He said, "This is Decker, boys. I'm coming into camp," and walked on in. He found John Brite, dazed and holding a .30-30 rifle with a broken stock. Coke Brite seemed to be a little clearer in his mind. Decker thought John was going to shoot him. John seemed to have no idea who Decker was, and both the Brite boys insisted to Decker that Baker had returned with a gang and was trying to kill them.

Decker went back, got his automobile started, and, with a neighbor, drove in to the office of the justice of the peace to tell what had happened.

The Brites started up the trail toward their house. An examination of the tracks made at a later hour showed that John was completely dazed. He had wandered around off the road, and had it not been for Coke's guidance would have had no idea where he was going.

When Decker arrived at the office of the justice of the peace the alarm was passed by telephone, and the sheriff and several deputies immediately started out for the scene of the killing. They arrived shortly before daylight, perhaps three hours after the shooting.

They found Seaborn had been struck with one bullet, apparently a high-caliber bullet such as might have been fired from a .30-30 rifle. Clark had been struck by one bullet which had also been fired from a rifle, and the course of it was most peculiar. It had shattered his spine so that the man had died instantly and without moving a muscle.

It was difficult to account for the position of Clark's body. He seemed to have been down on his knees when he was shot; his coat had been pulled up over his head; his revolver, fully loaded, was in his shoulder holster, and a blackjack, or sap (a club made of leather filled with lead shot), had been in his right hand when he died.

There was no bullet hole in his coat. The bullet had entered at the base of the spine and had ranged *upward* and across to come out by the right shoulder.

Martin Lange had been shot three times. There were two bullet holes in the forehead which followed an absolutely identical course. The two holes could have been covered by a fifty-cent piece, and the points of exit could have been covered by a silver dollar. He also had a wound in his leg which apparently had been made by a high-velocity bullet.

Baker stated that after he started running away up the stream, toward Decker's ranch, one of the Brites had said, "There's one son

THE COURT OF LAST RESORT

of a bitch getting away. Get him," and immediately a bullet had been fired that hit the "walk-log" which was used as a ford across Horse Creek, and Baker had seen the bark fly and the white wood underneath gleam in the moonlight as he jumped frantically into the stream and splashed his way across to Decker's house.

It may be noted in passing that there are two or three things wrong with that story. In the first place, if Baker had done that he would have had to cross over in the creek which was more than knee-deep and then climb a bank and a five-strand barbed wire fence, which, in his excitement, would have been almost certain to have torn his clothes. In fact, it would have been quite a job to climb over that fence in daylight. The second thing is that Decker insists Baker's clothes were entirely dry when he entered the house, and that although he looked afterward there was no puddle of water where Baker had been standing, or any sign of muddy footprints. The third thing is that no matter how hard they searched, and they did search hard, they couldn't find any place where a bullet had struck the walk-log and had knocked away the bark and exposed the white wood. They couldn't find where any bullet had struck it.

Now comes an interesting sidelight on the entire affair. The Brite brothers, clubbed almost to the point of insensibility, on foot and unarmed, had certainly no more than a three-hour start on the posse which was organized, in fact their margin was perhaps far less than three hours.

The sheriff started out as soon as it was light enough to see, taking up the tracks of the Brite brothers.

There are witnesses who claim that the sheriff gave very terse instructions to his men. "Shoot on sight and shoot to kill."

Decker stated that when he heard these instructions he backed out of the posse and refused to go ahead unless those instructions were changed.

The sheriff swore that he never said any such thing.

The justice of the peace, who was standing nearby, swore that he did.

Later on the sheriff is reported to have said to the district attorney, "These men will never be taken alive, and if they are taken alive they'll never reach Yreka, and if they do reach Yreka the mob will lynch them."

That quotation of the sheriff is taken from a letter written by the district attorney.

The sheriff had enlisted all possible aid and searchers kept pouring into the area.

Siskiyou County runs north to the Oregon line. The sheriff telephoned brother officers in Oregon, told them what had happened, and had them organize posses and start south so they could head off the Brites. These posses had Indian trackers who were searching every inch of ground, particularly along the ridges, hoping to pick up the trail of the Brites.

The sheriff and his posse were moving up from the south. The aid of an airplane was secured in the search, and bloodhounds were put on the Brite brothers' trail.

There followed a man hunt almost without parallel in the history of northern California.

The Brite brothers eluded this man hunt. They lived undetected in the hills. It took woodcraft of an exceptionally high order to enable them to escape detection.

They did more than that, as will presently be seen.

The district attorney, James Davis, was, in the meantime, collecting data in the case, and he didn't like what he was discovering.

The statement that Baker had given him a very short time after the shooting convinced him that even if everything contained in Baker's story was true, the Brite brothers had done exactly what he would have done under similar circumstances. Also he was far from convinced that everything in Baker's statement was true. He was, moreover, concerned with the highly inflamed public sentiment and the talk of lynching.

District Attorney Davis tried to give a word of warning to the sheriff, and it was then that the sheriff had made the statement above-quoted to the effect that the Brites would never be taken alive.

The district attorney went back to his office and started thinking things over, and continued to think things over for more than two weeks. Finally he went to the parents of the Brites and said, "I know that the boys are afraid to give themselves up because they feel they will be lynched. Now, if it would be at all possible for the boys to be at the end of the road at noon on a certain date, I will be there with a car. I will take the Brite brothers into custody myself, and I will take them out of the county to a place where they will have safekeeping, and they will not be lynched. They will have a trial."

The officers, of course, were keeping a very close watch on the Brites' house to make sure that the brothers didn't receive any help from their parents, so the chances of the Brites' parents getting word through to the boys appeared to be rather slim, but that was the only way the district attorney could think of to get his message to them.

At the time appointed, in the heat of midday, District Attorney Davis and one friend, Dr. Harris, a man who had confidence in him, and who believed in justice, drove up to the end of the road (the point of departure for all the searchers and the place to which they returned for more provisions, reinforcements, etc.).

The district attorney parked his car. Two men stepped out of the brush. "Are you the district attorney?" one of them asked.

"Yes."

"I'm John Brite. This is Coke."

The district attorney flung open the door of the car. "Get in," he said.

The two men jumped in.

"Get down on the floor," the district attorney said, and threw a blanket over them.

Davis then ran around the car, jumped in behind the steering wheel, started the motor, and took off for Folsom prison, near Sacramento, just as fast as he could make the car travel. Davis and Harris delivered the two prisoners late that night.

It was a triumph for law enforcement. It also marked the end of a feat of woodcraft which has seldom been equaled.

The Brite brothers had picked up the message from the district attorney. They had then been living in the hills for eighteen days, avoiding every posse that was searching for them, avoiding the bloodhounds, the airplanes, the Indian trackers, and meanwhile managing to exist.

After getting the district attorney's message they had back-tracked, coolly threading their way through the sheriff's posses (and it is to be remembered that these posses were not composed of mere amateurs, but of the best woodsmen and trackers the sheriff could impress into service), and, in broad daylight, these two men, with their lives in their hands, had stepped out of the brush at the end of the road, which was the outfitting point for all of the posses, and surrendered themselves to the district attorney and to Dr. Harris.

District Attorney Davis felt that he had taken the risks involved in the course of duty. As will presently be seen, he was a courageous public official who was willing to sacrifice his political career if necessary in order to do his duty as he saw it.

Dr. Harris was one of those men who represent the sterling backbone of any community. He went along as a citizen to give Davis moral support, and to see that there was a square deal.

Such was the state of public sentiment that if Davis's car had been stopped anywhere in Siskiyou County, the Brites would almost certainly have been lynched, and Davis and Dr. Harris, if spared the same fate, would have been roughly treated.

But, from the picture I get of these men, I think the only way a mob could have secured the Brites would have been over the dead bodies of these two citizens who had determined there would be a trial in court for the Brite brothers.

Davis is dead; and Dr. Harris, who was still practicing dentistry in Yreka when we started our investigation, recently passed away.

It is to be imagined how the sheriff felt when he learned that the Brite brothers were safely ensconced in the state prison at Folsom. The sheriff felt that these men had killed two peace officers, that they had made a monkey out of him by eluding his posses for eighteen days, and then, to add insult to injury, had calmly walked right through his cordon of searchers and surrendered themselves to the district attorney.

The position of the district attorney was then made plain.

He refused to prosecute. He said that the Brites, even if they had done everything that Baker said they had done, had acted in justifiable self-defense.

That statement was, of course, the district attorney's political death knell. Feeling was running high in Siskiyou County.

Moreover, District Attorney Davis felt that a previous lynching which had taken place in the county was a blot on its fair name and a violation of law. He felt that something should be done about it.

This was an unpopular attitude.

On September 5, 1936, there was an editorial in the Yreka *Journal* stating in part:

> How long is this comedy in the district attorney's office to go on? With the talk of lynching in the air does the district attorney think he is helping anybody's actions? After statements in the lynching case of Clive Johnson, his attempts to bring to justice those responsible, what end can he gain by placing gasoline on an already roaring fire of public indignation?

Yet when the Brites finally came to trial and asked for a change of venue on the ground of adverse public sentiment, there were a host of people who filed affidavits stating that there was no reason on earth why the Brite brothers couldn't have a fair trial right there in Siskiyou County. There had, of course, been some high feeling, but that had "died down now," and people only wanted to be fair. They wanted to let the law take its course.

The district attorney refused to prosecute. The grand jury filed an indictment, and a special prosecutor was appointed to prosecute the Brites on the ground that the district attorney had disqualified himself.

The assistant prosecutor, a man by the name of Correia, seems to have been anxious to discharge his duty as prosecutor, but nevertheless must have had some information to the effect that Baker had actually said what the Brites had claimed he said.

On December 31, 1937, after the Brites had been convicted of first-degree murder, Joseph Correia told the governor's investigating committee in part:

> I do not think they are personally to blame, for it may be society is to blame. We had a similar type here some time

ago, when he got drunk. They never had the roughness taken out of them. Of course, when they got into a scrape, they went the whole way, and saw that nothing was left. They are just naturally vicious. *As soon as they heard Baker's voice they just went after everybody that was around.* [Italics ours.]

District Attorney Davis made a statement which was given to the local press for publication. It is a statement which challenges attention. I think every prosecutor should read it and reread it, and then he should have it framed and hung over his office desk.

James Davis said:

It is the duty of a district attorney to be guided by his analysis of the truth or falsity of evidence as he finds it. His business is to seek out the truth, subject always to human error, and be guided by that truth as he sees it wherever it may point. As the attorney for the people, the constitutional rights of citizens must be regarded by him with care and discretion. He must view the situation in the light of substantial justice and whoever might be killed, whatever might be the roar of the mob, if a district attorney cannot withstand the onslaught of apparent injustice, although he may stand alone in his convictions, that district attorney is not worthy of his job. He takes the oath of office to uphold the constitution of this country, of this state, and all laws made pursuant thereto, and any other stand places him in a position of betrayal of his trust.

The district attorney stated that the first story Baker had told him, and on an occasion when he had examined Baker in great detail, showed that the Brites had acted in justifiable self-defense, but that by the time Baker had told his story to the grand jury he had changed certain facts and had added new factors so as to bring in the element of first-degree murder.

District Attorney Davis stopped there, however. He adopted the position that because Baker had told him his story while he was an attorney representing the State of California, he (the district attorney) couldn't give testimony as to what Baker had said.

As Davis subsequently stated in a published statement:

> The defense could not call me, however many subpoenaes they might have had, because facts learned by a district attorney in the performance of his duty are not admissible over the objection of the state, although practically all of the time of the trial I was present in my office and could have been called at any time by either party.

However, there were certain facts in the case which indicate there must have been either a suppression of evidence by someone, or that the investigative work of the sheriff left much to be desired. The physical facts simply didn't support the contention of the prosecution—not as those facts appeared in evidence.

It was the contention of the prosecution that all of the bullets had been fired from the Brite brothers' .30-30 rifle, including the two bullets which had gone through Martin Lange's head, and which they contended were fired in the perpetration of cold-blooded murder, while Officer Lange lay flat on his back on the ground, his legs shot out from under him.

Certain things are wrong with this contention.

In the first place, if one soft-nosed .30-30 bullet had hit a man in the bony part of the forehead, there wouldn't have been much left of the top of his head. In the second place, the idea that two such bullets could have followed a similar, identical, parallel course through a man's head, without ripping out all of the bony structure in the back of his head, is absurd.

Furthermore, if the bullets had been fired from a .30-30 rifle while Martin Lange was lying on his back on the ground by someone who was standing over him, the muzzle blast of the rifle at that close range would have left unmistakable evidence.

And, of course, no matter with what weapon he had been shot, if he had been shot as the prosecution contended while he was lying flat on his back on the ground, the bullets which had gone through his head would have been embedded in the ground directly under where the man had been lying, and not very deep at that.

Why weren't those bullets recovered?

It was a question that bothered us when we started investigating the case.

After we had been working on the case for some months we found that apparently the prosecution had hired a gold miner to go in there and carefully pan the soil so as to recover those bullets.

They hadn't recovered them.

Why?

Because they weren't there.

A good gold miner with a gold pan can recover a piece of lead the size of a pinhead from a cubic yard of soil. Here were two lead bullets which were supposed to have been embedded in the ground, and despite all of the gold-panning the bullets weren't discovered. There can be only one answer as to why they weren't discovered.

It is unfortunate that the trial court wasn't advised of this fact. Apparently the defense had no inkling of what had been done. Here was a vital fact in the case which was known to the prosecution. The information evidently never reached the court, the jury, or the counsel for the defense. Yet it was a fact which could well have been determinative.

The Brite brothers state that they can remember being aroused from their sleep. They can remember hearing Baker's voice telling some undisclosed assailant to "Pour it to those sons of bitches," and then men jumped on the bed and started beating them. They were clubbed into a state of insensibility, and when they began to recover consciousness they found themselves standing alone in camp with the bodies around them.

Is that story true?

In the case of John Brite it probably is true. In the case of Coke Brite it may or may not be true. There was considerable evidence that the men had used the .30-30 rifle as a club, and in so doing had not only broken the stock but had apparently left distinctive wounds on the face of at least one of the dead men.

The account of this clubbing shocked the Supreme Court when it was called upon to review the case, but I think the court failed to consider its significance.

Why would the men have used the gun as a club if they had deliberately used it as a murder weapon?

There is only one reason for so doing, and that would have been that the gun was empty.

Was the gun empty?

If the shells had all been fired from the .30-30 rifle, and if Baker had been telling the truth, six shots must have been fired; but when the officers went over the ground, picking up cartridges, *they could only find and produce in court two cartridges which had been fired from the Brites' .30-30*—that is, two empty cartridge cases.

Moreover, when the scene of the shooting was subjected to a detailed examination by daylight, it was clear *that at least one bullet had been fired from outside of the Brite brothers' camp and directed toward the camp.*

This bullet had cut across the bole of a small tree standing near the place where the Brite brothers had made their bed, and the scar was deep enough so that it was possible to tell the direction from which the bullet had been fired.

It had been fired from the brush back of the camp, aimed directly at the Brites, missing its mark by a matter of inches.

However, the most glaring inconsistency in the entire story, as our investigators discovered when we started examining the facts in the case, was that if Baker's story had been the truth and the whole truth, the Brite brothers' could never possibly have got up out of their bed. Moreover, the idea that two men having one gun between them could shoot two veteran officers and a civilian assistant before at least one of the officers could get in a single shot, is certainly preposterous.

Of course, virtually all of these matters were unknown to us when the Brite case was, so to speak, dumped in our laps.

Arthur DeBeau Carr, of whom mention has been made earlier, felt that there had been something wrong with the Brite case. He had reached this conclusion largely on the strength of the statements made by the district attorney in connection with his refusal to prosecute the case, and because of inconsistencies in the various statements made by Baker.

Baker obviously thought nothing of interpolating new significant facts in his testimony from time to time, facts which if true would inject a new element of premeditated, deliberate murder into the case.

For instance, at the time of the trial in December, 1936, we find Baker insisting that his memory of what had happened was much better than it had been on the second of September, 1936. As he expressed it, "Well, I am settled. I am over my scare. I can remember right at the present time better than I did then."

Then again at the time of the trial Baker was asked:

Q. Is your memory better than it was as to what happened on the thirtieth of August, on the night of the inquest?
A. Yes, sir, my memory is better.
Q. When?
A. Now, than that night. I had no sleep for three days and nights.
Q. Then, if you think you did make those answers, you might have been mistaken about them?
A. Well, that is the way I look at it at that time. I won't say that I did or I didn't.

However, the point is that Arthur DeBeau Carr went to two of his clients, Lon D. Morgan and Alf M. Perry, partners and publishers of the *Sacramento Shopping News*, and those clients decided to give Carr sufficient funds to publish a little "newspaper" that would point out some of the discrepancies he had noticed, and give his conclusions.

This publication, called *The Brite Star*, was printed and widely distributed. After our other articles in *Argosy* began to attract attention, Arthur DeBeau Carr sent us a copy and asked us to investigate the Brite case. We started an investigation and finally decided to read the transcript of the evidence.

When we read that transcript, certain things caught our attention, things which hadn't been emphasized in the trial of the case.

The Brite brothers had a rather good-sized dog called "Smoky," and Decker and the Brites both state that the dog was in the Brites' camp. Decker is very positive in stating that shortly before the shooting he heard him barking, the peculiar kind of growling bark that a dog makes when it is wrestling with a wounded deer or engaged in some sort of struggle.

Now, it was very peculiar that all through his testimony Baker never mentioned this dog. In fact, he seemed to go to great lengths to insist that no dog took any part in the affray. He even went so far as to state that his little dog had followed him up and was yapping with excitement. (If that was the case the dog certainly didn't follow him up to Decker's place, and if the dog had followed him up to the Brites' camp he would have followed him the rest of the way.)

However, we were struck with one significant statement which Baker made for the first time at the time of trial. He said that Coke Brite had jumped up out of the bed, or, as he expressed it, had "riz up" and had thrown himself on Officer Lange who had gone over backward, and that in the struggle that followed Officer Lange had shouted, "Take the brute off."

What brute?

It is quite obvious that up in Siskiyou County any officer who would have referred to a human assailant by plaintively asking bystanders for help to "take the brute off" would have been an object of ridicule from then on. Officer Lange wouldn't have said that about Coke Brite or about any other living man. In fact, from all we can find out about Officer Lange, he wouldn't have needed any help in taking Coke Brite off of him. Officer Lange was a husky, broad-shouldered, two-fisted, chunky individual who knew how to take care of himself in a rough-and-tumble and was perfectly willing to do so.

Moreover, how could the Brite brothers ever have got up out of a sleeping bag with two men standing on them, holding down the covers with their weight, pounding them over the head with blackjacks, two officers who were fully armed and prepared for any eventuality which might arise?

There is only one answer. A dog *must* have entered the melee.

Now we get back to the peculiar position in which Officer Clark's body was found. Apparently at the time of the shooting he was down on his knees. His posterior was elevated so that it was higher than his head. His coat had been pulled entirely over his head. There was a blackjack in his right hand. He had made no effort to draw his gun. He had been shot while in that position, elbows on the ground.

Reconstructing what must have happened there is virtually only one answer. A dog must have grabbed hold of the back of Clark's coat and was worrying him, had got him down to his knees, and then jumped over his back still holding the coat in his teeth.

Just as the dog jumped, someone had taken a shot with a .30-30 rifle, trying to kill the dog, and the bullet had gone into Clark's posterior, killing him instantly.

Who would have tried to shoot the dog?

Not the Brites.

Baker had finally told a story which made both brothers guilty of first-degree murder. He swore that they had declared that no goddamned officers were going to arrest them; that one of them had started clawing around in the bed as though in search of weapons; that the officers had jumped them and tried to "quiet" them by "tapping" them and telling them to be quiet.

When Baker had first told his story to the district attorney he had been a little more emphatic about what had happened. At that time he had said the officer had "beefed him [Coke] between the eyes." However, at the time of the trial he stated that Coke had "riz up" and "rode" Martin Lange right over the front of the car, that Seaborn threw Coke back and over on his back, or side, toward the head of the bed. Coke didn't fall "plumb down." He was in a stooped position; that he then grabbed the gun from under the bed and Baker had time to yell three times, "Look out, boys, he has got a gun."

Just as Baker yelled that the second, or perhaps the third time, the gun fired, and just as the gun fired, John "riz" and grabbed hold of it.

This very conveniently makes both brothers guilty of first-degree murder, but it introduces an element that is difficult to believe. What

were the officers doing all the time Baker was yelling twice, or perhaps three times (he had time enough to yell three times), "Look
out, he has a gun"?

According to the testimony in the case, neither Lange nor Clark
had fired a single bullet. Clark's gun was still in its holster; Lange's
was found lying on the ground near Seaborn's body.

Other witnesses stated that Seaborn had a gun, but the sheriff
denied this.

Seaborn's own gun was subsequently found, according to his
son, in Seaborn's baggage in his car.

What did actually happen?

Empty cartridge cases on the ground showed that the Brites'
gun had been fired only twice. The officers made careful search
and found two exploded shells, two empty cartridge cases that
had been fired from the Brites' gun. They never found more than
these two empty shells—if they did they didn't bring them into
court.

Who fired the rest of the shots? At whom were they fired?

How could anyone account for the position of Officer Clark's
body?

James M. Allen, who had been appointed as the special prosecutor, is now a superior judge in Siskiyou County. After *Argosy* started
publicizing the case, James Allen sought to explain the peculiar
position in which Clark's body was found by stating that at the time
he was shot Clark had been praying.

Actually in order to account for the position of the body Judge
Allen virtually had to concede either that a dog had entered the
affray and that someone, in shooting at the dog, had killed Officer
Clark by mistake, or he had to adopt some other theory that would
account for the unusual position of the body. It was lying a little distance away from where the Brites had been sleeping, and from the
course taken by the bullet it was apparent that the man's rump must
have been elevated, that he was on his knees and his elbows were
down on the ground.

What would put him in that position?

Praying?

It certainly is unusual for an officer, in the midst of making an arrest, in the course of clubbing a man over the head with a black-jack, to desist suddenly, withdraw a short distance, get down on his knees, put his elbows on the ground, pull his coattail over his head, stick his posterior up in the face of the man whom he had been try-ing to arrest, and at that peculiar time, and in that peculiar position, ask for divine guidance.

If we do not believe Baker's story about seeing the bullet knock bark off the walk-log, then we must place ourselves in a position of distrust-ing every part of Baker's story, because Baker could hardly have been mistaken about that graphic description of the flying bark and white wood underneath. He was either telling the truth, he was lying, or he was so confused all of his testimony is unreliable and of no value.

But even if Baker was mixed up on his logs, and was mixed up on nothing else, it then becomes apparent that at the very least seven shots were fired—one shot which killed Clark, one shot which killed Seaborn, one shot which went into Lange's leg, two shots which went into his head, one shot which was fired at Baker, and one shot which was fired by someone shooting at the Brites with a high-powered rifle such as a .30-30.

The Brites' .30-30 rifle was a repeater. It held six shots.

Anyone who knows anything about firearms knows that the two shots in Lange's head couldn't have been fired from a .30-30 rifle.

It is to be remembered that the Brite brothers also had a .32 cali-ber automatic.

Could the bullet holes in Lange's head have been made by the automatic?

An automatic has one distinctive feature. It immediately ejects an empty cartridge case as soon as the gun is discharged.

If those two shells had been fired from the Brites' .32 automatic, the officers would have found two empty cartridge cases of such dis-tinctive lines that there could be no mistaking the caliber and type of gun from which they were discharged.

The officers did not find any such cartridge cases.

At the coroner's inquest Baker stated that Seaborn grabbed Coke and threw him off of Officer Lange; that Coke grabbed his gun and

"*Martin Lange was on the ground, as I ran by Martin going up the Creek, Martin had gotten up; he was getting up on his hands and knees, and I pretty come running into him, and I hollered he has got his gun, watch him, boys, and about that time I heard a shot.*"

The implication of this is plain. Baker started to run as soon as he saw one of the Brites reach for a gun. He was already going up the creek as fast as he could go, and Martin Lange was on his hands and knees, and that was the time that Baker shouted, "Look out, boys, he has got a gun."

If that is true, Baker doesn't know who fired any of the shots, and his testimony, in which he stated that he saw Coke Brite pick up the gun and fire it and then hand it to John Brite so John could also fire it and make himself eligible for a place on the gallows, is unworthy of belief because Baker had his back turned and was running away as fast as his legs could carry him before *any* shot was fired.

At another time, however, in describing the shooting, Baker testified that when he started around the automobile, the last he saw of Officer Clark was when Clark was standing on the bed, over John, who was lying there twitching and twisting (evidently at this point John had been clubbed nearly into insensibility and Clark was standing over him); that he didn't see Officer Clark any more until the next morning when he went up there with the sheriff and saw him dead.

Baker had previously sworn that when the first shot was fired he could see both John and Coke, but that he couldn't see either Lange or Clark; that he had not started running until the first shot had been fired by Coke and the rifle had been given to John.

Then comes another and a startling contradiction. The witness states that "Mr. Lange was between this little ditch here and the car; down about this point, when I *walked* around to where he was standing *at the time the first shot was fired.*" [Italics ours.]

Note the peculiar connotations of this statement. The witness was walking, and at the time the first shot was fired he walked around to where Martin Lange was *standing*. Clark had apparently clubbed John into insensibility.

So here we have a peculiar set of contradictory facts.

Baker had also testified that when Coke "riz up" he grabbed the billy club with which he was being beaten, and jerked it clean in two.

This testimony was given after the officers had found a billy club broken in two.

It is also to be borne in mind that all of this action took place at night. While it was full moonlight in the open it was dark under the trees where the boys were camping. Yet Baker testified at various times to everything that took place with a wealth of minute detail.

There is no reason to discuss all of these contradictions other than to point out that the only story that was ever told of the shooting obviously left out one determining factor.

That factor probably is the dog. Or, to put it another way, the story that is told simply doesn't permit any logical explanation of how the Brite brothers could have got up out of bed, grabbed a gun and shot three men, at least two of whom were armed. It doesn't even give any explanation of how the Brite brothers could have got up out of bed at all.

Baker never varied from his statement that the Brite brothers had been lying there with blankets up over their heads, and that the officers had jumped on the bed and jerked the blankets back from the heads of the sleeping men.

The officers began clubbing the men. When Baker first told his story the clubbing was virtually unprovoked. When he told it the second time he said that the boys had said no goddamned officers were going to arrest them, and when he finally told it at the time of trial he had one of the Brites clawing around in the bed as though searching for some weapon.

But at all times the blankets were over the Brites' heads when the officers jumped on the bed.

In that case the officers were standing on the blankets. How were two men going to get up out of bed with two husky officers standing on the sleeping bag? It simply isn't done.

Moreover, Baker's picture of what happened is hardly respectful to the memory of two experienced veteran officers who knew how to take care of themselves.

It is obvious that if one considers all of this testimony at its face value, there is something lacking. There is no satisfactory explanation of the facts. One can't account for the position of Officer Clark's body. One can't account for the fact that two men using one rifle, changing possession back and forth, could kill three men, at least two of whom were armed, without either one of the armed men having time to fire a shot, particularly after Baker had had time to yell three times, and before any shot was fired, "Look out, boys, he has got a gun."

And, above all, one can't account for seven shots having been fired from a gun which holds six shots, yet leaving only two empty cartridge cases on the ground.

Add to that the fact that a gold miner panned the ground for bullets where the shooting took place, and couldn't find a single bullet, and one begins to get an entirely different picture from that which was presented by the prosecution.

The court and counsel for both sides seemed to have overlooked the damning significance of that one statement made by Baker to the effect that *after* the first shot had been fired he *walked* around to where Lange was *standing*.

This statement was made by Baker under oath at the time of the trial. It was more or less of an interpolation during the heat of cross-examination when counsel were trying to establish another point in the case, and that apparently was the reason its significance was disregarded.

If that statement is true, it becomes highly important. If it isn't true, then Baker was either lying or mistaken.

The prosecution naturally wanted to recover the two bullets which, according to its theory, had been fired through Lange's head while he was lying on the ground. By having a miner wash this ground in a gold pan the prosecution proved the bullets weren't there. In other words, it disproved its own case.

Having done so, the prosecution kept silent about this one vitally important bit of evidence which was known only to it.

If the defense had known of that point it is possible that the conviction of the Brite brothers might have been reversed by the California Supreme Court.

The Brites didn't know about it.

Apparently no one connected with the defense knew about it until *Argosy*'s investigators started digging into the evidence in the case, making an independent investigation some sixteen years after the shooting had taken place.

It's an interesting case.

When the facts were called to the attention of Governor Earl Warren, and of the California Adult Authority, a careful study was made of all of the evidence.

Since the conviction of the Brite brothers, the California Supreme Court had clarified the situation in regard to "premeditation" in connection with first-degree murder, and under that new definition it became clear that the Brites could hardly have been guilty of first-degree murder even if the strongest possible interpretation was put upon all of the evidence introduced by the prosecution.

The Adult Authority decided to place the Brites on parole.

As I write this they are out of prison, striving to adjust themselves to what is almost a strange world.

These men belong in the mountains, living off the country, prospecting, hiking, panning streams in search of elusive gold "colors."

Now they are trying to accustom themselves to "civilization," to routine and the discipline of a parole board, but at least they are out of the drab walls, the barred cells, the aura of prison.

I am hoping that one of these days they can return to the primitive, half-wild existence they know so well.

Even now, after all these years, they still have nightmares—the nightmares of two years in the "death house," waiting for a rope to choke the life out of them. Such an experience leaves indelible scars.

6

U p to this time the cases that had been submitted to us for investigation involved facts which could hardly be expected to occur in the life of an average citizen. However, let us consider the case of a man whom I will refer to as Richard Roe.

I don't think this man would object to having his true name appear in this account, but he has a young daughter, and for her sake we shall describe this man as Richard Roe.

Richard Roe was a typical average citizen. A highly skilled mechanic with a good job, a man who was popular, who had scores of friends. He loved to hunt and fish, and was a strong, red-blooded outdoor type.

He was married to a fine substantial wife, had a home, a child, and an established position.

He had been married long enough for the relationship to settle down to a take-it-for-granted basis on the part of his wife, who had perhaps become a little more absorbed in her duties as housekeeper and mother than as companion to her husband.

Richard Roe happened to meet an attractive, twenty-seven-year-old divorcee. She was a young woman who laughed easily and who was physically attractive to men.

It wasn't long before Richard Roe's acquaintance with this woman ripened into an intimacy which furnished him that degree of extramarital satisfaction for which he had been unconsciously searching.

Once the relationship had ripened into terms of physical intimacy, he found that his home, his wife, whom he really loved, his hunting, his fishing, his circle of masculine friends, and his surreptitious but more or less regular visits to the young woman in the case, rounded out a happy life.

One Thursday night in midwinter he started out for a weekend hunting trip with friends. They went to a hunting club some two hundred miles from home, where Richard Roe had a most enjoyable week end. There was the masculine companionship which he so loved. There was the thrill of hunting in the crisp air. There was food, fellowship, sleep, and lots of outdoor exercise.

Returning to his home town at a late hour on Sunday night, he decided that before going home he would slip in to see his girl friend.

He parked his car, locked it, slipped quietly into her apartment as he had been doing on so many occasions during the past eighteen months—and found her lying nude on the bed, quite dead, a scarf wrapped around her neck.

The woman had evidently been dead for some time.

In stunned silence he stood over the bed. He had been very much attached to this girl, although both were simply "playing around." They liked each other, and understood their relationship.

Richard Roe had entered the apartment in happy anticipation. Now, having switched on the light, he found himself looking down at a dead body.

In the midst of staggering shock, his own predicament loomed menacingly.

He dared not announce his discovery because he couldn't account for his presence in that room at that time of night by any possible excuse which would not have cheapened his position in the community, exposed him to public ridicule, and in many instances, contempt. Moreover, it would have had a disastrous effect upon his wife and daughter.

Richard Roe switched out the light. There was only one thing to be done. He must get away from there, and get away fast, and under such circumstances that no one could ever prove he had been in that apartment.

Richard Roe tiptoed out of the place, looking furtively over his shoulder. He unlocked his car, jumped in, and drove away.

At two o'clock Monday afternoon the woman's body was discovered.

Police had very few clues to work on, but they started trying to reconstruct something of the woman's life.

A young, attractive woman cannot entertain a man in her apartment over a period of a year and a half without people noticing and commenting. The talk will be in whispers, but it will exist.

Now that the woman was dead, witnesses began to come forward with bits of gossip. Little clues began to build up. One witness contributed this, another witness contributed that. The police began to get a description of the "man in the case."

Finally they were able to get the key clue which resulted in a positive identification.

The police picked up Richard Roe for questioning.

At first he denied everything. Then, seeing that he was trapped, he admitted the affair, and then admitted his presence at the apartment at approximately eleven P.M. Sunday night. He told a straightforward, convincing story and the police released him.

But there were no other clues forthcoming. The police began to think things over, and finally Richard Roe was arrested for the crime.

The resulting trial was, of course, a tragedy so far as Richard Roe's family was concerned, and a tragedy for him.

A jury convicted him.

There was strong evidence of his innocence. He could give an iron-clad alibi from Thursday until around nine or ten o'clock on Sunday evening.

There was a great deal of circumstantial evidence to indicate that the woman in the case had been killed on Friday night.

She had a job, seemed to like it, and was a regular, steady worker. Whenever she hadn't been able to go to work she had notified her employers by telephone.

She had quit work on Friday evening and had been escorted to her apartment by two women who worked with her at the same factory. Except for the person who murdered her, she was never seen alive by anyone after that time. She did not report for work on Saturday morning, nor did she call in to say she would be absent. The clothing that she had worn to work on Friday was neatly folded on a chair by the bed.

Saturday afternoons she habitually went to visit her mother in a nearby city. It had been her plan to do so on this Saturday afternoon. She did not go, nor did she telephone her mother. The mother said this was the first time that her daughter had ever failed to visit her without telephoning to let her know that plans for the regular weekend visit had been changed.

In this case, of course, the medical evidence became a matter of prime importance.

Unfortunately the doctor who first examined the body had made a cursory examination. He had had limited experience examining the corpses of murdered persons to determine how long they had been dead, and while he gave it as his opinion that the woman had been dead only a few hours when he saw her, his testimony was such that it appeared he had done little to give his opinion any real evidentiary value. The jury, however, accepted this opinion.

The coroner's physician had viewed the body on Monday evening at about seven P.M. He guessed that death had occurred some twelve to twenty-four hours earlier, but admitted under cross-examination that the woman could have been dead for perhaps seventy-two hours.

It was the mortician who gave the best evidence in the case. The mortician testified that he had cared for several thousand bodies, but he had never seen a body as decomposed as was the case here, unless the person had been dead for at least eighty hours.

Richard Roe was convicted. The case was appealed to the State Supreme Court, and the State Supreme Court divided four to three on whether he was guilty. The majority of the court held that he was. The minority opinion was written by the chief justice of the court who set forth reasoning which, in the light of later developments, proves to have been remarkably logical.

This chief justice, in his dissenting opinion, said that Richard Roe had "found himself enmeshed in a set of circumstances which raised a *suspicion* of his guilt, but each of these circumstances is consistent with his innocence. There is no rule at law or at logic that *several* suspicious circumstances, *each one of which* is consistent with the innocence of an accused, becomes proof of guilt when they are *considered together*. Four or five times *nothing* is *still nothing*. In this case it is impossible to find a single fact cited against the accused which is not consistent with his innocence."

It is indeed unfortunate that there was no expert medicolegal examination of the physical evidence while it was still intact. There was, however, a sufficient compilation of medical facts to enable us to submit the problem to Dr. LeMoyne Snyder, who, after a careful examination, issued a statement in which he advanced a very positive and definite opinion that the victim had died on Friday night.

Similar facts were submitted to Dr. Richard Ford, acting head of the Department of Legal Medicine at Harvard University, and while Dr. Ford's opinion was not couched in the forceful language of that given by Dr. Snyder, it indicated that he had reached substantially the same conclusions. Both men deplored the fact that there had been no adequate examination of the physical facts.

However, tragedy had struck into the life of Richard Roe. His affair with the woman in the case developed, of course, into sensational news which was known to everyone. He had now become a convicted killer. His conviction had been sustained, even if by a divided court, and there was nothing for him to do but to go to prison. And so he became a felon, donning a prison uniform, and being assigned a prison number. He moved into a cell to await the long, weary passing of the years before he could once again be permitted to emerge as an individual, tainted with a felon's record, his life, his home, his career, completely destroyed.

However, Richard Roe had a vigorous, aggressive lawyer. Ordinarily our so-called Court of Last Resort does not concern itself with cases where the prisoner is represented by counsel, but we made an exception in this case because we definitely felt that no procedural rules should prevent us from doing everything we could for Richard Roe.

We co-operated with his attorney, and he co-operated with us. We made an exhaustive investigation of the facts in the case, and came up fighting mad. We went to the Board of Pardons and we went to the Governor.

In view of the dissenting opinion of three members of the Supreme Court, in view of the additional facts which had been uncovered, it should have been a simple matter to get a pardon for Richard Roe, but it turned out that it wasn't so simple.

In many instances when a prosecutor has presented a case to a jury and secured a favorable verdict, he is reluctant to consider the possibility that such a verdict could have been erroneous, or that an innocent man was prosecuted. In many instances there are other behind-the-scenes activities, political pressures brought to bear, and there is, of course, the worst handicap of all—official indifference.

It is necessary for pardoning officials to take positive action in order to have a prisoner released. Officials are always busy. Every day brings its emergencies. So long as no positive action is taken in relation to a pardon, things run along in the even tenor of their ways and the "law takes its course." There is, therefore, every incentive to political inertia, and, unfortunately, all too little incentive for definite, positive and immediate action.

And so in the case of Richard Roe, the weeks lengthened into months and dragged along in endless monotony.

However, the forces of publicity were at work, his lawyer was a fighter, and a very strong public opinion began to crystallize into demand for action.

At length, after Richard Roe had been in prison for four years, the Governor issued not a pardon but a commutation of sentence to time served. This was in the nature of a compromise, something of a sop to all parties concerned, but it resulted in the release of Richard Roe, and it automatically prevented him from claiming damages from the State for false imprisonment.

A few weeks later, Richard Roe, his wife and child, drove three thousand miles to my ranch in California to stop in for a couple of hours' visit to tell me how much they appreciated the work that had been done in the case, and then to drive all the way back, where he resumed his life in the community in which he had lived prior to his conviction.

That is one of the interesting things about Richard Roe. His steady, dogged determination to fight things out and not to hide from facts.

A man of lesser caliber would have sought to fade into oblivion. He would have tried to take an assumed name and a new life in a new community. A woman who had less sterling common sense than Richard Roe's wife would have left him.

He went right back into the life of the community. He went right back to the same highly skilled work on the same job he had held down prior to his conviction. He had made a mistake in his companionship with the murdered woman. He admitted that mistake, but he was looking the world straight in the eyes and carrying on.

That attitude is entirely in keeping with his character.

I well remember some of the things he told me during his brief visit at my ranch; things which had to do with the reaction of the public in his case, and things which show what public opinion can do when it is properly aroused.

The day Richard Roe was released from prison he went back home where his wife and child were waiting for him. The phone started to ring, people whom he had never heard of before began to call up to congratulate him and express their gratification that justice had been done. People dropped in to pay their respects. A man came to the door carrying a tape measure. He explained that he was a tailor, that he was unable to make any cash donation to help Richard Roe reestablish himself in society, but he was going to take measurements and donate a suit so that Richard Roe wouldn't have to start his new life wearing prison clothes.

Later on in the evening the phone rang incessantly. Finally Richard Roe had to sit right by the phone because the minute he'd hang up there would be another party who had been waiting for the line.

It was, he said, after two o'clock in the morning before the phone finally ceased ringing so he could go to bed.

There had, of course, been quite a bit of publicity. His picture had been published and there were not only people who knew him but people who knew what he looked like. He told me that for days afterward when he would go out people would look at him, turn around, do a "double-take," come up and ask him if he wasn't Richard Roe, then shake hands with him and wish him all the luck in the world.

That was an inspiring example of how people can and will pull together, and of the underlying charity and good will which characterizes the average citizen.

And there was something about Richard Roe that inspires confidence. He had taken a long drive to come to my ranch to thank me. He stayed for an hour and a half or two hours. My ranch is rather isolated and people who come to see me often stay overnight. Nearly always they stay for meals. It's a long way down there and a long way back. Therefore, we think nothing of having a guest at meals—sometimes one—sometimes eight or ten.

Around dinnertime I told Richard Roe that we were expecting him and his family to stay over for dinner.

He smiled and shook his head. He wouldn't think of imposing on me. He had driven three thousand miles primarily to thank me, and he was going to drive three thousand miles back. He was ready to start. He just wanted me to know how grateful he was and he wanted to give me personal assurances of his gratitude.

People like that somehow do a lot to restore a person's faith in human nature.

7

So far we had encountered cases of what might be termed accidental, wrongful convictions.

However, it was only to be expected that we would run onto a case where a man had deliberately been framed for murder. This is, of course, the favorite theme of the fictionists, and it holds public interest because it does happen in real life.

In the case in question it was necessary that there be a "fall guy," someone on whom the murder could be blamed, and the most appropriate victim who could possibly be selected to play the role of "fall guy" was one Louis Gross.

This story goes back to November 17, 1932, when the body of Mortado Abraham was discovered by the victim's son in Highland Park, Michigan. (Highland Park is contained within the city of Detroit.) The man had been shot through the forehead with a .38 caliber bullet while he was asleep.

Police proceeded upon the theory that the motive for the shooting had been that Abraham was "in the way." His attractive wife, according to the police theory, might well have been the second corner of a romantic triangle, and detective work proceeded along those lines.

The people involved were, for the most part, Syrian. The murder had taken place in a Syrian neighborhood, a tightly knit little community where it was difficult to get information, and more difficult to get it straight. There were "interpreters" in the neighborhood who were only too willing to "co-operate" with the police. Other persons didn't seem to want to cooperate at all.

Police began to uncover some evidence which they seemed to feel supported their theory, when one of the suspects suddenly "remembered" that Louis Gross had confessed to the suspect that he (Louis Gross) had killed Mortado Abraham.

Louis Gross was a Jewish peddler who made a living peddling odds and ends to the Syrian neighborhood. He was a small-time operator and his reputation was not of the best. There had been three previous convictions for larceny and attempted larceny.

The police finally arrested Louis Gross and he was charged with first-degree murder.

The case went to trial before a jury. Everything about the trial was completely mixed up. Gross admitted that one of the suspects in the case had offered him a sum of money to get Mortado Abraham out of the way, and that Gross had refused. The man whom Gross named promptly stated that this story was made up out of whole cloth, that Louis Gross had stolen two rugs which he had sold to Mortado Abraham for a down payment; that Abraham had found out the rugs were stolen and had refused to pay the balance due; that Gross had killed him in revenge.

The witnesses hurled charges and countercharges, and, of course, the fact that Louis Gross had had a previous record didn't help him any. There was only one salient fact on which everyone was in accord: that someone had shot Mortado Abraham with a .38 caliber gun while he was asleep. All other facts were contradictory and contradicted. Everyone called everyone else a liar.

The police apparently were satisfied with their case against Louis Gross, and accusations, counteraccusations, conflicting statements, weird theories and surmises were batted back and forth around the courtroom like a tennis ball during a championship match.

The weary jury tried to unscramble the situation as best it could. It handed Louis Gross a verdict of guilty of the charge of first-degree murder.

Louis Gross went to the penitentiary.

Thereafter certain persons influential in the Syrian neighborhood took quite an interest in the case of Louis Gross. So did certain police officials, to the extent, at least, of seeing that the case was closed with the conviction of Louis Gross, and that Louis Gross would remain where he was for the rest of his life.

In Michigan, at this time, it was necessary for a prisoner to raise sufficient funds to pay the court reporter for a transcript of the testimony before he could appeal his case. Louis Gross did not have any funds and he didn't have any way of raising funds. Protesting his innocence, he went to prison to serve the mandatory life sentence imposed on him by the court.

The severity of sentences varies greatly in different states, and a life sentence particularly may mean one thing in one state, something quite different in another. Michigan, having abolished capital punishment, tries to see to it that a life sentence for murder means a life sentence. As the district attorney of Wayne County (which includes the city of Detroit) expressed it, "A life sentence usually means that the defendant in question is confined until he is dead."

Years passed. Louis Gross tried to find out how much it was going to cost to get a transcript in order to try and raise money. The court reporter looked back through his notes and made a startling discovery.

The pages of shorthand notes covering the trial of Louis Gross had disappeared from his book. They had been neatly torn out. So far as the official records were concerned there was absolutely no evidence in the case of Louis Gross. There was nothing to transcribe.

Louis Gross appealed to the office of the prosecutor, a successor of the one who had presented the case against him.

The situation was unusual, and one of the deputies made an investigation, became convinced that Louis Gross had been wrongfully convicted, and so reported to the prosecutor. The prosecutor, looking into the case, found out that not only had the shorthand records of the court reporter disappeared but that the files in the police department had disappeared, that the shorthand testimony given at the preliminary hearing had disappeared, and that here again pages had been removed from the shorthand notebooks of the official reporter. It seemed obvious that persons who knew where to look and how to look, and what to look for, had completely eradicated all records except the record of conviction and the sentence. Exasperated, the prosecutor went to the locked files in his own department to see what he had on the case, and found that someone had looted those files. They, too, had disappeared.

The prosecutor vowed that he was going to do something about this. He was going to insist upon a detailed investigation. He didn't care particularly about Louis Gross but he was indignant over the manner in which the official files had been looted.

Unfortunately, the prosecutor was coming up for re-election, and a solid block of organized voters, determinedly supporting his opposition, retired him from office.

The new prosecutor who came in was uninterested in Louis Gross or the mystery of the missing files.

So Louis Gross remained in prison and more time passed. A slow, steady procession of marching months which, ripening into years, buried him alive under a blanket of time.

From time to time he protested his innocence and the fact that he had been framed.

His statements were greeted with skeptical smiles.

Louis Gross contracted prison tuberculosis and was moved to the hospital. There wasn't very much chance for him.

Then he met Rabbi Sperka.

Rabbi Sperka, an alert, quick-thinking, energetic man, began to examine the mystery of the missing records. The more he investigated the more puzzled he became, but he had no one to whom he could turn.

Then he read about the Court of Last Resort in *Argosy*. He looked up what we were doing, and he wrote to me.

On the surface it was just another routine application, but I answered his letter, and the more I corresponded with Rabbi Sperka, the more impressed I became with his sincerity and ability. So then I started writing to Louis Gross. I asked Louis Gross what assurances he could give us that, apart from the legal aspects of the case, he himself was worthy of activity on our behalf. His previous record had caused us to take a very dim view of his case.

I received in return a letter which, written in all good faith, nevertheless contained one of the most unique character references I have ever encountered. "I have been living in one cell block for fifteen years with no complaints," said Louis Gross. "That is my character reference."

Dr. LeMoyne Snyder lives in Lansing, Michigan, so the next opportunity I had to break away and go East I stopped over in Lansing to look up Dr. Snyder, and, together, we drove down to the penitentiary at Jackson to see Gross.

There wasn't much to see.

Gross, thin, emaciated, had just about given up all hope. He knew that the cards were stacked against him and there wasn't very much he could say. "I am innocent," he said.

They all say that. We asked him for facts in connection with his case, circumstances that might be of some help, something that would give us a peg on which to fasten our investigation.

There weren't any. It was the word of Louis Gross, a four-time loser convicted of murder, against seemingly reputable citizens. There wasn't any opportunity to analyze the testimony because the shorthand notes had all disappeared.

We went to call on Rabbi Sperka.

Rabbi Joshua S. Sperka of the Synagogue of B'nai David in Detroit is one of the busiest men I have ever met. Not only does he administer the affairs of his synagogue but in addition does voluntary chaplain work among the Jewish prisoners in Michigan's penitentiaries, and it is to be remembered that the state prison of southern Michigan at Jackson is the largest penitentiary in the United States, probably in the world.

We met the rabbi in the synagogue. After that preliminary conference we had several more which took place in his home.

It was my first experience with a Jewish rabbi. It was the first time I had seen a man of Jewish faith ministering to the spiritual necessities of his charges. The visits to his home made a lasting impression on me.

The phone rang almost constantly. People came to the door. It was quite easy to see that the demands on the rabbi's time were such as to more than take up every minute which he could possibly devote to his work. Yet there was no evidence of strain, no impatience, no nervousness, only a gentle tolerance.

I think it was that gentle tolerance which made such a lasting impression upon me.

The next thing which impressed me was the affectionate co-ordination of the Jewish home. When I commented on this, the rabbi assured me that his home was not exceptional, that I simply had heretofore not been privileged to see the Jewish home life behind the scenes.

Be that as it may, I have never been in a home where there was more real affection, more intelligent co-operation on the part of all concerned. The family was a functioning unit. There was no necessity for discipline as we ordinarily consider the word. The children were willing and cheerful. Permeating the whole atmosphere of the place was this attitude of gentle patience, this tolerance of the vicissitudes of life.

I remember that on one occasion, and only on one occasion, did the rabbi comment on the subject of intolerance and persecution. His comment was in answer to a direct question from me. At that time he told me, in a calm, matter-of-fact voice, about the first pogrom he had ever seen. He was a boy in school in Warsaw and word was passed through the quarter that an anti-Jewish mob was on its way, armed with clubs and stones.

He remembers the sound of slamming doors and shutters as the entire quarter closed up and bolted itself in. The separate slamming noises blended into one muffled roar so that it sounded like distant thunder.

And then the rabbi went on to describe the acts of violence which followed, acts which had been inspired simply because of a racial and religious intolerance, acts which the government not only allowed but which were encouraged by the parties in political power.

There was something so utterly incongruous in the thought of persecution of the exponents of any religious faith while I was sitting in the atmosphere of the Sperka home, listening to the rabbi recount in his gentle voice, without embellishment, without anger, and apparently without resentment, facts of physical violence inflicted against his race and creed, that I became ashamed that we could tolerate such things in a modern civilization.

I had, of course, read about all the Hitler atrocities and had been revolted. But these atrocities had been during war-time, ordered by a crazed mind, and they had not been brought directly home to me. To think that people as sweet and as thoroughly lovable as the Sperkas could be the subject of persecution simply because of their religion came as a revolting shock.

Rabbi Sperka saw my attitude and hastened to assure me there was nothing like that in this country. Of course, there was a problem, he admitted—a psychological problem. It was necessary to make the children proud of the fact that they were Jews. Not ostentatiously proud, not belligerently proud, but to give them a quiet assurance which would keep them from developing an inferiority complex when they were held up to ridicule on the part of their schoolmates.—Oh yes, there was a certain amount of that—one couldn't escape it. It was one of the facts of life which had to be taken for granted. It was a mental persecution but it wasn't particularly significant unless it warped the outlook of the children. That, of course, was the main thing to be guarded against.

Then Dr. Sperka changed the subject and we talked about other things.

I remember that on one occasion, while listening to the numerous telephone conversations, the ringing of the doorbell, the appointments which were being made, and the attempt to sandwich them in with other appointments, I asked Rabbi Sperka how he kept from becoming a nervous wreck. I told him that I worked pretty hard myself, that I was nervous, and admitted it.

He smiled and said, "If your work were that of ministering to the spiritual needs of people who are looking for strength, you would find that there was no nerve strain."

I never left Rabbi Sperka's house without having more faith in the world in general. I never left the man's presence without carrying away an abiding conviction of his absolute sincerity and of the importance of the work he was doing.

Perhaps I have mentioned our contact with Rabbi Sperka in more detail than would have been the case if it weren't for the uneasy feeling that here in this country, as elsewhere, there is a soil in which someone might try to plant the seed of religious intolerance.

We need to be on our guard lest some crazed mind in our own country might find it politically profitable to nourish seeds of prejudice. And for that reason I have tried to give a picture of Rabbi Sperka as we met him and as we came to know him.

Rabbi Sperka was convinced that there should be an investigation of the Louis Gross case. We had about decided to let Gross go because of his past record, but Rabbi Sperka patiently pointed out that a man should not be condemned because of past sins for which he had made atonement and expiation.

Louis Gross had been in prison for some fifteen years for a murder. If he hadn't committed that murder, the true facts should be brought to light.

I explained that it was almost impossible to try and find any way of opening an investigation, but the rabbi simply smiled patiently and reminded us that justice was, after all, on our side, and that in the long run right usually was triumphant. Ways would open up, he was confident of it.

In a conversation with Harry Steeger, Dr. Sperka expressed himself along the same lines, and then went on to state that despite the enthusiasm which we investigators had for the Court of Last Resort, he didn't think we fully appreciated its significance or the extent to which it was destined to grow. He wanted us to realize that what we were doing was a *most* important work—work in the cause of justice and on the side of right. He wasn't any visionary, impractical dreamer—he was a clear-headed thinker, and he knew that we were going to succeed in our work because he knew that people were hungry for just this sort of thing.

And so, somewhat against our will, Dr. Sperka imbued us with his faith that "something would happen," and we started a full-scale investigation of the case of Louis Gross, fifteen years after the case had been concluded and long after all of the records in the case had completely vanished into thin air.

We found that in June of 1943, Louis Gross had petitioned the Michigan courts for relief. We found that this strange situation was disclosed by the record:

> THE COURT: Now I understand that you have made a thorough search of the records, the stenographer's records, and you find that the stenographic notes of Mr. Harry Kenworthy, who was the official reporter at the examination of Mr. Gross, as well as the official reporter at the time of the taking of the statements in the Gross case, both in Highland Park and in the prosecutor's office, are also missing.
>
> MR. DE COURSEY: That is right, Your Honor.
>
> THE COURT: And our Mr. Robson was the official court reporter of this court.
>
> MR. DE COURSEY: That is right. The prosecutor's number of the transcribed record of the Gross examination was A-1758. That file is the only one missing from the package containing the examinations of that time, and the book of shorthand notes of Harry Kenworthy, being book No. 196, in which the shorthand notes of the Gross examination were, is also missing from the books in the basement of the County Building.
>
> THE COURT: I have had Mr. Robson's stenographic notes brought to this courtroom and I examined them myself, and all the stenographic notes that he took for that particular year, and some months prior thereto and some months subsequent thereto—all the notes that he took are there except the Gross notes, the Gross murder case notes, and they have been systematically taken out, as there has been a systematic rifling of all records in both this courthouse and the prosecutor's office and also the Justice Court in Highland Park. Not only have the notes disappeared, all statements have disappeared, and even

the circuit court file, together with its cover, has disappeared from the county clerk's office.

MR. DE COURSEY: That is the jacket containing the complaint and warrant, and information.

THE COURT: There is nothing before the court in the way of any official records at all, except the motion for new trial filed by Mr. Gross, which leads me to only one conclusion: that whoever did this knew what he was doing, and had access to the files and records in the county clerk's office as well as the basement of the County Building, had access to the records in the prosecuting attorney's office, which should be kept under lock and key, as well as here, and had access to the records, the transcripts and papers in the possession of the Highland Park police department and the Justice Court in Highland Park, and the person or persons who took them certainly knew what they were when they took them. A more systematic theft could not be perpetrated on the people of the state or upon Mr. Gross. I am not naming anybody, but I have my own opinion.

The court had, however, finally decided that there was nothing it could do and relief was denied. Louis Gross was returned to prison to serve out his life sentence, until nine years later when he told his story to Rabbi Sperka, and Sperka started working on the case.

Shortly after we began to investigate we were given a tip. We were told that a captain of the Highland Park police had been removed because of his activities in connection with an investigation of the conviction of Louis Gross. One Captain Cross it seemed had enjoyed the confidence of the Syrian settlement. The Syrians all felt that he was an honest man, and when some of the more influential Syrians had told Captain Cross that the conviction of Louis Gross was a complete frame-up, the officer had started an investigation. Because of it, we were told he had been removed from office.

That had been fourteen or fifteen years earlier.

What had happened to Captain Cross?

We tried to find out.

It was quite a search. Dr. LeMoyne Snyder took charge of this aspect of the case and finally advised me that Captain Cross had gone to Florida, had left Florida, had retired and was now living in a log cabin in the north woods of Michigan.

Finally Dr. Snyder wired me that he had an address for Captain Cross and would I go with him and find out what Cross knew about the case.

Once more I went to Lansing, picked up Dr. Snyder and we drove up into the wild north woods, following directions on a rude map which Dr. Snyder had, until, after turning off the highway and jolting along over a timber road, we finally came to a neat cabin.

Captain Cross and his wife were there. They had just returned from Florida the day before and were busily at work opening up their cabin.

Captain Cross was only too willing to talk. His story is rather a sad commentary on our administration of justice.

Captain Cross had specialized in Syrian cases. He did this not because of any particular aptitude but because he was honest and because the Syrians knew and respected him. They came to him with confidences which were extended to him and to no other member of the force.

He started finding out what he could about the Syrians. He studied their religion; he talked with them at great length about their philosophy; he formed friendships—and then Captain Cross was transferred to the state police. He was on the state police in 1932 when Mortado Abraham was murdered. He didn't return to the metropolitan police until a year or two after Louis Gross had been convicted and sent to the penitentiary.

Some of the influential Syrians who had given Captain Cross many a tip were glad to see him back. They called him into private conferences in back rooms, they whispered words to him that they were afraid to say out loud. The whole Louis Gross case was a frame-up. Louis Gross was not guilty of the murder. He had been convicted to save someone who really was guilty.

So Captain Cross started an investigation.

It could well have been that which caused all of the records in the case to vanish.

Captain Cross had been working on the case only a short time when one of the political heads of the municipal government called him into conference.

"Captain," this man said, "I understand you are working on the Louis Gross case."

Captain Cross admitted that he was.

"Lay off of it."

"I have reason to believe that Louis Gross was improperly convicted."

"You heard what I said. Lay off of that case."

"I think that Gross was framed."

"I told you to lay off of it."

"I already have some information indicating that Gross is innocent, information pointing to the real murderer."

The executive stood up signifying that the interview was over. "I told you to lay off of it," he said. "That's all you need to know."

Captain Cross looked him in the eye. "All right," he said. "I am not going to lay off of it. I think an injustice was done and I think I can clean the thing up."

Captain Cross walked out of the office. Within thirty days he was retired from the police force, very much against his will, but nevertheless he was retired.

The salary of a police officer is not particularly munificent, and if the man is honest he doesn't have an opportunity to put much aside for a rainy day. Captain Cross had a living to make. The problem of making it during the years of the depression absorbed all of his time. He would have liked to have done something more for Louis Gross but he lacked official authority on one hand, time on the other. He was fortunate enough to get a job at one of the automobile plants and the hours there were long.

Years passed. Captain Cross retired and went to Florida. Then he began to think of the north woods of Michigan and he finally acquired this cabin. He spent summers there, and winters in Florida; occupying a simple cabin in the north woods in summer, a modest house in Florida where he and his wife could live simply and unostentatiously far removed from the winter resort prices. He was living simply but happily on his retirement income.

By this time we knew, of course, there was something radically wrong with the Louis Gross case. We began to have some inkling of where to look and what to look for, but we didn't have the faintest idea of how we were going to find it.

We also began to realize that we were running up against trouble.

Dr. Snyder and I went into Highland Park to take a photograph of the house where the murder had been committed and to look the premises over. We were spotted as soon as I unlimbered the camera, and there was a certain amount of hostility manifested toward the investigation. We got out of there before things came to a head, but it was obvious that persons with considerable local influence did not want the Gross case looked into.

By this time *Argosy* had started to publish facts about the case and it was evident that the Court of Last Resort was going to do what it could to get to the bottom of things. That, of course, caused a commotion in Highland Park and in Detroit.

The Detroit *Times* published an account of our investigation, and, in order to get a local angle on the story, went to the office of the prosecutor, Gerald K. O'Brien, asked him what he knew about the case and called his attention to the work that was being done by *Argosy's* investigators.

That was when the break which had been predicted by Rabbi Sperka occurred.

In virtually every case that we have investigated we have found that the attitude of the prosecutor's office has been one of either active or passive resistance. For the most part this resistance takes place behind the scenes. It consists of little whispers which are passed out here and there at the right time and to the right persons who have the proper political power. Our investigations nearly always are conducted against this background of official coldness and indifference that at times amounts to behind-the-scenes sabotage.

The situation was different in Detroit.

Gerald K. O'Brien, the prosecutor, is, as we came to know him later, a tough, two-fisted fighter who is anxious to convict the guilty, but who is fully as anxious to see that the innocent are liberated.

When he heard what the reporter had to say, he sat up and took notice.

"If there is any chance that Louis Gross was wrongfully convicted," O'Brien said, "my office wants to find it out. If *Argosy* Magazine is conducting an investigation I will join with it and I'll do everything I can at this end. I'll start investigating right now."

Gerald K. O'Brien was as good as his word. He called in two of his ace investigators and told them to go out and see what they could uncover about the case of Louis Gross and the murder of Mortado Abraham.

Those men went down into the Syrian community. They were a couple of hard-bitten, capable men who had had plenty of police service, who had the brains necessary to elevate themselves to the rank of investigators. They knew most of the answers and all of the questions.

They went down to investigate the murder of Mortado Abraham, and they came back to get their guns. "We think we are going to need them," they reported to O'Brien.

O'Brien admitted to us that things had been rather tough. People had started pushing his investigators around until the two had abruptly decided that even when clothed with official authority the investigation of that murder was no job for an unarmed man.

Thinking this over, I realized what a formidable job it would have been for us to have gone in there without any official authority and tried to carry through a complete examination of that case.

Gerald K. O'Brien directed the investigation personally, and it wasn't long before he came to the conclusion that there was something very, very fishy about the conviction of Louis Gross.

One of the persons who was supposed to have some real knowledge of the facts was persuaded to take a lie detector test.

As Gerald O'Brien told us about it afterward, the needle went over so far and so fast the machine all but jumped out of the window. The witness promptly decided he didn't care for any more tests.

O'Brien went into conference with us, found out what we knew about the case, and became convinced that Louis Gross was innocent.

Thereupon O'Brien did something that is practically without precedent in the annals of prosecution. He himself went into the Wayne County Circuit Court, and before Judge Thomas F. Maher filed, as the public prosecutor, a motion asking that Louis Gross be granted a new trial. He advised us of his action in a letter to the publisher of *Argosy* Magazine in which he said:

DEAR SIR:

I have filed a motion for New Trial, in the Louis Gross case, before the Honorable Thomas F. Maher, of the Wayne County Circuit Court.

As Prosecuting Attorney of Wayne County, I believe it is my duty to protect the innocent as well as prosecute the guilty. This motion will be heard, in all probability, before the next issue of *Argosy* Magazine goes to print.

I wish to commend the *Argosy* Magazine, Mr. Erle Stanley Gardner, and the whole staff of the magazine for the splendid work they have done in the Gross case.

It is my earnest hope that the Circuit Court will grant the Motion that has been filed.

Sincerely yours,

s/ GERALD K. O'BRIEN
Prosecuting Attorney

The application for motion for a new trial came up. Gerald K. O'Brien made a ringing declaration of the principles of his office. He wanted to convict only the guilty. He was firmly convinced from an investigation made by his office, and from one made by the members of the Court of Last Resort and with which he was fully familiar, that Louis Gross had been wrongfully convicted. He was, therefore, asking the court to entertain a motion for a new trial. If permission were granted, he was going to ask for a new trial, and if that should be granted he was then going to move to dismiss the case against Louis Gross because he felt he was innocent and the wrong man had been arrested.

Judge Maher listened intently and nodded his head. Permission was given. The motion was filed and granted, and Gerald K. O'Brien then made his motion to dismiss, and it also was granted.

Louis Gross walked out of prison a free man. There was no necessity for any pardon. In the eyes of the law he had never been convicted of this crime. He had served sixteen years of his life but the conviction had been set aside, a new trial was granted and the case against him had been dismissed.

There was, of course, more to it than we are free to publish at this time. Gerald K. O'Brien has information in his files pointing not only to the murderer but to a very sordid series of facts which brought about the conviction of Louis Gross as a "fall guy." We think we know how it happened that the records disappeared, and there are indications that certain shares of corporate stock changed hands as the result of this case.

We can't disclose that information at the present time for obvious reasons. Louis Gross is a free man, but the murder of Mortado Abraham has never officially been solved—as yet. One of these days we may hear more of this case.

In the meantime, it is impossible to leave it without making some comments on the attitude of Gerald K. O'Brien.

One of the things which has caused us very deep concern in connection with our work on the Court of Last Resort is that we may start the pendulum swinging to the other extreme. As we develop a series of cases where innocent men have been wrongfully convicted of murder, there is always the possibility that citizens who are called upon to do jury duty will expect the prosecution to produce proof which amounts to a mathematical demonstration.

Under practical conditions this is impossible.

However, if this complete lack of co-operation, or, in some instances, this behind-the-scene whispering campaign of some prosecutors continues, it is absolutely certain that the general public is going to become highly suspicious of our entire law enforcement machinery. The results may well prove embarrassing to prosecutors all over the country.

If a few more prosecutors would be more interested in justice and less in political advancement, if a few more would take the attitude of Gerald K. O'Brien, it would be one of the greatest steps which could possibly be taken in restoring the confidence of the general public in the cause of justice on the one hand, and in the integrity of prosecutors on the other.

Too frequently there is the feeling on the part of the citizen, a feeling which unfortunately is sometimes justified, that a prosecutor is too much concerned with his "record." Too many of them want to go before the people proudly exhibiting a record which shows a high batting average of convictions.

This is an entirely erroneous' attitude. A prosecutor is a public official. He is charged with implementing the enforcement of law, and, as Gerald K. O'Brien can bear witness, there is nothing he can do which will promote public confidence that can compare with concentrating on justice first and a batting average second.

O'Brien told me that he had never anticipated the deluge of publicity that would accompany his action in the Gross case.

Papers all over the United States, and in many foreign countries, commented on it. It caused a lot of talk, and above all it gave jurors such confidence in the integrity of O'Brien that he had to be doubly careful. Knowing his attitude, jurors began to regard him not so much as a prosecutor but as a judge, an impartial arbiter in the cause of justice. If O'Brien was prosecuting a man and wanted a conviction, then the man must be guilty.

I only wish that we could have a few more prosecutors like Gerald K. O'Brien in this country. I think it would do more to help the cause of justice than any other single factor I can think of at the moment.

And I wish we had a few more men like Rabbi Joshua S. Sperka. The country needs them.

8

One of the most puzzling, complex, baffling problems that faces an investigator who is trying to check up on a murder case is to uncover what actually did happen.

Time after time the investigator is forced to rely on speculation when he knows that there *should* be some definite proof which would furnish a measure of guidance.

Take the Vance Hardy case, for instance.

On May 3, 1924, Louis Lambert was running a soft drink business in Detroit, Michigan. This was during the days of prohibition, and prohibition was not popular, particularly in Detroit. There seems to be reason to believe Lambert's soft drink business was a front for a "speak-easy."

This was the heyday of the organized gang. At that time Detroit's ten-man homicide squad was hopelessly overworked. Homicides were running at the rate of one a day. It was a physical impossibility for the police force to keep up with such a deluge of crime. Murders were taking place faster than they could be investigated and other crimes were running them a close race. It was an era during which law and law enforcement were at an all-time low.

On this third day of May, 1924, which was a Saturday, Louis Lambert went to the branch bank as was his custom. It was located within a short distance of his business, and down the street a few hundred yards was a branch of the Hupmobile factory.

By the time the factory closed on Saturday the bank would be closed, so many of the employees made it a practice to drop in at Lambert's place for a sociable drink and to have their pay checks cashed. Lambert needed a large amount of money on hand to cash all of these checks, and every Saturday his procedure was the same. He'd go to the bank in the morning and secure an ample supply of cash.

On this Saturday morning death was waiting for Louis Lambert.

Down the street a short distance, a woman who was running a bakery shop saw a Studebaker car, with the side curtains in place, pull up to the curb and park. Three men got out and sat around waiting and watching.

Lambert went to the bank. The men got in the car and started the motor, whipped the car into a U-turn and started along the street toward the bank.

Louis Lambert left the bank. The car, fully enclosed with the side curtains drawn, pulled up alongside Lambert. Someone opened a door, a shot was fired, Lambert staggered, would have fallen but eager hands reached out from the automobile and grabbed his coat, pulled him half into the car, and the car sped away, Lambert's legs sticking out over the running board.

One of the bank employees, who had been watching Lambert cross the sidewalk, grabbed a gun which was kept for protection against holdups, ran out to the sidewalk and started to shoot.

The persons in the Studebaker returned this fire. Lambert, his legs still dangling, was whisked away.

Several minutes later the Studebaker was driven into an alley in a residential section of Detroit, where it was abandoned. Three men jumped out of the car and started away at a jog trot.

Bruno Marcelt was in the kitchen of his house. The kitchen windows opened on the alley. His wife was away, and he was at the moment engaged in changing diapers on his baby. He looked out of the window, saw the three men running away, and then a moment later saw the dying Lambert get out of the car, stagger for a few feet down the alley and fall.

Marcelt rushed out to see what he could do.

Lambert said in a half whisper, "The River Gang got me," or it may have been "The River Front Gang got me," or it may have been "I believe the River Gang got me."

It is difficult to remember exactly what was said at that time, but the gist of it was that Lambert knew who had been responsible for his death and designated the murderers as either the River Gang or the River Front Gang. (This is a highly important point in the case, although it was overlooked at the time.)

Marcelt and a neighbor saw the three men running away. That is, they were proceeding at what Marcelt repeatedly refers to as "double-time."

Marcelt and the neighbor started to follow. They never got close enough to have a good look at the men whose backs were turned toward them. They probably were never closer than a hundred and twenty feet.

One of the men half-turned, brandished a gun and said, "Get back or you'll get some of the same."

That discouraged pursuit. Marcelt and the neighbor turned back; the three murderers went away. An ambulance came for Louis Lambert, and that night he died in a hospital.

At that time Vance Hardy was apparently a rather likeable, fast-thinking, fast-working young chap who was following carnivals, hanging around race tracks, and looking for suitable opportunities to make a fast dollar. He was undoubtedly on the way to becoming a first-class candidate for state prison. However, he was jolly, full of fun, made friends without any effort, and saw no reason to settle down.

One of these friends was a man whom we'll refer to now only as Benny.

Benny was in many ways one of the most interesting men we investigators for the Court of Last Resort have ever met. Benny was a holdup man, a professional stick-up artist who had been making a living for years by the simple process of holding up people who had money and taking it away from them.

He had an unusually keen mind and he profited by the experience he had. By the time he became a veteran stick-up artist he knew just about all of the angles. He had even gone so far as to classify prospective victims by age, race, nationality, etc., so as to know just how to go about engineering an effective stick-up.

Twenty-six years later Benny was to sit down in a room and unburden himself to us, and his conversation was taken down on a tape recorder. It is a most fascinating and interesting story of crime as seen through the eyes of a criminal.

Benny particularly emphasized the necessity of a good job of casing rather than "going on a blind." In casing a place, Benny and his confederates learned the background and habits of every man and woman in the place that was to be held up. They knew just how to approach each individual person, and when the going was tough and there was police pursuit they knew how to discourage this pursuit.

Benny was an expert, daring automobile driver. He knew every alley in Detroit, and his favorite getaway was to take to the alleys, roaring through them at high speed, taking the corners on two wheels, throwing his car so adroitly into a skid that he could make a complete about-face and be going in the opposite direction almost within the winking of an eye.

It was Benny who bewailed in his conversation with us the unfortunate tendency of certain citizens to become heroes.

The hero, Benny explained, was one of the greatest menaces to the holdup profession. A hero was usually a youngster, over the age of fifteen, but usually under the age of twenty-two. He hadn't as yet learned that the place of an innocent bystander in a holdup was to stand with his hands elevated. The young, hot-blooded, impulsive individual wanted to become a hero. He would, Benny explained sadly, at times even "go so far as to grab for the gun."

"That makes for trouble," Benny said. "It makes for bloodshed and that gives the business a bad name. . . . I just don't believe in this too much heroism, Mr. Gardner. I don't believe in this hero business. When crazy men go to stick up a place, a man who has any intention of becoming a hero should think twice. It's sometimes nice to be a hero and have your pictures in the paper, but if you have to pay for it with your life it's too great a price—and it's bad for business."

On the other hand, when some other gang had engaged in a holdup which hadn't gone off as smoothly as anticipated and guns had blazed, and the newspapers were filled with pictures of the victim and angry editorials against the bold criminals, Benny and his cohorts rubbed their hands in glee.

To the uninitiated it would seem that during a period of such publicity, the gang should lie low, but actually the exact opposite was the case.

As Benny explained it to us, during such times prospective victims in a holdup were cowed into submission by the horrible example which had been made of a fellow citizen who had been so foolhardy as to resist.

At some length Benny went on to explain the simple tenets of the holdup profession. The stick-up men really didn't want to kill. They wanted to work out a smooth plan by which they could get the money and make an escape. If they could do that without firing a shot the holdup was perfect. If they had to fire a shot that was potentially bad business.

And there was, of course, a special technique to be used in holding up women. According to Benny, if you terrified a woman she promptly proceeded to faint or to have hysterics. If she fainted, when she came to she started to scream, and if she had hysterics there was absolutely nothing you could do with her. In the holdup business there is nothing worse than a screaming woman (unless it's a "hero"). It was, therefore, necessary to verse oneself carefully in the little acts of gallantry by which a woman could be made to understand that it was only her employer's money that was being taken, and, after all, the holdup men were rather considerate young chaps.

Benny's pet taboo was Chinese. You simply couldn't stick up a Chinese, he explained. They just *wouldn't* hold up. That was all there was to it. You tried to stick up a Chinaman and he wouldn't hold up.

A book could be written about Benny and what he told us about the inside of the holdup racket, Benny insisting vehemently that it took a lot more brains to stick up a bank than it did to run one.

The point is that Benny and Vance Hardy became acquainted in a casual sort of way, and Benny took a liking to young Hardy.

At that time, however, both of them insist that Benny had no intention of cutting Vance Hardy in on his racket, and that Hardy knew nothing about the manner in which Benny was making his livelihood. It was simply a casual contact which was fast ripening into a friendship, a friendship which it seems certain could have brought no good to Vance Hardy as matters existed at the time.

Benny had some friends who had been unfortunate enough to be apprehended by the police and convicted. They had been sent to Marquette prison, and had managed to evade prison censorship of correspondence so as to let Benny know that if guns could be left at a specified place they felt certain a prison break could be engineered.

Benny was always ready to oblige a friend.

He secured the guns and, by means of wires, fastened them to the underside of an automobile. Then he planned the trip up to Marquette. To work in with his plans it was necessary that this trip seem utterly and completely innocuous. Therefore Benny decided to take a couple of people along with him who had no police records, people in whom the law could not possibly have any interest.

Benny found two men who answered his purpose. One of them was Vance Hardy. He suggested to Vance that he was going to have to make a trip up to the northern part of the state, and inquired if Vance wanted to go along "just for the ride." Vance did.

There is considerable mystery about what happened immediately after that. It is one thing on which Benny refuses to take us into his confidence. He won't even discuss it. However, the best guess is that the inmates of Marquette prison hadn't been quite as successful in evading censorship as they had thought. Apparently the prison officials knew that guns were to be brought up by Benny, and they weren't playing it quite as wide open as Benny thought. After he arrived in the vicinity of the prison he must have received a tip-off that all was not well. Perhaps there was some signal which was to have been given indicating that it would be all right to proceed. When this signal was not forthcoming Benny became suspicious.

In any event, it seems certain that when the car started out there were guns wired to the undercarriage where they were out of sight. By the time the police sprang their trap and triumphantly pounced on Benny, the guns had mysteriously disappeared.

The police were baffled. They were also angry. They had detected the conspiracy to bring in the guns. They had nabbed the man whom they felt certain was the gunrunner but they didn't have any evidence. They were in no mood to exchange pleasantries or to discuss constitutional rights. So far as Benny's two companions were concerned the police didn't waste any time or any sympathy listening to stories about having merely gone along on a sociable trip for the ride.

The police arrested all of these men and took them back to Detroit.

As to what happened after that we have only the story of Vance Hardy and of Benny.

As Benny expressed it to us, "The police were sore because they thought they had a cinch case. When they picked us up they found they didn't have any evidence. They took us back to Detroit and threw us in the can and charged us with murder. Not any particular murder—just murder. Then they brought in a whole procession of people who had been in a position to identify suspects of different murder cases and had them try to identify us. Every ten or fifteen minutes we were dragged out and put on display in the hope that some witness would identify us in connection with some murder. The police didn't care what murder. It went on hour after hour."

Finally, according to Benny, Bruno Marcelt pointed to Vance Hardy and said in effect, "That looks something like one of the men I saw running away. One of them was about his build and complexion."

That connected Vance Hardy with the Louis Lambert murder.

Bruno Marcelt, according to his own subsequent admission, didn't feel that he could make an identification. He had only said that Vance Hardy was about the same build, and had a "ruddy complexion" similar to that of one of the men he had seen a hundred and twenty feet away on that day when Louis Lambert was murdered.

He kept insisting to the police that all he could say was that Hardy was "something like" the fellow, and that he couldn't positively identify him. He hadn't seen the man plainly enough.

By this time the police were desperate. They slapped charges of murder against Benny and against Vance Hardy. Benny was able to convince the jury that on the particular day in question he had been in the company of some reputable citizens at a party, and introduced enough evidence to beat the case. Vance Hardy had only one alibi witness, his sister, who insisted that Vance Hardy had been having dinner with her in Louisville, Kentucky, at the time of the Lambert holdup. She said he attended the Kentucky Derby on that day.

Vance Hardy was convicted.

Vance Hardy had insisted and he continued to insist that he was innocent. He went to prison filled with bitterness and was far from being a model prisoner. He engaged in a jail break and made an escape. Upon being recaptured he was thrown into solitary confinement and kept there.

Solitary confinement is a punishment intended to be meted out to desperate criminals over a period of a few days at a time. A few weeks represents the extreme limit that a man is supposed to be able to endure this form of punishment.

Vance Hardy was placed in solitary confinement for ten years.

There seems to be but little question that Hardy would have died in solitary confinement if it hadn't been for the fact that a new warden took over the administration of the prison. Vance Hardy, at that time near death, was released from solitary.

There are certain other forms of punishment amounting to torture which can be meted out to prisoners when they are in solitary confinement. These punishments leave no visible mark upon the prisoner, and it is always easy to deny that they were inflicted. One of the better known of these punishments is to force the prisoner to stand up in front of a barred cell door. His arms are pushed through the door at about the height of his shoulders and just over a crossbar. Then a pair of handcuffs are snapped on the prisoner's wrists on the outside of the door.

The prisoner stands there hour after hour. He has no alternative but to stand there. His feet ache. His muscles become a network of screaming torture. The bite of the handcuffs on the bones of his wrists makes excruciating pain. There is nothing a man can do about it. If he tries to take the weight off his feet, the pressure of the steel manacles becomes unbearable. He can't even shift his position. He simply stands there, and stands there, and stands there.

Apparently Vance Hardy endured this form of torture day after day, day after day.

Prisoners can cite many instances of men who went completely mad, and of others who died under this form of torture. Vance Hardy endured it.

Once a week he was permitted to walk down the corridor to take a shower bath. That was his only form of recreation, his only form of exercise. The cell was not quite dark, but a minimum of light was admitted through a small window near the top of the cell, and, because there was nothing on which he could use his eyes, he found himself going blind. In fact, from all we can gather, Vance Hardy would have lasted only a few more weeks when there was a change in prison administration and he was returned to a more normal confinement.

Gladys Barrett, Vance Hardy's devoted sister, felt positive that Hardy was innocent. There may have been some doubt in her own mind as to the accuracy of the alibi she gave him. Hardy had been visiting at her house in Louisville, but whether it had been on the day of the crime or at about the same time, is a question. She always insisted that it was on the day of the crime, but when Alex Gregory ran her on a lie detector, there were indications on her graph which made Gregory feel that she might be mistaken as to the exact date.

Later on, further doubt was thrown on her statement by investigations of the Michigan Corrections Department, Division of Pardons, Paroles and Probation. Gladys Barrett had insisted that the day of the murder was the day when the Kentucky Derby was being run, and investigations indicated that such was not the case.

However, Gladys Barrett maintained that her brother was innocent, and her reactions on the lie detector showed that she had a genuine and complete confidence in his innocence. If he had been implicated in any way in the crime his sister certainly didn't know about it, and, on the other hand, had every reason to believe that he could not have been implicated.

Gladys Barrett devoted her entire life to seeing that the injustice against her brother was rectified.

It was a long, uphill fight. All of her earnings went into that fight, and she accomplished nothing.

She secured counsel, and Vance Hardy went into court asking for a new trial on certain technical grounds as well as on the claim that Bruno Marcelt had been forced by the police to make the identification which had resulted in his conviction.

This brings us back to Bruno Marcelt.

Years after Hardy was convicted, Gladys Barrett found herself working in a munitions plant. One of the men whom she saw from time to time had a familiar face. It was Bruno. Marcelt, also employed in the same place.

Gladys Barrett made his acquaintance. She interrogated him concerning his identification, and to her Marcelt confided that he hadn't been able to make a real identification of anyone; that the police had brought pressure to bear by calling for him in the small hours of the morning, placing him in the "tank," treating him just as they would treat a criminal, and giving him to understand he'd get the works if he didn't cooperate. This had been on the day of the trial.

Marcelt had felt that if he didn't identify Vance Hardy things would go pretty bad with him. The other witness who had been with Marcelt at the time stated flatly that he couldn't identify Hardy and was promptly sent to jail for contempt of court.

Now obviously there was some other sequence in here that didn't appear in Marcelt's story. The witness must have been defiant, or must have disobeyed some order or process of the court, but the fact remains that as far as Bruno Marcelt was concerned, he felt that this neighbor had been sent to jail for contempt of court because he had failed to identify Vance Hardy.

Bruno Marcelt identified Vance Hardy.

In telling Gladys Barrett about this, he admitted that he certainly couldn't be positive Vance Hardy was the man. He doubted that he was the man. He wanted to rectify the wrong he had done. Gladys Barrett said she'd get a lawyer and Marcelt could sign an affidavit.

So Marcelt signed an affidavit and Gladys Barrett proceeded to try and get a new trial for Vance Hardy.

Thereupon certain things happened.

According to Marcelt's story, a deputy prosecutor sent for him and said, in effect, "What's this about your affidavit? Did you tell the truth at the time of trial, or are you telling it now? Both of these statements can't be correct. If you are telling the truth now then you committed perjury at the time of the trial and can be punished. If you told the truth at the time of trial then this affidavit of yours is perjury, and if you don't repudiate it you can be prosecuted."

It may or may not have been a threat. It may have been merely a statement of law, but Bruno Marcelt felt it was a threat.

Marcelt repudiated the affidavit.

He was able to do this because the affidavit had been written in longhand by the attorney Gladys Barrett had brought to call on Marcelt, and he had signed the statement the attorney had prepared. Marcelt was able to repudiate this affidavit by saying that he hadn't read it, and that it wasn't in his language. The attorney insisted that he had written it out just as Marcelt had told it to him and had carefully read it back to him before he signed it.

The question became academic because Marcelt repudiated the affidavit.

Vance Hardy went back to prison. The motion for a new trial was denied.

Gladys Barrett kept on fighting—if you could call it fighting. It would perhaps be better to say that she kept on beating her head against the stone wall of official hostility and indifference.

The liberation of Louis Gross had caused quite a commotion in the Michigan state prison, and, as usual, after a case in one prison has been brought to a successful termination, we were deluged with applications on behalf of other prisoners who were confined in the same institution.

Gladys Barrett submitted an application on behalf of her brother. She did more. She called on Dr. LeMoyne Snyder in Lansing. She wrote letters individually to the various members of *Argosy's* committee. And, in addition to that, she sought and obtained personal interviews.

There could be no question of Gladys Barrett's sincerity. She believed that her brother was completely innocent of the crime charged. She had devoted the last twenty-five years of her life to waging a singlehanded crusade against injustice.

There is something compelling about a situation where a woman has used all of her meager earnings to right a wrong. Gladys Barrett didn't know very much about law. She knew nothing about legal procedure. She didn't know how to spend her money most effectively to get the best results for her brother. She accepted advice from various people, and whenever she could get money together she would spend it ineffectively, making applications to officials who considered Vance Hardy a number and Gladys Barrett a nuisance.

The point is that she spent all of the money she could save up for expenses. She went without new clothes. She made her old clothes last, repairing them over and over. She went without proper food. She worked, and worked hard, at whatever wages she could get, denying herself all of the luxuries and many of the necessities so that she could save a few pennies here and there until they had grown into a sufficient reserve to enable her to sally forth once more and again vainly strive to get a new appraisal of her brother's case.

So when Gladys Barrett appealed to us, the picture she presented was so filled with human heartache that we were sympathetically inclined.

There was, moreover, the feeling of Dr. Russell L. Finch, the prison physician, that something should be done for Hardy. Dr. Finch was a close personal friend of Dr. LeMoyne Snyder; and Vance Hardy, who by this time had been assigned as a nurse's assistant to Dr. Finch, had interested the doctor in his case.

So, at Dr. Snyder's insistence, we decided to investigate the Vance Hardy case, at least to the extent of talking with Bruno Marcelt.

There could be no mistaking Marcelt's sincerity. We felt certain that Marcelt had either been forced to make an identification of Vance Hardy, or that he thought he had been forced. At times, Marcelt, searching his memory, would feel positive that Vance Hardy was not the man he had seen running away from the scene of the crime. At other times he would feel that there was a certain superficial resemblance, and that was as far as he could conscientiously go, either one way or the other.

In the city of Detroit there probably were two hundred thousand men who fitted those same specifications of description, so, of course, from a legal standpoint it would make but little difference whether there was this resemblance.

Marcelt was a conscientious individual. He had grown in intellectual stature with the years, and held a position of responsibility. He had learned to exercise his best judgment in matters calling for thoughtful consideration, and, above all, he had learned the importance of knowing he was right in his facts before making up his mind.

As a result of all this, the testimony he had given in the Vance Hardy case had been preying on his mind. Opposed to the twinges of his conscience, however, was the feeling that in the event he tried to change his testimony he would promptly be arrested and sent to prison for having perjured himself at the time he gave his testimony at the trial.

Dr. Snyder was able to point out to Marcelt that the statute of limitations granted him immunity from any prosecution for perjury because of testimony he had given at the former trial; that now he was not only free to tell the truth but that it was his duty to do so.

Marcelt, however, was still mindful of what he had felt was a very distinct threat made by the deputy prosecutor should he make any sworn statement which departed in any way from the testimony he had given at the time of trial.

So Tom Smith and Dr. Snyder went to the office of Gerald K. O'Brien and put the matter before the prosecutor himself.

O'Brien acted with characteristic, straight-from-the-shoulder vigor. He sent word to Marcelt that he wanted him to tell the truth regardless of what it might be; that if he told the whole truth now and was certain about it there would be no prosecution on the part of his office because of the former testimony.

So Marcelt told the truth.

I was present at the time Marcelt was interviewed. In fact, the whole committee, Raymond Schindler, Alex Gregory, Dr. LeMoyne Snyder, Tom Smith, Harry Steeger and I sat around the table. There was a microphone on that table connected with a tape recorder. We didn't want any misunderstandings this time as to what Marcelt said, or as to whether someone had put words in his mouth.

He sat in front of the microphone and started to tell his story, at first somewhat self-consciously, using rather stilted language. Then, as he began to think of the mental torture he had endured over the years, the words came pouring forth, one word following another with such rapidity that it would have been impossible for any stenographic reporter to have taken down what he said. But it was all recorded on tape.

It was the anguished cry of a man whose conscience had given him no rest for years because he had let the exigencies of the situation force him into making what amounted to a positive identification at a time when it actually shouldn't have been positive, in fact when he shouldn't have made any identification at all. All he had seen was a group of three men running away from the scene of the crime. One of the men had briefly turned toward him—at no time had Marcelt been closer to these men than a hundred and twenty feet. He had never had a close look at any of the men.

I have the tape recording of that interview. Sometimes when I want to illustrate a point about identification evidence, I play back that tape. It is easy to understand the weight that had been on Marcelt's conscience all of those years—twenty-six years—when one listens to this tape.

It so happened that at about this time a radio company wanted to put one of our cases "on the air." It was felt that in view of Marcelt's attitude and his tape-recorded statement there couldn't possibly be any better case with which to start than that of Vance Hardy. So we decided to make a complete tape recording of the factual background of the Hardy case.

It was a good thing we did.

We went out to the scene of the crime, taking along a sound technician, a microphone and spools of tape. We arranged a "setup" so that only the microphone need be out on the sidewalk, while the tape-recording machine was concealed in a nearby storeroom.

During the intervening twenty-six years the scene of the crime had changed to the extent that the streets had now become main thoroughfares for automobile traffic. A traffic signal had been installed and the intersection where Louis Lambert had met his death was indeed a busy one.

It was planned that Tom Smith would carry the microphone and show me the location of the crime, pointing out to me where Lambert had entered the bank, where he had stepped off the curb, where the automobile had spun into a U-turn, etc. In this way the invisible radio audience would get a good picture of the locale.

We had just started our recording, and, naturally, had collected something of a crowd, when a man, walking up, asked one of the radio technicians, "What's all the excitement about?"

"Nothing in particular," the radio man said, trying to get rid of as much of the crowd as possible. "Just some people investigating an old murder case which occurred here some twenty-six years ago."

The man became visibly excited. "What murder case?" he asked. "Who was killed?"

"Louis Lambert," the technician said. "Why? Why are you interested?"

"Because I saw it," the man said. "I saw the whole thing."

So, as Tom Smith and I were going through the act, just as Tom was saying, "Now Louis Lambert had come down this street and stepped up on the curb about where you are now standing, Erle. The bank is right behind us, and that door . . ." the radio technician said in a hoarse whisper, "There's a man here who says he saw the crime committed. Do you want to talk with him?"

"Gosh, yes," we said. "Bring him over."

And so the witness, whose name we didn't even have at the

moment, was brought up in front of the microphone and proceeded to tell his story.

It was a peculiar interview. I was asking questions, feeling my way, trying to size the man up, not at all certain but what he might have been "planted" by someone who wanted to see that Vance Hardy was going to remain in prison for the rest of his life, and that this man, telling a story in front of a crowd and directly into a microphone would make an identification which wouldn't be any better than Bruno Marcelt's had been, but which, under the circumstances, would be infinitely more damaging to Hardy's case. The dramatic background, the fact that the interview was being recorded, that there was no opportunity to cross-examine the witness properly, all made it necessary to move cautiously. Trying to size up the type of person with whom I was dealing, I was watching for that first indication of overeagerness which would indicate someone had "planted" him with a story to tell.

During all of this time the traffic signal was changing from red to amber, amber to green, then back to red once more. Cars were speeding along, sliding to a stop, waiting, then, as the signal changed to green, the sound of fifteen or twenty motors being revved up all registered in the microphone.

It was a momentous interview.

The witness had been a newsboy selling papers on the corner at the time of the murder. During evenings he worked for Louis Lambert as a pin boy in Lambert's bowling alley. As Lambert had emerged from the bank he had said good morning to him, and those had probably been the last words Lambert had spoken to anyone before he fell mortally wounded and was dragged into the automobile. Moreover, the witness had seen the three murderers while they had been loitering around, waiting for Lambert to show up.

Of course, the witness hadn't known that these men were planning to commit a murder. There was, therefore, no reason for him to notice them particularly, but nevertheless he had noticed the man who seemed to be the dominant, outstanding figure, the one who Marcelt had felt had the same general physical make-up as Vance Hardy.

And, later on, when Hardy had been arrested and tried, just to satisfy his own mind the witness had gone up to court to get a good look at the accused to see if he was the man whom he had seen in the group waiting for Louis Lambert to emerge from the bank.

He was convinced that Vance Hardy was not that man, but he had said nothing to anyone.

This witness said he had never been interviewed by the police and that he had never volunteered to tell his story. This statement that he was making in front of a breathless crowd of a hundred or a hundred and fifty people was the first time he had ever told the story to investigators.

The witness then went on and told us something which we had generally understood was the case but which we hadn't been able to prove.

Louis Lambert had received a shipment of whisky which had been twice watered. During those days of bootleg activities and gang wars, a person was naïve indeed to expect a shipment of the "pure quill." Good whisky was watered, diluted, flavored, spiked and adulterated. But this particular shipment had been so adulterated that the customers for whom Lambert was supposed to have ordered it refused to accept it. Therefore Lambert maintained that he wasn't going to pay for it. This had caused hard feelings, and a day or two before the murder a grim committee had entered Lambert's place of business to tell him that he was either going to pay "or else."

The theory of the prosecution had been that Vance Hardy, who concededly didn't know Louis Lambert at all, had held up Lambert and killed him simply in order to obtain possession of the large sum of money which Lambert had just drawn out of the bank, that the motive for the crime was robbery and nothing else.

If it could be shown that Lambert's death was the result of a bootleg war, and that the motivation had been revenge, it not only tied in with rumors we had heard, but it would account for Louis Lambert's statement when Marcelt had gone over to pick him up: "The River Gang got me."

Therefore the testimony which this witness gave us, standing there on a busy street intersection, became of the greatest value, and the fact that all of the dramatic highlights of that interview were permanently engraved upon recording tape was in every way a break for Vance Hardy.

Alex Gregory gave polygraph, or lie detector, tests both to Vance Hardy and Gladys Barrett, and was able to reach very definite conclusions. Vance Hardy had no guilty knowledge of the murder of Louis Lambert. Gladys Barrett was sincerely convinced that Hardy was innocent, and she had no knowledge whatever of any circumstance which would indicate his guilt, although Gregory felt that Gladys Barrett was being more positive in her statement about Vance Hardy having been at her house on the exact date of the crime than the circumstances would justify. She was, perhaps, doing a little wishful thinking on this point. Hardy had probably been with her at about that time, but when she stated she was sure of the exact date she was rationalizing. That was Gregory's best opinion from reading the charts made by the polygraph.

Bruno Marcelt was under the distinct impression that he had been the only one at the trial who had made any sort of an identification of Vance Hardy.

There may be some question as to this. There was perhaps an identification made by a man who had seen only the hands of one of the murderers when they had reached out and dragged the dying Lambert into the car. This man, according to Vance Hardy, had identified him by saying that his hands looked to be the same.

However, no one will know exactly what happened at the time of the trial because here again the records had all disappeared.

In the present case, however, there was probably a different motivation than that which took place in the Louis Gross case.

There had been a custom in Detroit which had existed for some years of permitting verdicts to be received in the absence of the trial judge when the verdicts were returned late at night. The verdicts would be received by the clerk and held until court convened the next day, when they would be entered in the court record. The Supreme Court eventually declared that this practice was unconstitutional and granted a new trial to one of the prisoners who had been so convicted. Of course, there were hundreds of other prisoners who would be entitled to a release under similar circumstances.

It is, perhaps, no mere coincidence that in some of these cases where the judge had not been on the bench when the verdict was received, the records disappeared, so that there was no way of establishing officially the fact that the defendant was entitled to a new trial.

There was considerable evidence that the Vance Hardy case was one of these in which the verdict had been received sometime in the evening after the judge had left the bench and gone home, and the procedure in connection with the verdict had been substantially the same as that which had been held by the Supreme Court to entitle the defendant to set aside the conviction and have a new trial.

Human recollection being what it is, establishing what had happened twenty-six years earlier was rather difficult. Some members of the jury who convicted Vance Hardy had felt positive that the judge had been on the bench when the verdict was received. Others were equally positive that the verdict had been received in the absence of the judge. In any event, someone had deliberately torn the pages out of the shorthand reporter's notebook so that it was impossible to determine what the official records had to say on the subject.

In view of Marcelt's positive statement that no one else had identified Vance Hardy; in view of Hardy's own statement of what had taken place at the trial; in view of Marcelt's repudiation of his so-called identification; in view of the records shown by Gregory's exhaustive polygraph tests, plus the fact that we learned another police polygraph expert had previously given Vance Hardy similar tests and had come to the conclusion that Hardy was innocent; in view of the testimony of the witness who had been interviewed at the scene of the crime and who had given us such pertinent information to the effect that Lambert had been killed as the result of a bootleg war, we felt entirely justified in asking the Governor for a pardon for Vance Hardy.

In Michigan there is a peculiar procedure in regard to pardon. The governor has the sole right of pardon, but before he can issue a pardon it is necessary that an application be referred by him to a board which makes a preliminary investigation. If the board feels the prisoner is not entitled to a pardon, that is all there is to it. If the board feels there is some doubt in the matter, a public hearing is given and any person who may wish to interpose an objection is privileged to attend that hearing. At the conclusion of the hearing the matter is referred back to the governor. The board is the same body which grants paroles, fixes sentences, etc.

It would seem that the object of this statute was to prevent the surreptitious granting of pardons, and to give any person who wanted to appear and be heard the opportunity to do so. However, the legislation is relatively new and no one knows exactly what it does mean.

One thing that as a practicing lawyer I would say it did *not* mean was that the board should act as a reviewing tribunal and retry the case as a court would.

However, the Michigan board acted on the theory that they were to hold a hearing similar to a court's, and the results were ludicrous to say the least. Judges sometimes permit themselves to become bogged down in a welter of red tape, but when laymen start assuming judicial prerogatives and masquerading as they feel judges would act or should act under similar circumstances, they are all too prone to invest themselves with a ponderous misconception of the laws of evidence. Not knowing what the law of evidence is, they strain at absurd technicalities on the one hand, and entirely overlook fundamental safeguards on the other.

Because evidence of the so-called polygraph examination is not admissible in the courts, the board refused to consider Gregory's conclusions in connection with the polygraph as evidence, and the same was true of the police polygraph expert. And, incredible as it may seem, the board even went so far as to intimate that because the prosecutor had not considered the possibility that Lambert had been killed as a result of a bootleg war when the case was originally tried, it would be inequitable to allow Vance Hardy at this late date to demonstrate that such was the case.

On the other hand, a police officer who had kept notes on the case as to what he thought the witnesses had testified to, or were going to testify to, was permitted to testify in great detail as to the contents of his notes, the notes virtually taking the place of an authenticated court record of the transcript of testimony.

The board did demonstrate pretty conclusively that Gladys Barrett was mistaken in fixing the date when Vance Hardy had been with her by referring back to the Kentucky Derby. The records showed that the Kentucky Derby was not run on the date of the murder. It was quite probable that Hardy could have been with his sister for the purpose of attending the Derby, but he certainly couldn't have gone to it on the exact date of the murder.

Investigators for the board also uncovered one witness who came as a distinct surprise to all concerned. It was a witness who stated positively that he had seen the men in the murder car and Vance Hardy was *not* one of those men.

Having given the matter mature consideration, the board filed its opinion, holding that it was incumbent on Vance Hardy to prove himself innocent by evidence, stating that he had failed to do this, and then, treating all of the conclusions, all of the arguments, all of the self-serving declarations of the police as being entitled to the weight of evidence, elevating the notes of a police officer to the dignity of official evidence; and finally commenting by implication that it wasn't cricket for Vance Hardy to try and establish a different motivation for the murder than that which the prosecutor had felt must be the case at the time the matter was originally tried.

Vance Hardy's application was denied.

Once more Gladys Barrett had been rebuffed. Once more her brother, his hopes raised high, had been sent back to prison.

We had talked with Governor G. Mennen Williams and with his legal advisor. We felt pretty certain that Governor Williams, under the circumstances, would have pardoned Hardy if he had had an opportunity to give the matter his personal consideration, but he certainly wasn't in a position to go against the direct recommendation of the board, particularly in view of the new legislation in connection with pardons which had been so recently enacted in Michigan.

Members of the Court of Last Resort felt that the decision was so flagrantly against the dictates of justice that the Michigan courts of law, even though bound by the strict letter of the law in regard to evidence, would give the relief which the board had denied.

So our committee went to two Detroit lawyers, Sidney Sherman and David Martin, men who are considered leaders of the bar in their field; able, conscientious men who had long been familiar with the work that was being done by the Court of Last Resort, and who had expressed a willingness to co-operate at any time they could do so.

We presented the facts to them.

They agreed to serve without compensation, to institute formal proceedings, asking for a new trial before Judge Joseph A. Gillis, the same judge who had previously heard and denied Hardy's motion for a new trial.

These lawyers were inclined to think the case had been a close one, that Judge Gillis had been somewhat on the fence, and that the motion for new trial had been denied largely because the affidavits of the jurors seemed to be about equally divided as to whether the judge had or had not been on the bench. If new evidence could be presented, the lawyers felt that Judge Gillis would grant Vance Hardy a new trial.

Tom Smith and I had previously interviewed Judge Gillis in connection with the Hardy case, trying to find out exactly what had been in his mind when he had denied Hardy's motion for a new trial.

That visit had been highly interesting. We had dropped into Judge Gillis' court about eleven o'clock. He had agreed to go to lunch with us as soon as he had finished his calendar. He was trying some contested criminal cases.

I thought that we had probably misunderstood the jurist; and that what he had meant was that he was trying *a* contested criminal *case*. I hadn't felt that it was possible for a man to dispose of more than one of them in the course of an hour.

When we entered court we learned our mistake.

The calendar had been partially disposed of. There remained some *twenty* cases to be cleaned up before the judge was able to go to lunch.

Some of these cases were mere routine, the court accepting a plea and meting out sentence, but at least a dozen of them were contested cases.

It seems absolutely incredible that a judge could dispose of that many before lunch. (As it turned out, lunch was delayed an hour or so, waiting for the judge to get through with his calendar.)

However, Judge Gillis did just that, and I think he made a remarkably good job of it.

A case would be called. Judge Gillis would summon the attorneys, the defendant, the prosecuting attorney, and all of the witnesses to stand up before him. The witnesses would raise their right hands and be sworn all at once. There were no technicalities, no particular attention paid to the framing of questions. Usually the judge framed them all.

He would look at the complaint in the matter. He'd point his finger at the prosecuting witness. He'd say, "All right, now just what was it that happened on the second of June? Just tell me the story."

The witness would tell him in his own language. The judge would break in from time to time with questions, hurrying him along, getting rid of side comments and extraneous matters, looking for the real meat in the case.

Then he'd turn to the defendant. "All right, what have *you* got to say about this?"

He'd listen to the defendant's story, say, "You got anyone who can back up your story?. . . All right, let's hear from *him*."

The judge would then listen to whatever corroboration there was for the defendant's story. Then he'd turn to the prosecuting witness. "Anybody else see this thing besides you?" he'd ask, and that would pave the way for a brief recital from any of the other witnesses on behalf of the prosecution.

It's surprising how quickly a story can be told when the judge encourages a witness to speak right up and tell it in ordinary language, without having any formalized courtroom procedure in which an attorney asks a question, another attorney objects to the question, there is considerable argument on the merit of the objection, the judge makes a ruling, the witness answers the question yes or no, then the attorney asks him to elaborate his answer, and so forth on down the line.

Judge Gillis is, in many ways, a controversial figure. He is an individualist. He reminds one very much of an umpire in a ball game calling out a close decision at home plate. He isn't going to please everyone and he just doesn't give a damn whether he does or whether he doesn't. He calls the shot the way he sees it and lets it go at that.

Listening to those cases in court I was remarkably impressed with Judge Gillis' knowledge of human nature, his quick perception, his ability to ferret out the weak spot in a case, his ability to get the facts out of a witness, confine a garrulous witness to the pertinent facts in a case, encourage a tongue-tied witness to tell his story.

And as an attorney I was very deeply impressed with the decisions themselves. As nearly as I could tell the judge was deciding every one of the cases right.

Defendants find it's hard to lie to Judge Gillis. He looks them in the eye, grins sardonically, and the best rehearsed lies become stumbling recitals. Moreover it's a lot easier to get at the truth when you hurry a man along so that he doesn't have a chance to depend on a carefully rehearsed story.

Personally I don't like to see such a congestion of cases that a judge has to rush them through in this manner. On the other hand, when attorneys are given all the time they want, they haggle and quibble endlessly. I will say this, if I had to participate in a case on such a crowded calendar I would as soon have it heard by Judge Gillis as by any jurist I know anywhere in the country.

And that's quite a concession from me because I don't believe that judges as a rule should take over the trial of cases. I think that a defendant is entitled to his counsel and to his day in court, and that he is entitled to the technical advantages which the law gives him in connection with evidence. If he's to be convicted for a technical violation of the law he should have the advantage of the technicalities of the law in his favor.

When I first saw what Judge Gillis was doing I was prepared to resent that procedure. By the end of an hour I was nodding my head approvingly.

Talking with him afterward I learned that he feels the process of justice is altogether too complicated, and a lot too expensive. He likes to see that the poor man gets justice; that he gets it swiftly, expeditiously and inexpensively.

In a magazine article someone referred to Judge Gillis as the poor man's judge, and I think he's more proud of that appellation than of any of his judicial honors.

Judge Gillis talked frankly with us about the Vance Hardy case. It had been a close decision. He felt that the question of whether the judge was or was not on the bench when the verdict had been returned was something that Hardy had to establish by a preponderance of the evidence. As far as Judge Gillis was concerned the evidence was as near equally balanced as it could possibly be in such a case.

Conferring with Sidney Sherman and David Martin, LeMoyne Snyder, who is an attorney as well as an M.D., put all of our information at the disposal of these attorneys. It was agreed that if some bit of new evidence could be discovered, particularly on the question of whether the judge was on the bench when the verdict was returned, Judge Gillis would ride along with us.

Tom Smith started work.

It was a pretty hopeless task. He was following a trail that was twenty-six years old. Most of the jurors in the case, like most of the witnesses, had either disappeared into oblivion or had passed away.

Then Tom learned of a relative of a surviving juror. The juror was traced to the northern part of Maine, where, as winter was setting in, he would probably be isolated until early summer. And because of the passing of time in the case there was always the possibility that early summer would be too late.

Bob Rhay, who has charge of the records and correspondence of the Court of Last Resort, who sifts through the original cases, condenses them into brief notes, tabulates and answers the dozens of letters which are received every day, is an aviator of considerable skill. He thought that by chartering an amphibious plane it would be possible to make a landing on a lake which was near where the juror lived, yet which because of certain thermal conditions in the springs which fed the streams that flowed into the lake remained ice-free after most of the surrounding lakes and streams had frozen.

It was a race against time. He flew to Maine and there picked up a local pilot and a local notary public, and flew over miles of wild, snowbound woods, until they located just about the one lake anywhere in the country which was free of ice. Then they managed to get to the juror, who remembered the case perfectly, who was absolutely positive that the judge was not on the bench when the verdict was returned. They secured an affidavit from this juror, got back to their plane, and took off with fingers of ice already beginning to clutch at the edges of the shore line.

Attorneys Sidney Sherman and David Martin prepared an application for a new trial on behalf of Vance Hardy, and went into Judge Gillis' court.

Everyone who listened to these attorneys was impressed with the thoroughness of their preparation. They had studied the case forward, backward and sideways. They were acting without fee, purely because of their interest in the cause of justice, and because they sincerely felt that Vance Hardy had been wrongfully imprisoned. They made a masterful presentation of the evidence.

Judge Gillis heard all the arguments, read the affidavits, and decided that Vance Hardy was entitled to a new trial upon technical grounds. Then he went out of his way to state that he had become interested in this case after we had talked with him; that from confidential sources of his own he had learned definitely that Louis Lambert was killed not for purposes of robbery but as a means of revenge in a bootleg war; that he seriously doubted whether Vance Hardy knew anything whatever about the murder, and that, in his opinion, Vance Hardy was entitled to a new trial.

There was, of course, no possibility of securing a conviction in a new trial in view of the fact that Bruno Marcelt, the state's star witness, not only would not identify Vance Hardy but would have stated if he'd been questioned that his previous identification had been made under duress, and that his present best judgment was that Hardy was not the man he had seen leaving the scene of the crime.

So the prosecution dismissed the case and Vance Hardy walked out of the courtroom a free man.

Circumstances had prevented my leaving my California ranch on the date set for the final hearing on the motion for a new trial in Judge Gillis' court, but I knew that the matter was in able hands, that lawyers Sherman and Martin had left no stone unturned, and that they felt satisfied Judge Gillis' decision would be favorable. LeMoyne Snyder, who had been working with the case for many months, was on hand, as were Tom Smith and Alex Gregory, and I had been in close touch with all of these people in their conferences immediately prior to the court hearing. We felt that under the circumstances we could almost guarantee that at long last Vance Hardy was "going to get a break."

However, for various and obvious reasons we didn't communicate our hopes in the matter to Gladys Barrett. After all, she had had her hopes raised so many times only to see them dashed to pieces, that this time we simply told her we were going to do the best we could.

However, the morning of the hearing someone brought her an orchid and told her to pin it on for luck.

Immediately at the close of the hearing, as soon as Vance Hardy walked out of court a free man, Gladys Barrett telephoned me in California. Her voice was broken and quavering with tears and excitement. She tried to stammer out the story but she was incoherent with happiness.

However, she didn't need to tell me in words. Just the tone of her voice and her happy sobbing was all that was required. I passed on my congratulations over the telephone and told her I was certain her luck had turned, that at last she had won her long fight for her brother's freedom, and from now on she could occasionally buy herself some new clothes.

That was when she broke down completely. "Mr. Gardner," she sobbed, "I'm wearing an orchid. . . . Think of it! . . . Me, wearing an orchid! . . . It's the first time I've ever had an orchid in all my life."

She certainly was entitled to it.

9

It must not be thought that all of our cases resulted in triumphant vindications of our judgment, or in demonstrations of a defendant's innocence.

We encountered a good many cases where we felt certain that the defendant had been wrongfully convicted, but where there was no opportunity to prove our point. In other words, we couldn't get any more evidence than had been available at the time of the original hearing.

As every lawyer knows, it is an axiom of law that it is impossible to prove a negative. Unless we could find some new, positive piece of evidence tending to make it definitely appear there had either been false testimony or a wrong interpretation placed upon evidence which had been collected, there was nothing we could do.

On the other hand, there were many, many cases where a preliminary examination indicated promise, and we'd start digging away at the facts with all the diligence of a dog scratching away at a rabbit hole, only to find out either that the facts in the case had been misrepresented to us, or that, after all, the defendant was guilty.

It is, of course, natural for a prison inmate to lie about his conviction. In the first place if he is guilty it is second nature with him to lie, and in the second place he has, as far as he individually is concerned, everything to gain and nothing to lose.

A man is convicted and the main evidence against him is perhaps circumstantial, or hinges upon some one point, one circumstance, the testimony of one witness. The defendant goes to prison and has plenty of time to think. He begins to canvass all possible explanations, all of the stories he might have told which would have accounted for and explained away this bit of evidence.

It is surprising how adroit a man can become at doing this. In the course of time he works out an explanation, and rehearses that explanation until he believes it himself. He can recite it so convincingly that it sounds perfectly logical and true.

Most of the time which we were able to donate to work on the Court of Last Resort was consumed in separating the wheat from the chaff. In far too many instances what looked like good hard wheat turned out to be chaff.

One typical case which comes to mind is that of T. R. McClure, a personable, twenty-one-year-old Negro who was wanted for murder in the state of Ohio. He wasn't apprehended until two years or so after the commission of the murder. This young man was extremely plausible. He had no prior record, and the story which he told caused us a great deal of concern. He insisted that the prosecution had been able to convict him only by putting on a ballistics expert who had engaged in a lot of "double talk." He had been sentenced to death in the electric chair.

At that time Ohio was not particularly sympathetic with the Court of Last Resort. However, as it turned out, many of the officials in the prison felt that McClure had been wrongfully convicted and his pending execution bothered them.

We started an investigation, trying only to find out about the claim that the evidence on ballistics had been a mass of double talk.

Almost immediately we ran into difficulties. It speedily became apparent that there was someone, or that there were several someones, who didn't want the McClure case investigated, and who particularly didn't like the idea of the Court of Last Resort looking into the thing. Obstacle after obstacle began to be put in our way.

Finally, however, we stopped trying to get a transcript of the evidence from persons who should have been glad to see that we had it, went to the court reporter and had his notes of that portion of the evidence transcribed. We were startled at what we found.

In identifying bullets there are generally two types of characteristics by which an expert reaches an opinion.

First there are the "class characteristics." These have to do with the number of grooves and lands in the barrel of the revolver which fired the shot, the degree of twist, the spacing, the direction, etc. These vary with different revolvers so that an expert, having a bullet on which the marks of the grooves and lands are plainly indicated, can usually tell with certainty the make of revolver from which the bullet was fired.

Individual, or microscopic characteristics, are something else. They represent the *individual* scratches on the bullets which are caused by blemishes, tool marks, etc. in the *individual* barrel of the weapon from which the bullet was fired. These translate themselves into numerous small scratches which are visible under a microscope, and which are truly the individual characteristics of the barrel in question.

Where the bullet has not been too badly defaced or distorted it is possible to use an instrument known as a comparison microscope, and, by using a test bullet fired from any weapon which is suspect, determine definitely and positively whether the two bullets were fired from the same gun.

The comparison microscope has two eyepieces, which, by means of prisms, transpose a section of one bullet so that it appears directly over the section of the other. The bullets are mounted on little spindles which can be rotated by means of a micrometer, and the investigator merely rotates the bullets patiently and carefully until he comes to a point where suddenly all of the individual scratches on the test bullet match with those of the so-called fatal bullet. In that event he knows that the two bullets were fired from the same gun; or he can continue his rotation until he knows that there is no point at which the scratches will coincide, and then he knows definitely and absolutely that the bullets were not fired by the same weapon.

It is, therefore, apparent that the class characteristics relate only to the make and caliber of a weapon, whereas the individual characteristics are the means by which a bullet can be literally "fingerprinted."

In the McClure case it appeared that after the defendant had been arrested the officers tried to trace a certain gun which he had and which he had pawned in a pawnshop. They were able to find this weapon and McClure readily admitted that this had been his gun.

The police turned this over to a ballistics expert, who fired test bullets through it and compared them with the fatal bullets.

The prosecutor called the expert on ballistics to the stand and this is an excerpt from his testimony:

Q. Then did you make an examination, a microscopic examination of the test shot pellets with any one or two of the pellets turned over to you by Dr. Gerber?

A. Yes.

Q. Under the comparison microscope? Did you do that?

A. Yes, I did.

Q. Describe to us briefly the procedure and technique adopted or used by you in making this comparison microscopic examination of these pellets, how you mounted them, and so forth.

A. We first mounted the test shot pellet on a gun we have on the stage of the microscope, that would be fixed on a base, flexible, on this mounting, that was set on the right-hand side, the right-hand microscope. We took one of the pellets submitted by Dr. Gerber and mounted that in a similar fashion on a mounting in a stage on the left side of the other microscope, and then we set the comparison piece, the comparison bridge connecting the two microscopes, and in lining those two up,—we could revolve this mounting to which the pellets have been fastened—we could revolve those around until we came to a point where we had the land impressions, the two edges of the complete land impressions. We have the two edges included in this optical field for the evidence pellet, and the same way for the test pellet, and in that way, with a microscopic magnification, we could tell whether the two land impressions were of the same width.

Q. What did you find as to that?

A. We found that the land impressions were of identical width.

Q. In addition to noting the width of the land impressions under the microscope, did you examine for the existence or non-existence of similarity or non-similarity of the microscopic engravings on the land impressions?

A. Yes, I did.

Q. Tell us what you observed about that.

A. Well, I observed that there was some microscopic engravure that was similar. However that was insufficient to be of a positive identification nature. There was a lack of microscopic engravure on the evidence pellets, and it was insufficient, although there was some similarity, it was insufficient to say the two were identical in microscopic engravure.

Q. So, as a result of your examination microscopically, you are telling this Court there was some similarity between the microscopic markings, but not sufficient enough to enable you to definitely conclude that the two pellets had been fired from the same gun, is that correct?

A. Yes sir.

Q. The class characteristics, however, were alike?

A. Yes, the class characteristics were.

You may examine.

Cross Examination

Q. In your testimony, you cannot swear those pellets were fired from the same gun?

A. No, sir.

Q. That was turned over to you by the Coroner?

A. No, sir.

Q. They could have been fired from some other gun of the same make?

A. Smith & Wesson.

Q. Is that correct?

[Objection]

A. As long as I cannot say it was from the same gun, I cannot say it was not fired from another gun.

Q. Another gun, other than Smith & Wesson?

A. It is possible, but not very probable. I mean, we might, when we compare the guns officially—the land impressions made from another type of gun may look to be just as wide, however, when we do magnify them, under the microscope, where even the width of a hair looks like a great distance, we do readily throw out those that are not alike.

Q. Now, by those pellets that are marked State's Exhibit 5, that were turned over to the Coroner, it is impossible to say to this Court whether those pellets were fired from that gun?

A. That's right, sir.

In other words, about all this testimony amounted to was that the test bullet and the fatal bullet had both been fired from weapons of the same make and caliber.

It will be noted how scrupulously careful the expert had been to state that he could not make a positive identification based upon the microscopic or individual characteristics alone, but how he did state generally that the two bullets were identical in class characteristics.

Unless this had been further explained by cross-examination it is quite evident that a jury, hearing that testimony, might well have felt that both bullets had been fired from the same gun.

Apparently the attorney representing McClure preferred to let well enough alone. There is, in fact, in this transcript every evidence that the cross-examiner was feeling his way with great care, as though he had been walking through a shallow ford and expected with every step to strike quicksand.

McClure was not tried by a jury but by three judges, a procedure which many attorneys (most prosecutors) have advocated.

Theoretically this gives a man the benefit of an expert appraisal of evidence and eliminates the emotionalism and inexplicable prejudices which are so frequently encountered when cases are tried before a jury. Actually in my own experience I am a strong advocate of the jury system.

Take this McClure case, for instance. If the attorney for the defense didn't dare to go into the matter of the ballistics evidence any further, why didn't the judges go into it? Why, in the name of reason, didn't someone bring out the fact that any real expert confronted with two bullets, one fatal, the other a test bullet fired from the suspect's weapon, in the absence of any complicating circumstances, finding that he could not match up the individual or microscopic characteristics of a bullet, would know absolutely and definitely that the two bullets were *not* fired from the same weapon?

Why didn't someone ask the expert about that?

No one did.

McClure was sentenced to die in the electric chair.

We started to investigate the case, and the more we investigated it the less we liked what we uncovered.

In the first place, McClure was a bright young Negro lad who should have developed into a useful member of society, and he probably would have if society had given him very much of a chance.

As it happened at that time, however, society was engaged in the usual sordid undercover activities which are so frequently a part of the law administration in big cities.

Crooked police officers were engaged in taking graft from the community in which McClure lived. Small houses of prostitution were permitted to run, just so they weren't too large. Small gambling games were permitted to run, just so they didn't get too noisy. The whole slimy combination of police corruption and underworld activity went hand in hand, creating the environment in which McClure managed to find his cheap lodgings.

Young McClure was personable. He was well liked, and it wasn't long before women took a fancy to him. He was being supported in part and from time to time by their earnings. He was sucked into the gambling environment, and soon formed associations which made this young impressionable lad feel that "only suckers worked."

It was quite apparent that young McClure had drifted around in a cesspool of this police-inspired, police-encouraged vice until he himself had become tainted. If the law enforcement officers tolerated and encouraged these little houses of prostitution, these petty gambling games so as to make graft money, why shouldn't McClure get in on the ground floor? There was only one answer to this question as he asked it of himself.

So young McClure took to sleeping until late in the morning, hanging around the gambling houses, and picking up "easy" money.

During the years which had elapsed since the murder was committed, the city had had a somewhat belated twinge of civic conscience and had started a clean-up in the district where McClure lived. The clean-up had disclosed ugly facts, and at least one of the police officers who had been taking money from the district had been convicted and sent to prison. All of this, however, was too late to do young McClure any good.

Dr. LeMoyne Snyder tried to get hold of the fatal bullets themselves so that an independent, thoroughly competent, unprejudiced ballistics expert could make an examination.

What happened was, in Dr. Snyder's opinion, a runaround.

We felt that under the circumstances the execution of young McClure should be postponed. We wanted time to investigate.

The date of the execution rolled around, yet there was no official word from Governor Frank J. Lausche of Ohio.

Dr. Snyder made a personal one-man, last-ditch fight to get McClure's execution postponed. He did everything he could but to no avail. Members of our investigating committee sent telegrams to Governor Lausche. The Governor intended to let the execution take place on schedule.

LeMoyne Snyder, on the day set for the execution, addressed a luncheon club in Lansing, Michigan. The members of the club had asked LeMoyne Snyder to tell them something of the activities of the Court of Last Resort. Dr. Snyder told them about the McClure case and what was happening.

That which followed is an interesting and inspiring illustration of the underlying spirit of fair play which characterizes the people of the United States.

Without Dr. Snyder's knowledge, a member of the Michigan Supreme Court, who had been appealed to by a prominent business-man who attended that luncheon, personally telephoned Governor Lausche, and then, to cap matters, Governor G. Mennen Williams personally asked Governor Lausche to postpone execution.

This last request made Governor Lausche furiously angry. He felt that Dr. LeMoyne Snyder was trying to get Michigan to dictate the official course of conduct in the state of Ohio. It wasn't until Dr. Snyder finally got through to Governor Lausche on the telephone, just a couple of hours before the execution, that Governor Lausche learned that the action of G. Mennen Williams had been entirely self-inspired, that Governor Williams was not even of Dr. Snyder's political party, and that what had happened was a spontaneous uprising of sentiment in the state of Michigan.

That caused a lot of thinking and eventually some action.

With less than an hour from the time young McClure was scheduled to be strapped into the electric chair, Governor Lausche granted a thirty-day reprieve.

We redoubled our efforts to find out something about the McClure case, and the Ohio runaround functioned perfectly.

It was reported in the press that members of the trial court, indignant at the tactics of the Court of Last Resort, had announced that we were going to be brought before the court and charged with contempt. Personally I didn't wait for the reactions of any of the other members. I advised Governor Lausche that I would not only be glad to subject myself to the jurisdiction of the Ohio court and see what they wanted to do about a contempt charge in an open hearing, but that I would waive extradition and would personally pay my own fare back to Ohio.

Needless to say there was no official action from the court. Apparently members had been misquoted in a newspaper interview.

However, things started going around and around—mostly around.

It seems that the exhibits in the McClure case, including the bullets, had been released to the prosecutor. The prosecutor was only too willing to let Dr. Snyder *look* at the bullets, but to permit them to be taken to a ballistics expert for an official examination—that was something else again.

The Ohio Pardon and Parole Commission stated that it would be glad to give Dr. Snyder permission to take the bullets to the laboratory of a recognized ballistics expert provided the prosecutor would consent. The prosecutor would not give his consent unless the board told him to. The board would make no such order.

We wanted to take Alex Gregory to the prison and give McClure a polygraph test. The Ohio Pardon and Parole Commission stated that this could only be done after permission had been obtained from the Governor. The Governor felt that he could not give permission to make this examination unless it was requested by the Ohio Pardon and Parole Commission.

Looking back on it in the light of after-developments, I am now satisfied that someone in the state of Ohio was putting out a lot of political poison, and that Governor Lausche actually felt we were not trying to do a public service but were trying to cut ourselves a piece of cake.

However that may be, the second date fixed for the execution of young McClure speedily approached. And we had gotten nowhere.

It is for this reason that ordinarily we do not investigate capital cases. There is not time for any publication of facts in the magazine, and we cannot marshal public sentiment which, after all, is the only weapon we have when we are confronted with official indifference or political influence.

However, it soon became apparent that if young McClure should be executed under the circumstances as they then existed, there was going to be a flare-up of public sentiment which would have terrific repercussions. There had been enough local publicity to cause considerable comment. And so finally permission was granted for us to give McClure a test on the polygraph.

It will be recalled that the lie detector is a scientific instrument which measures simultaneously the respiration of the individual, the electric resistance of his skin, and the blood pressure.

Just as an electric cardiogram must be evaluated by an expert in order to be any good, the graph of the so-called lie detector must be examined by an expert. Moreover the situation is not that simple. In making the graph certain conditions must exist. In the first place there must be a carefully selected list of questions. The individual temperament of the subject must be appraised and the conditions must be approximately ideal. There must be the full co-operation of the subject, and there must be no distracting noises, no particular change in the tone of voice in which the questions are asked. Above all, no attempt at third-degree. The person who gives the polygraph test must have a completely detached attitude of scientific investigation. He must be interested only in ascertaining the truth or falsity of certain matters as determined by the subject's reaction.

I am definitely not in favor of ever having the polygraph brought into court or used as part of courtroom procedure. On the other hand, when a man of the caliber of Alex Gregory gives an individual a test on the polygraph I will unquestioningly accept his conclusions.

If Gregory doesn't know, or can't determine, he'll say so. If he says a man is innocent, that man is pretty certain to be. But, above all, if he says a man is guilty, I know that Gregory has given him every benefit of the doubt. If he ever makes a mistake it is certainly not going to be an error which will result in forfeiting a man's freedom or costing him his life.

But if we ever let down the bars, if the polygraph ever becomes accepted as an official instrument of inquisition, if men are required to take a polygraph test, or if polygraph experts are permitted to go into court to testify as to their findings, a whole flock of "experts" will spring up like mushrooms. A few of them will be competent, scientific investigators. Most of them will be men who have neither the ability to reach scientific conclusions, nor the integrity to withstand the numerous temptations with which a polygraph expert is daily confronted.

Once the official circles in Ohio had given us an opportunity to run McClure on a polygraph, curiosity began to manifest itself to find out just what was going to happen. The time was only a few days prior to his execution, and, as above mentioned, there had been an enormous flare-up of public interest in the state of Ohio.

Also, I think that by this time there was beginning to be a feeling on the part of some of the Ohio officials that we were, after all, only trying to do them a favor by getting at the truth, and were not necessarily trying to liberate young McClure or to court publicity. We wanted to know what the facts in the case were.

The Ohio Pardon and Parole Commission called a session at the penitentiary to await the results of the examination.

McClure, plausible, convincing, likeable, had convinced some of the chaplains and other people of his innocence. They were certain that he wasn't lying, but was telling a plain, straightforward story.

Moreover, there was the transcript of that evidence of the ballistics expert, and the cold hard fact that every attempt to have these bullets examined by an impartial, thoroughly qualified expert had been effectively blocked. Perhaps each person who had taken part in the big runaround felt he was within his rights. There certainly had been no evidence of concerted action. The fact remained that with a man's life at stake, with the testimony as disclosed in the record, we were unable to have an examination of these bullets by such a fully qualified, nationally known laboratory expert. Such an expert would, of course, have to take the bullets into his own laboratory where he could conduct an impartial scientific examination. We found ourselves unable to satisfy this condition. We had the permission but we couldn't get the bullets.

Finally, however, T. R. McClure, smiling confidently, assured that he was at length going to be "vindicated," faced Alex Gregory and settled down for the polygraph test.

To the uninitiated these tests seem unbelievably simple. Some of the questions are so absurdly irrelevant that it seems a shame to waste time asking them.

The fact remains, however, that this type of interrogation, the mixing of innocuous questions with others that are pertinent, the whole sequence of interrogation, is predicated upon certain rules of applied psychology which have been carefully thought out.

Alex Gregory asked his list of questions in a monotone.

McClure answered those questions, but as he did so the machine, recording changes in his respiration and blood pressure, began to build up a highly significant graph.

Midway through the examination Alex Gregory knew that McClure was guilty.

But Gregory kept on with his examination. He repeated the questions. He watched the needles on the machine as they traced out a telltale graph of deception. He changed adjustments. He changed his approach. He tried again. And every time he got the same answer.

Then Alex Gregory spread the graph out in front of young McClure. He showed the boy exactly where his blood pressure had responded to every question. He showed where McClure had been trying to deceive us on certain facts which we knew about, and where he had shown a telltale emotion in connection with other facts that were as yet unknown to us.

Gregory now knew as a result of studying this graph that McClure had committed two robberies and that he had committed the murder.

Confronted with that devastating evidence, young McClure's self-confidence drained away. He sank back in the chair and confessed.

"You're right," he said. "I did it."

And then McClure went on to tell his story, the story of the right man who had been convicted on the wrong evidence. He confessed to the robbery and murder for which he had been convicted, and he confessed to the other robbery which the polygraph record had indicated. Also he confessed to the crime of forging and cashing a government check.

As a result, we were able to explain the ballistics evidence. McClure, it seemed, knowing the gun with which the crime had been committed was not the pawned weapon, had calmly steered officers to the pawned weapon and identified it as his, knowing that a ballistics test would show that the fatal bullet had been fired from another gun. And of course that's exactly what happened.

McClure, it seemed, according to his confession, had wanted to leave Ohio and go to Detroit. He owed a substantial sum of money to a certain individual in Ohio. McClure said he went to this man and told him he wanted to go to Detroit.

The man shook his head. "Not while you're owing me that money."

"How can I pay it?" McClure asked.

According to McClure's confession the man furnished McClure with a gun and told him to "pay up."

We are always very careful to explain to persons whom we interrogate that we are not representing them in any way; that we are, so far as we are able, representing the public; that they cannot tell us anything "in confidence"; that since we are appealing directly to the American public we must take the American public into our confidence, and that anything told to us must be for publication. Prisoners cannot confide in us as they would in an attorney.

Therefore Gregory went to the door where the Ohio Pardon and Parole Commission was waiting.

"Gentlemen," he said, "if you care to step in here I think Mr. McClure has a statement to make in which you will be interested."

They were very much interested in McClure's statement.

A few days later McClure went to the electric chair, and a few people in Ohio breathed a sigh of relief. The lethal electric current effectively sealed the lips of Theodore R. McClure and the case is "closed."

No steps were taken so far as we know to interrogate the person McClure named in his confession as having furnished him with the gun.

Governor Lausche and the officials of the Ohio Pardon and Parole Commission belatedly recognized the work we are trying to do, and I will say one thing, Governor Lausche has more than made up for his official reluctance in the McClure case.

Not only did Governor Lausche advise us that whenever we had any other case in Ohio we could count on the full co-operation of all the officials in that state, but he has on occasion expressed himself on the Court of Last Resort and on his experiences with it so that other governors who might well have been dubious have been impressed and have given us their co-operation.

As for McClure, he had convinced several persons of his innocence, then had met his Waterloo when he placed his magnetic personality up against a scientific investigator.

He held no hard feelings.

"You can't blame a guy for trying," he said as he was being led to the electric chair.

(AUTHOR'S NOTE)

Some time after the conclusion of the McClure case I was invited by my friend Dr. Alan R. Moritz, the noted authority on legal medicine, pathology and medicolegal investigative technique, to address a special class on Homicide Investigation at the Western Reserve University. While there I had an opportunity to become familiar with the work being done by the Cleveland police, and, more particularly, with the Homicide Bureau.

I was very much impressed with what I saw.

Captain David Kerr, the Chief of the Homicide Bureau, assured me that, in his opinion, the three judges who convicted McClure had paid absolutely no attention to the ballistics evidence, but had acted entirely upon the other physical evidence in the record.

As it turned out, there was sufficient additional evidence to indicate McClure's guilt very conclusively. We did not have this in our hands when we launched the investigation. Our attention was attracted to the case by McClure's plea and the nature of the firearm identification evidence.—McClure, of course, knowing that the gun which he had used in committing the murder was not the gun which had been tested by the police, very shrewdly concentrated upon that one point in enlisting our aid.

If I had known as much about the competency of the Cleveland homicide bureau as I know now, I could personally have spared myself a great deal of worry. Cleveland is, I think, one of the most civic-minded communities in the United States. The support it has given its police in investigative work is far above the average, and it has furnished its coroner, Dr. S. R. Gerber, with what is probably the best-planned, most efficient coroner's laboratory in the country.

In short, as things exist today, Cleveland is one of the last places where one would look for an investigative blunder in a homicide investigation.

But we didn't know all this when young McClure appealed to us for aid.

10

It didn't need any pressure whatever to get Governor Okey L. Patteson of West Virginia to recognize the work that the Court of Last Resort was doing.

Robert Ballard Bailey was under sentence of death in the state prison at Moundsville, West Virginia. He was scheduled to have the dubious honor of being the first person executed in the new electric chair which had been installed when West Virginia changed the method of execution from hanging to electrocution.

Warden Orel J. Skeen had doubts about the guilt of Robert Bailey.

Not only were there some peculiar things in connection with the evidence in the case itself, but the prison grapevine beat an insistent tattoo about the prison. The grapevine insisted positively and absolutely that Robert Bailey was innocent.

Bailey also had what should have been one of the most convincing alibis in the world. The city police of Charleston, West Virginia, gave him that alibi.

At the exact moment when witnesses insisted that Robert Bailey was perpetrating the murder, the city police were trying to apprehend him on a charge of drunken driving.

The witnesses fixed the time of murder at only a few minutes after three-thirty in the afternoon. The police definitely fixed the time of pursuit at three-thirty in the afternoon. The police insisted that Robert Bailey was staggering drunk. The eyewitnesses to the murder said that the murderer, whom they identified as Robert Bailey, was cold sober. There could be no mistake about the Robert Bailey whom the police were chasing. Not only did the police recognize him but they riddled the back of his automobile with bullet holes, and when Bailey's automobile was located it was perforated with the bullets which had been fired by the police.

However, Bailey had a head start on the police. He was driving on some rather tricky roads. He had the courage of desperation, and the happy-go-lucky willingness to take chances which is the result of having imbibed too much alcohol.

There were plenty of witnesses to identify Bailey as the drunken driver. These witnesses all knew Bailey. The witnesses who identified Bailey as the murderer were fewer in number and were strangers to him. It could well have been a case of mistaken identity.

Robert Bailey was a peculiar character. He seemed to have been born to be behind the eight ball. When he was sober he was quite all right, but occasionally he would get drunk, and then he would do peculiar things, crimes that had no rhyme or reason. He couldn't explain why and neither could anyone else. He was just as apt as not to have a dozen or so drinks, then try to steal a wheelbarrow from a contracting job in plain sight of a watchful and hostile overseer.

He always got caught. There was no finesse about these crimes. By the time he'd sober up he'd find himself in jail faced with a charge so absolutely, utterly ridiculous that both prosecutor and judge would lose patience with him and decide they'd teach him a lesson. He had, therefore, served two previous terms in West Virginia penitentiary for crimes so foolish that it almost seemed as though Bailey liked it in the penitentiary and was trying to take a short cut to get back in whenever the law let him out.

The murder of which he was convicted was not like Bailey at all. Somebody who probably was known to a West Virginia housewife picked her up, apparently to give her a ride home. This was in broad daylight shortly before three-thirty in the afternoon.

At exactly three-thirty, a witness, who knew the woman in question, saw her riding in an automobile with a man. She identified the man from a quick glimpse as being Robert Bailey. She was very positive about it being three-thirty. She had a certain personal reason for being conscious of the time, and at the exact moment she had seen the couple in the automobile she had been looking at the clock on a public building, a clock which was one hundred per cent accurate and which showed the hour to be exactly three-thirty P.M.

Later on, farther up the road, a motorist who was following a car saw the legs of a woman protruding from the car. A little farther on the woman either fell or was pushed from the automobile, which was going rather slowly.

The automobile kept on going. The motorist stopped to give aid, and a bystander, who had been walking along the road, also stopped to help.

At about this time a car came along the road from the opposite direction, going back toward the city, and a man stopped and got out. The bystanders asked him if he would take the woman to the hospital or to her home, and he said he would do so, that he knew who she was and would be glad to do what he could.

The man who had been following the automobile was convinced that this was the same car from which the woman had been thrown. When he looked at the back of the car as it moved away it looked familiar to him, and from that he was satisfied that this was the same car.

He identified the driver of that car as Robert Bailey.

He insisted, however, that Bailey was sober; that his speech was perfectly normal, that he smelled no liquor on his breath, that Bailey was able to help him load the woman in the automobile, that his co-ordination was perfect, that he engaged in the very delicate and tricky task of helping to get the rather heavy woman lifted from the road and into the front seat of the automobile.

At that exact moment municipal police insist that Robert Bailey was drunk, and Bailey admits he was. His associates who were with him say he was drunk, and other reputable witnesses say he was staggering drunk; that he was, moreover, at a point some miles removed from the scene of the crime.

The motorist who had identified the murderer as Robert Bailey fixed the time with definite certainty because he was on his way

home from work and he knew exactly when he had left the job—
shortly after three-thirty P.M.

No matter how you looked at it, it was a thoroughly cockeyed
case.

And Robert Bailey was sentenced to be electrocuted.

Bob Bailey, always noted for doing the wrong thing at the wrong
time, in the worst possible manner, awakened from the drunken
sleep in which he plunged on his return home. He had a recollection
of having been pursued by the police and of having been shot at.
He went out and looked at his automobile, and, sure enough, found
that it was perforated with bullet holes. He knew he was in a jam.
Thereupon, running true to form, he did the worst possible-thing.
He grabbed his wife and child and ran away, waiting for things to
blow over. He insists that he knew nothing whatever about any murder charge, but only knew he had been quite drunk, that he had fled
from the pursuing officers, that he was a two-time loser, and that if
they caught up with him things would go hard with him.

On the other hand, the newspapers in Charleston saw in the case
a marvelous opportunity for editorial comment. Here was a ne'er-
do-well two-time loser who had run afoul of the law on various and
sundry occasions, who had received clemency at times, who had
failed to respond to treatment, who was definitely not an asset to
the community. Apparently he had finally culminated his criminal
career by committing a murder.

The newspapers went to town.

Bailey, hiding in an isolated district in Florida, was, he insists,
ignorant of all this hullabaloo. According to his story he was merely
waiting for things to blow over.

Things didn't blow over. The wind blew, but it blew the flames of
public indignation into a fever heat of prejudice.

Eventually Bailey was located. He was arrested and, according
to his story, that was the first he knew of any murder charge. No
one believed him. He was brought back, prosecuted, convicted of
murder in the first degree, and sentenced to death by a judge who
promptly sat down and wrote a letter to the Governor asking him at
least to commute the sentence.

All in all it was quite a case.

Bailey perfected an appeal and the higher court turned him down.

Warden Orel J. Skeen, who has the courage of his convictions, who is a firm upstanding Southern gentleman, who believes in a square deal for all of the inmates in his institution, couldn't believe that Bailey was guilty.

He had come to know Bailey pretty well while he was confined in the institution. He didn't think Bailey was of the type to commit this crime, and the prison grapevine told him Bailey was innocent. Warden Skeen was increasingly reluctant to strap Bailey in the electric chair and pull the switch which turned on the current, yet there was no other alternative.

Then Skeen thought of Tom Smith.

Tom Smith, it will be remembered, had been the warden of the Washington State Penitentiary at Walla Walla, and as such had come to know all of the wardens pretty well. These wardens are all members of the Prison Association and meet at conventions once each year.

When Tom Smith left his position as warden to engage in work for the Court of Last Resort there was quite a bit of comment among the various wardens; and Skeen, who had known Tom Smith personally and liked him, recalling his new activities, picked up a telephone and put through a call for him no matter in what part of the United States he might happen to be.

As it happened, Tom Smith, Dr. LeMoyne Snyder, Alex Gregory and I were in Lansing, Michigan, working on the Vance Hardy case.

Tom Smith received Skeen's telephone call there on a Thursday afternoon, and, after a brief conference, agreed to get in touch with Skeen the next day. Robert Bailey was scheduled to die in the electric chair during the early part of the following week.

Smith, Gregory and I drove all night, arriving in Moundsville, where the penitentiary is located, in the very, very small hours of the morning.

Harry Steeger caught a night plane out of New York and was there by morning to meet us.

We talked with Warden Skeen and then we went to talk with Robert Bailey.

Bailey was thin, emaciated, and apprehensive. The thought of the electric chair loomed large in his mind. He couldn't hold food on his stomach. He couldn't sleep. The man was on the point of becoming a nervous wreck.

Gregory, however, felt that there was a strong possibility Bailey could take a polygraph test, and that his responses could give us a valuable clue. Bailey was only too anxious to try it. He was anxious for anything, any last chance, any straw at which he could clutch.

I sat in the room with Gregory while he put Bailey through a polygraph test.

The test indicated that Bailey was innocent of the crime of which he had been convicted.

Because of Bailey's nervous condition, however, because of the seriousness of the situation, Gregory wanted to be sure. He asked me to leave the room and spent a long session during the afternoon giving Bailey test after test.

At the end of that time Gregory pronounced that in his opinion Robert Bailey had no guilty knowledge of the murder.

That presented us with quite a question.

It was a long drive over to the state capitol, but we arose early Saturday morning and drove down there so we could interview the judge who had tried Bailey's case.

The judge was in a peculiar position. He didn't want to talk for publication, but, reading between the lines of his conversation, we got a pretty good picture of the situation and how the judge felt about the case. He also gave us a carbon copy of the letter he had sent to Governor Patteson.

It was then just before noon on Saturday. The days were beginning to get hot, and we knew that everyone who could arrange to do so had planned to leave the heat of the city and go out to the country. It would be impossible to do anything officially before Monday morning. But Robert Bailey was scheduled to die during the first part of the following week. Steeger had to be in New York on Monday morning. We had left a red-hot situation in Michigan, and Tom

Smith, Alex Gregory and I had to be back in Lansing at least by Monday morning.

Orel Skeen called up Governor Patteson's secretary, Rosalind Funk, and explained the situation to her.

Rosalind Funk, as I was to learn later, had been the Governor's secretary for some time. She knew what was important and what wasn't, and she knew how Governor Patteson felt about matters.

While Orel Skeen was talking with Mrs. Funk, I felt the chances of our seeing Governor Patteson before Monday were about one in a thousand, and we had to be in Michigan Monday morning.

Warden Skeen hung up.

"What did she say?" I asked.

"She said it was important enough to warrant her getting in touch with the Governor personally. We're to call back in ten minutes."

Ten minutes later Mrs. Funk relayed what the Governor had said. It came as a great surprise to me.

Governor Patteson had planned a week-end trip, but Mrs. Funk conveyed his words to us as she had taken them down in short-hand. "These gentlemen are prominent men. Their time is valuable. They're devoting that time gratuitously to the interests of justice. I think Robert Bailey is guilty. I've examined the transcript in the case, and have seen no reason thus far for taking any action. I believe it's a case where the law should take its course. But if these gentlemen are willing to sacrifice their week end on this case, I'm willing to sacrifice my week end. I'll meet them at my office at the State Capitol at one-thirty this afternoon."

Governor Patteson is one official who takes the responsibilities of his office seriously, and who tries to be fair regardless of personal or political considerations. He extended us the most courteous treatment, and had the most open mind of any official we had so far encountered. He was dignified in his official position, yet managed to extend to us the hospitality of his state so that I always picture West Virginia as one of the most truly friendly states I have ever visited.

We filed up to the Governor's office at one-thirty. The electrical current in the building had been shut off and the air conditioners weren't working. It was hot and oppressive in the Governor's office, but he sat in there and listened to what we had to say. He asked questions. We were there from one-thirty until nearly five o'clock; then Governor Patteson called in the press and announced that under the circumstances he had decided to grant a reprieve in the Bailey case, that we had signified our desire to make a further investigation, that he was going to assign a member of the West Virginia State Police to be with us at all times so that our investigation would be clothed with official authority. Bailey was not going to be executed as long as there was any doubt as to his guilt, and we were going to be given every opportunity to complete our investigation.

It is not possible at this time to give all of the ramifications of the investigation in the Bailey case. The case is still open. But I mention these matters in order to show the caliber of the chief executive of West Virginia. It was a refreshing experience.

We embarked upon an investigation of the Bailey case, and in many respects it was one of our most exasperating cases. The facts did not fit, and it's impossible to put them together. For instance, the witness who, sometime after Bailey's arrest, identified Bailey as being the man who was driving the car from which the victim was pushed, was equally positive in his assertion that the car Bailey was undoubtedly driving that day was not the car that the witness saw being driven by the murderer.

The woman victim in the case, picked up at about three-forty-five outside of Charleston by this person who had been identified by the witnesses as Bailey, with the promise that she would be taken home or to a hospital, apparently never was taken to her home and certainly not to a hospital. She was found shortly before midnight lying by the side of the street in Charleston, a place where it was almost impossible for her to have lain undiscovered for more than an outside limit of thirty minutes. Her neck had been broken. She was still alive. She was taken to a hospital and there died.

She is reported to have stated to members of her family that the man who was responsible for her injuries was "Bob the glasscutter." Robert Bailey was a glazier.

There were various bits of contradictory evidence. One of the woman's shoes was found at the place where she had either fallen or been thrown from the automobile. Yet when the victim was found in the alley late that night, the driver of the ambulance is positive that she was wearing both shoes. At almost every point in the case we were confronted with contradictory evidence.

At the end we became convinced that the evidence in the case presented a cockeyed picture. It didn't establish Bailey's guilt beyond a reasonable doubt. We picked up the prosecutor in the case and went to Governor Patteson to make a report showing exactly what we had uncovered.

Governor Patteson heard that report and promptly commuted the sentence of Robert Bailey to life imprisonment, stating that in the present condition of the evidence he was far from satisfied with the verdict, that there was a reasonable doubt to say the least as to Bailey's guilt, and he called on the state police to institute a new investigation of the murder right from the beginning.

Presumably that investigation is being made at the present time and therefore there are certain aspects of the case which should not be discussed. However, from a practical standpoint, our investigation just about covered every available fact, and until new facts are brought to light by the course of time, and through uncovering new witnesses, it is possible that the case of Robert Bailey will remain *in statu quo.*

There was one rather interesting sidelight in the Bailey case. It will be remembered that when we first contacted Governor Patteson he was pretty well convinced that the law should take its course. Warden Skeen, marshaling his reasons for asking us to come in and make an investigation, mentioned among other things the fact that the prison grapevine stated Bailey was innocent. The Governor was skeptical of the accuracy of this grapevine.

Warden Skeen said, "Don't ever underestimate that grapevine, Governor. I don't know how those men get the information they have. I don't know how they reach the conclusions they do. They have unlimited time, of course, in which to think, and they'll digest and redigest every bit of information they get."

The Governor's smile was good-naturedly skeptical.

"Well," Skeen said, "let me give you a specific instance. You remember when you rang me up and asked me if I would accept the position as warden?"

The Governor nodded.

"If it's a fair question," Skeen went on, "how long before you placed that telephone call had you decided that I might make a good warden?"

"About two hours," the Governor said.

Skeen nodded. (Apparently there had been a political situation where two factions each had been plugging for one individual as warden, and Skeen had not only been a dark horse but a last-minute choice.)

"When I assumed my position as warden of the penitentiary," Skeen said, "I found that they had been making book in the prison on the next warden, and that as early as ten days prior to the date you called me up, the betting had been two to one that I'd be the next warden."

"Why, I hadn't even thought of you in that connection at that time," Governor Patteson said.

Skeen smiled. "That's the point I'm trying to make."

The Governor thought that over. The smile of good-natured skepticism left his face.

Veteran wardens never discount the prison grapevine. Nor do they discount that telepathic something which is a definite intangibility, yet which is of major importance in the administration of prisons; that is, the peculiar feeling of tension or lack of tension which one gets as soon as one enters the walls.

Sometimes things are rolling along smoothly. It's impossible to tell what gives this impression. There is simply a lack of tension. Perhaps it's in the way the men move. Perhaps it's in their walk, the swing of their hands, the way they hold their heads. No one knows. No one has ever been able to classify it.

But at other times there will be the feeling of tension. An experienced prison man stepping inside the walls knows instantly that all is not well. Men may be moving around as usual, but there's a seething cauldron of trouble boiling a devil's brew beneath the surface. You can *feel* it. It's there, it's a very definite factor.

There is, of course, some sort of telepathic emotional force which permeates any body of men who are held so closely confined. Let something important happen in a prison and the word seems to spread instantaneously and without the need of oral communication.

Men in confinement are subject to peculiar emotional stresses, and when these stresses get bottled up too long without any outlet one never knows what is going to happen.

I remember standing on a prison wall with the warden of one of the penitentiaries, watching the men down in the enclosed yard batting baseballs around. It was a big yard but there were times when the baseballs banged against the walls.

"Rather tough on baseballs," I said.

"They cost a lot of money," the warden admitted, and then went on, "But it's one of the best investments we can make in the prison. As long as we have the men down there taking out their animal spirits in good healthful exercise, out in the sunlight, we don't need to worry about some of the other problems quite so much. The more we can keep them outside, the more we can keep them engaged in athletic sports, the more we can keep them interested in good healthful competition, the better off we are."

Opposed to that are other prisons which are classified as "high security units," where men are constantly watched, where no spontaneity is permitted, where exercise is regimented almost as rigorously as the rules of confinement. One never knows when some untoward minor occurrence in a prison of that sort is going to transform the inmates in a split fraction of a second from automatons into yelling, bloodthirsty devils, grabbing the nearest guards to serve as hostages, wrecking everything they can get their hands on, starting on an orgy of destruction which must burn itself out emotionally before the men can be brought back to any semblance of control.

Those prison riots are terrible things. Officials who have been through a full-fledged prison riot are never quite the same afterward.

A riot is mass hysteria. Just as a woman may give way to hysterics, so does the collective body of prison inmates become a wildly yelling group of emotional maniacs. They don't know what they're going to do. No one knows. They're savage animals until the twisted, warped emotions burn themselves out.

Men who have been repressed, subdued, regimented, punished, build up an emotional tension. Wise prison officials try to furnish some safety valve, some channel of escape so that the tension never reaches the point of explosion.

That's the reason for prison clubs, debating societies, athletic contests, prison newspapers.

The "tighter" the prison, the more inflexible the rules, the more strict the discipline, the more chance there is for riot if any fortuitous circumstance ever gives the men a chance.

It only needs a little thing, perhaps a blow, a wild demoniacal yell, and then as though things had been rehearsed to a split second of timing, taut nerves give way all at once to spontaneous pandemonium.

Escapes may be planned and rehearsed. Riots are as spontaneous as a dust explosion in a factory.

Recently in visiting one of the "high security" Eastern prisons, I found that the warden had gone back and examined records over the years on the three riots the prison had experienced. They had all taken place on the third Friday in the month.

Why?

No one knows.

11

By this time our work was attracting national attention and letters were pouring in.

Henry Franklin, a young vigorous attorney of Peterborough, New Hampshire, who had had an FBI training, and also parole experience, wrote in with a practical suggestion. He wanted to organize an auxiliary committee of lawyers, who had been connected with the Federal Bureau of Investigation, to help us in our work.

We told him to go ahead, to start out with a small, compact committee of men whom he knew and had worked with.

So now we have a subcommittee of able attorneys who are also familiar with investigative work. They are:

E. Cage Brewer, Jr.
Brewer & Brewer
Box 306
Clarksdale, Mississippi

Philip V. Christenson
Christenson & Christenson
1st Security Bank Building
Provo, Utah

John C. Firmin
322 Niles Building
Findlay, Ohio

Henry H. Franklin
Blodgett & Franklin
Savings Bank Building
Peterborough, New Hampshire

Thomas E. Heffernan
1415 Coast Highway
Corona del Mar, California

Marshall W. Houts
311 Waverly Drive
Tulsa 4, Oklahoma

W. Logan Huiskamp
Boyd, Walker, Huiskamp & Concannon
609 Blondeau Street
Keokuk, Iowa

Paul F. Kelly
333 Pine Street
San Francisco 4, California

Donald A. Rosen
407 Van Nuys Building
210 W. 7th Street
Los Angeles 14, California

I have met most of these men personally. They are alert, vigorous young men who know their law, and understand how to investigate a crime.

One thing is certain. The FBI, under J. Edgar Hoover, has reached a high-water mark in the training of the highest class of investigators this country can produce. For the most part a man who has served the FBI is absolutely tops.

We have used this "Franklin Committee" (Henry Franklin is its chairman) in several cases. The results have demonstrated its great value, and it has greatly increased our efficiency.

Moreover, it is to be remembered that these are, for the most part, young lawyers who have not as yet achieved financial independence. Their time is their chief asset. Therefore an offer on the part of these men to donate their time means a major sacrifice.

Some of these men haven't been called on yet, because we haven't had any cases in their part of the country which we felt could be handled to advantage.

Three of them, however, have been called on in cases of major importance, cases which haven't yet been completed so we can't report on them at this time. These men have given a great measure of their time not only willingly but eagerly.

Then there are the readers themselves.

Thousands of these readers have sent in letters of encouragement, suggestions and comments. Some of them have gone further. One of them, a very busy man who is in the high income bracket, consistently devotes a part of his time to this work, following our investigations, calling on governors, trying to interest other citizens and getting them to watch the actions of their governors in connection with the cases we publicize.

Nowadays, whenever members of our group travel, they find men who seek them out to tell them how important they feel this work is and how much they want to do to support it.

All of this means a great deal. It means the public is waking up.

However, this awakening public interest carries with it a whole new set of responsibilities and obligations.

For instance, the number of new cases has simply engulfed us.

Tom Smith, who had been driving day and night trying to keep pace with the investigative work, decided that it was a job calling for more vitality than he had to give. He reluctantly tendered his resignation.

Looking around for another investigator we decided that Marshall Houts, with his legal training, his background of investigative experience and training in the FBI, would be an ideal person, and, after some consideration, Marshall Houts decided to come with the Court of Last Resort on a full-time basis.

It would be interesting to tackle the vast pile of material that has accumulated in the Court of Last Resort and figure out how many man-hours have gone into separating wheat from chaff in relation to the number of man-hours that have been spent in trying to liberate individuals we feel have been wrongfully convicted.

This doesn't necessarily mean that *all* of these cases are what is known in the vernacular as "bum beefs." Some of them are, some aren't. All too frequently we hear some story of an injustice which makes our blood boil with indignation. Weeks later, after we have spent time and money on an investigation, we find that the prisoner lied to us about certain phases of the case and withheld information about others. That, of course, human nature being what it is, is to be expected. But there is not nearly as much of this as we had anticipated. Prisoners seem in the aggregate to be far more ethical in such matters than any of us had expected.

When we first discussed the program with penologists they predicted that every prisoner who wanted his freedom, and all of them do, having everything to gain and nothing to lose by appealing to us, would appeal to us in the most heartrending terms possible.

Actually it is interesting to note there is a sense of honor among these men. Quite frequently we receive letters from prison inmates commending us for the job we are doing, suggesting that we investigate the case of some other prisoner, but taking pains to tell us that they themselves are not material for the Court of Last Resort, that in their cases the conviction was justified.

But merely because we find a case where *we* are satisfied a man has been wrongfully convicted doesn't mean we can tell the public about that case. There are some cases where the possibility of error is so apparent we go ahead on the original facts. But whenever possible, we try to conserve our energies for those cases where there is some *positive* fact indicating the innocence of the defendant. This doesn't necessarily mean a *new* fact, it means something that is a definite factual indication of innocence.

It is no good to say, for instance, that John Doe was identified as being the person who perpetrated a crime, that he tells us that the identification was erroneous and that we have decided there are so many indications this was the case that we feel John Doe should be liberated.

We have dozens of such cases. They represent probably the most puzzling and exasperating problem in the whole field of criminal justice. It is in the field of eye-witness identification rather than in the field of circumstantial evidence that the most tragic injustices occur.

But in the case of John Doe, unless there is something we can do to *prove* there was a mistake in identification, our hands are bound. The jury originally had all of the evidence before it. It had the advantage of listening to the people on the witness stand and of forming its own conclusion as to whether those people were or were not telling the truth, whether they were or were not mistaken. For us to come along at a later date and suggest that John Doe be released simply because we do not agree with the verdict of the jury would weaken our program and expose us to ridicule.

John Doe, quite naturally, sees this problem from a different viewpoint. He is innocent. He was wrongfully convicted. He is serving life imprisonment for a crime he didn't commit. It is only natural that he should feel his case should receive our consideration, someone's consideration, everyone's consideration.

Unfortunately the person who makes the sort of identification which *should* be entitled to the greatest weight is often made to cut a sorry figure in the courtroom.

That person is sincere and honest. He says, "The light was poor. I had only a fleeting glimpse of my assailant. I was excited at the time. I *think* that this defendant is the person who held me up. His appearance is in every way similar to that of the culprit."

The attorney for the defense pounces upon this unhappy witness when it comes time for cross-examination. "It isn't what you *think* that counts," he yells, "it's what you *know!* Are you willing to *swear* that the defendant was the same identical man who held you up?"

"I *think* he is the same man."

"Do you *know* he's the same man?"

"I think that he is, but I can't be absolutely positive."

"Then there *is* a doubt in your mind, perhaps a rather nebulous doubt, but nevertheless a doubt?"

"Well, if you want to put it that way. I *think* he's the man. That's the best I can do."

And so the attorney for the defense smiles at the jury and says, "Well, gentlemen, you have taken an oath to acquit this defendant if there is a reasonable doubt in your mind as to his guilt. Now here's the complaining witness in the case who admits there's a doubt in his own mind. You can't expect him to remove a doubt from your mind while there's a doubt in his mind."

On the other hand, some person who has made up his mind he's not going to be trapped on cross-examination, that he isn't going to let any smart lawyer get the best of *him*, sits on the witness stand with tight-lipped determination and says, "I know it was poor light. I may have been excited at the time, but I saw my assailant and that's the man—the man sitting right there next to you—the defendant in the case. He's the man."

How frequently does this happen?

No one knows.

Police know that many, many times they get descriptions from victims of the assailant, and when the assailant is finally captured and the crime is definitely pinned on him, it is found that the description given by the victim was absurdly erroneous.

Many, many times there are erroneous identifications which only the police know about. They pick up some person for questioning. They don't have very much against him. They invite the victims of recent stick-ups to "take a look."

Suppose one, or perhaps more, of the victims identifies this man. Then another man is picked up and *he* has some of the loot in his possession, and again the same victims identify this new suspect. Suspect number one is turned loose. He gets out of there fast. Suspect number two doesn't know there had ever been another identification. Quite naturally, the police don't tell the lawyer for the defendant, and the witnesses, now convinced that they are *positive*, don't say a word.

Sometimes it even works the other way.

In the Boggie case the police picked up the man who seemed to be guilty. Three witnesses identified him. Then it seemed the man had an alibi so the police turned him loose. The witnesses became firmly convinced that they *must* have been mistaken. The man had an alibi, didn't he?

Later on police picked up Boggie and felt they had a good case against him. After some hesitancy the witnesses identified Boggie, who it will be remembered, turned out to be innocent.

I have had a professional criminal, whose confidence I had won, tell me that two or three times he had found himself confronted by persons whom he had robbed, and that they failed to identify him. On the other hand, another person positively identified him as being the culprit in a case with which he had nothing to do.

There is one other fruitful source of mistaken identification.

Let us suppose that a prominent citizen is held up on the streets of one of the big cities in the United States. He goes to the police and reports the holdup.

The police want to show him that they are on the job. They ask him for a description of the man. The citizen was emotionally upset at the time. He was probably frightened. The light was far from good. He is probably still under an emotional tension when he is at police headquarters.

"How big was he? How tall was he?" the police ask.

The citizen searches his mind.

"About the same as that fellow over there?" the officer asks, pointing to one of the detectives.

"No, a little smaller."

"About like that other fellow?"

"Something like him."

"All right. Five feet eight inches," the officer says. "Now how about weight? About like this fellow?"

"No, more like that other chap."

"Weight a hundred and sixty-five."

Then they take the citizen into a rogues' gallery where they bring out a series of photographs, where they consult charts labeled *Modus Operandi*, etc.

They begin to show the citizen pictures.

About that time one of the officers says, "Say, I've got an idea. Richard Roe was just released from San Quentin about two weeks ago, and this is exactly the kind of a job that he'd pull. It's just the way he works."

"By George, that's right," the other man exclaims. "Say, now, look here, I think we've got this thing solved. I think we know your man."

He goes to the file and brings out pictures of Richard Roe.

The man starts to shake his head.

"Now, wait a minute," the officer warns. "Let's not be hasty about this. You may have to change your opinion. I think if you could see this man you'd recognize him as the ringleader of the crowd. Remember that this picture was taken four or five years ago and that pictures sometimes don't look too much like a man. Now just don't go off on a tangent on this thing. Study that picture carefully. Look at it in a better light."

The citizen keeps studying the picture. He doesn't think it's the man. The officer asks him why not, asks him to point out any particular where the picture doesn't fit.

Eventually the citizen makes what is called a "partial identification."

Then he goes home. Two weeks pass, then a grinning detective calls him on the phone. "I think we've got your man. Come on and you can identify him."

The citizen drives up to headquarters. He is shown a shadow box with five men in it. The man in the middle is Richard Roe. The citizen immediately feels a flash of recognition. He's seen *that* man before. His face is familiar. It was in connection with all that holdup business. He nods emphatically. "That's the man."

How much of that identification is predicated upon a recollection of the face of the man who held him up, and how much of it upon the fact that he studied the photograph so carefully that he became familiar with a photographic likeness?

You don't know. The officers don't know. No one knows. The witness himself doesn't know.

The officers do know that dozens and dozens of times they have persons make positive identifications where in the light of subsequent events it conclusively appears that the identification was based entirely upon the previous study of a photograph. People make positive identifications of individuals who couldn't by any stretch of the imagination have participated in the crime.

This field of mistaken identification is fruitful of miscarriages of justice. However, if juries are to be distrustful of circumstantial evidence and can't depend on eyewitness evidence, what can they depend on?

The answer, of course, is that we must accept eyewitness evidence but must be careful to judge the intellectual integrity of the person making an identification.

For instance, the August 9th, 1952, issue of *The Saturday Evening Post* contained an article, "I Was Accused of a Sex Crime," written by a businessman who had been driving home from work on an afternoon in April, 1950. He had been slowed down by a traffic jam, and a motorcycle patrolman crossed the avenue in front of him, headed for two girls who were at the side of the avenue waving and shouting.

It turned out that the motorcycle officer mistakenly believed that he had seen this man's car pulling away from the curb, that the two young girls were appealing for help because a man had made an indecent exposure in front of them.

The two girls "identified" the businessman as the person who had made the indecent exposure.

The businessman was arrested. He was tried. He was convicted. Every effort he made to prove himself innocent was brushed aside. The authorities simply closed their minds because they were so convinced this was the culprit. When the man who actually was guilty wrote letters to the authorities telling them they had the wrong man, they promptly branded these letters fakes and went so far as to accuse the convicted man's daughter of having written them. They arrested her. A handwriting "expert" testified that she had written these letters.

The whole tragedy of errors came to an end when the man who was guilty, harassed by his conscience, surrendered and finally was able to convince the reluctant authorities that he was the guilty person.

There are literally hundreds of cases where there seems to be good ground for believing the identification evidence was erroneous. We have corresponded with quite a few prison inmates who have been convicted of crimes of sexual violence, where I am very well satisfied that there was a wrong identification.

Unfortunately there are other factors which enter into an identification of this sort.

In the sex crime which was reported in *The Saturday Evening Post*, it appeared that the police had given the two young girls an opportunity to see the defendant and study his appearance before they were asked to identify him in a line-up. In other words, they made a "preliminary identification."

Quite frequently a person who is to be placed in a line-up is shown to the witness who is to be asked to identify him, before the line-up, usually without the knowledge of the suspect.

A few years ago there was a very interesting case in Detroit. A girl's body was found lying on a city dump. She had been stabbed by a knife in the back. The course of the knife wounds had been upward, rather than downward as one would have expected had the assailant been pursuing her and stabbing with the knife.

Police were baffled. However, they finally secured a tip that a young man, who was operating a near-by service station that night, had been seen with a knife.

By that time the police were rather desperate and they ran down this clue for all it was worth. They located the knife. They apprehended the man and finally secured a confession.

The man was tried for first-degree murder. The attorney who was representing him was puzzled by the fact that in two respects the man's confession did not match the physical facts in the case. For one thing, if the man's confession had been the truth, the course of the knife wounds would have been down rather than up.

It was a small point, the type of point which a prosecutor could sneeringly refer to as a "technicality," a "last desperate straw," at which a guilty defendant was vainly clutching in an ecstasy of desperation.

The jury apparently had but scant sympathy for the defendant and he was on his way to a conviction for first-degree murder when it happened that, in running down another crime, the police stumbled on the purse that had belonged to the dead girl. Since this purse was in the possession of a person who quite evidently had been perpetrating a series of crimes, the police made further search and found a knife which more nearly matched the stab wounds in the girl's body than the knife possessed by the service station operator.

The upshot of it was that the judge had to interrupt the deliberations of the jury to explain that the real culprit had been apprehended, and that the man who was being tried was actually innocent of the crime, despite the fact that his confession had been obtained.

In cases of this sort there is a mistaken tendency to blame the prosecuting attorney simply because he is presenting the case the police have worked up.

There are, of course, prosecutors who take an unfair advantage just as there are defense attorneys who shamelessly try every trick in the book.

In some jurisdictions the judges really control the presentation of cases and the attorneys are relegated to a more secondary position. In most of our state courts the judges sit back as umpires or referees and the attorneys handle the cases, the prosecutors trying to get the jurors to convict, quite frequently seeking to arouse prejudice against the defendant by sneering sarcasm, by thunderous denunciation, while the defense attorneys try to arouse sympathy by such devices as the aged mother, the weeping wife and the innocent children who must not be left "fatherless."

Most people lose sight of the fact that it is the sworn duty of the prosecutor to present the case the police have made against the defendant. All too frequently when there has been an erroneous conviction the people blame the prosecutor instead of poor investigative technique.

In this Detroit case there had been a "free and voluntary" confession.

That, of course, is a disturbing factor. Some people do not have the mental stamina to hold out against hours of repeated questioning.

We ourselves had one very interesting case where there was an erroneous identification and where it was claimed there was a confession by a man who, as it turned out, was innocent. Actually this was probably not a complete confession but was a statement containing some facts which the police considered incriminating and which as it turned out were false.

This was in the case of Silas Rogers, who was recently pardoned by Governor John S. Battle of Virginia.

According to the story Rogers told us, he had made this statement because of police brutality. According to his story, the police had beaten him to a point where he hardly knew what he was saying.

However, there are other cases where it would seem that there is no actual physical violence, but where the mind of the suspect simply doesn't have the stamina to keep contradicting assertions.

If we are to take away from the police the power to question a suspect, to confront him with the evidence against him, and ask him to try and explain it; if we deprive them of the opportunity to expose the attempts at explanation as falsehoods, and finally to trap the prisoner into such a position that he realizes further subterfuge is hopeless and he throws up his hands and says, "All right, I did it," we are going to impair the efficiency of the police to such an extent that criminals will have a field day.

On the other hand, far too many confessions are obtained by physical violence; and there is the question of what, for want of a better name, I shall call "mental violence."

There are ways of beating a person's mind into submission just as effectively as his body can be beaten into submission.

We are, at the present time, investigating another case in which there was a "confession." That is the strange case of Lefty Fowler in Oklahoma. Fowler was convicted of murdering Helen Beavers. The entire circumstances surrounding his conviction are such that it is difficult to believe he is guilty. It seems to us, in our judgment, that there was far better evidence against another suspect than against

Lefty Fowler. For some reason, the investigation against this other suspect was abruptly dropped, and Fowler was apprehended. So far we have never been able to find any really significant circumstance that caused the authorities to concentrate on Fowler other than the fact that he knew the dead woman and had quit his job shortly after the murder.

Fowler confessed not once but three times. He insists that he was frightened into making these confessions. None of them really conforms to the physical facts or explains how the murder was committed. The first two confessions are so wide of the mark as to be almost absurd. The third confession eliminated some of the contradictory facts of the first two, but contains absurdities of its own. It was taken down in shorthand and winds up with this statement purporting to come from the lips of Fowler:

"Gentlemen, there is your confession, that's what you wanted and it was a nice piece of work. I'm proud of you. . . . Will you shake hands with me. I am glad to know you."

Alex Gregory has given Fowler a very careful examination with the polygraph and is absolutely convinced that Fowler did not kill Helen Beavers and has no guilty knowledge of her death.

It was rumored that there was another girl in the car with Helen Beavers at the time she was killed, and finally the investigators of the Court of Last Resort located this young woman.

Under questioning this woman told our investigator that she was with Helen Beavers at the time of the murder, that she herself managed to make an escape. She was obviously in abject terror for her own life. Her story was corroborated by certain physical facts. I feel certain that the authorities, using her testimony, could have convicted at least one of the two persons she says murdered Helen Beavers.

However, the authorities convicted Lefty Fowler. They are quite satisfied with the case the way it is.

We are far from satisfied.

The State Bar of Oklahoma asked me to attend their annual convention at Tulsa to explain the work of the Court of Last Resort. I did so, and following my talk it was quite generally agreed that if we had any case in Oklahoma the lawyers would investigate the facts.

The State Bar as a unit could not, because of the nature of its organization, act in individual cases, but we were assured that where it seemed a case had merit there would be plenty of volunteers to see that justice was done.

So when we had investigated the Fowler case and made the facts public, three of Oklahoma's most prominent attorneys stepped forward and announced they were going to represent Lefty Fowler in filing a petition asking for a full pardon.

This committee of lawyers consists of Hicks Epton, president of the State Bar of Oklahoma; Floyd Rheams, one of the most prominent and influential members of the Tulsa Bar, and O. A. Brewer, generally conceded to be one of the most clever courtroom strategists in the state.

To secure the combined services of these outstanding attorneys a client would have to be a very wealthy individual. He could rest assured that his wealth had secured for him just about the best combination of legal brains available in the state.

But Lefty Fowler has no money at all. Yet, because the Oklahoma attorneys are interested in the cause of justice, Fowler finds himself on equal terms with the wealthiest oil magnate in the state.

Because the Fowler case is, as I write this, officially pending before the Pardon and Parole Board of the State of Oklahoma, and as there is some possibility the matter may still be pending at the time this book is published, I will skip many of the controversial details.

Quite naturally the action of the three representatives of the Oklahoma Bar, in coming to the rescue of a penniless prison inmate, caused widespread newspaper and editorial comment within the State of Oklahoma.

Thanks to that comment and questions asked the interested parties by enterprising newspaper reporters, some of the statements, which had been made to us by Fowler, and which were so weird and bizarre that we would have discounted them if it hadn't been for Gregory's polygraph examination, have now been substantiated.

For instance, Fowler told us that originally he had been arrested on the charge of being drunk. He had been sentenced, and was in jail serving that sentence when another man was thrown into the cell with him.

This man managed to smuggle a flask of whisky into the jail. He had it in his hip pocket. He seemed intoxicated and urged Fowler to drink with him.

According to the petition filed by the committee of attorneys with the Pardon and Parole Board, this person, who was committed under the name of Virgil Havens, made Lefty Fowler a proposition.

Let us quote from Fowler's petition:

> He (Virgil Havens) offered Lefty a drink which was refused. He next made Lefty a proposition. He had a lawyer coming down to get him out of jail and he would have his lawyer pay Lefty's fine if Lefty would drive his car to Chickasha. He was still a little drunk and didn't want to take a chance on driving it himself. Lefty agreed to this. A short time later, a man whom Havens introduced as his lawyer, entered the cell and secured the release of the two men. Lefty subsequently learned that this "lawyer" was . . . of the Oklahoma Crime Bureau.

Now it is significant that on the police judge's docket, under the heading of "City of Waurika versus Virgil Havens" appears this statement:

> This man was a secret detective out of Jake Sims' office at Oklahoma City, who pulled a fake drunk to get in jail with Lefty Fowler to secure his release and plan a second arrest by . . . State Highway Patrol.

Now why did all this take place? Why all the cloak-and-dagger stuff? What did anyone expect to gain?

Fowler was in jail. If the authorities wanted to rearrest him for the murder of Helen Beavers, all they had to do was to go and arrest him. If they wanted him taken to Duncan, all they had to do was take him there.

But notice what Fowler claimed happened.

A cellmate, who was a member of the Oklahoma Crime Bureau, posed as a drunk purely for the purpose of getting Lefty Fowler to drive a car which would enable the State Highway Patrol to arrest him at a certain predetermined point.

Why?

Moreover, we find this law enforcement agency having a detective posing as an attorney, an attorney who was supposed to befriend Lefty Fowler by paying his fine.

Why?

It is, of course, a dangerous practice for an officer of the law to pose as an attorney for any purpose whatsoever.

Why was it necessary to have an "attorney" call on Lefty Fowler? Why was it necessary to have Lefty Fowler released and put into a situation which was quite obviously a frame-up so he could be rearrested?

Was all of this cloak-and-dagger stuff part of a third-degree, an attempt to terrify Fowler so that he would think his life was in danger?

According to Fowler's petition:

> Lefty and Havens got into Havens' car. Lefty was driving and proceeded north on Highway 81 toward Duncan. Four miles south of Duncan, . . . in highway patrol car number 63, sirened Lefty to a stop. At this point, Havens jumped out of the car and yelled "run!!" What would have happened if Lefty had run is pure speculation. Fowler has his own ideas and says that this incident had considerable influence on his subsequent actions.

The trooper who had made this arrest subsequently testified that the arrest was "on the investigation of murder," although, according to Fowler's petition, he further stated he had "stopped the car for reckless driving." The trooper admitted under cross-examination that the car was not stolen, that he had never found out whom the car belonged to, and that he made no further investigation concerning the car, and that no charges other than murder were ever lodged against Fowler.

Now then, we come to a startling situation. The car apparently belonged to a relative of the prosecutor, and the car, with out-of-state license plates, had been furnished as part of an elaborate plot or scheme for the purpose of arranging for this second arrest.

What was the object of this second arrest? Why was it so carefully engineered? Whose idea was it?

The whole experience gave Fowler a mental picture which was far from reassuring when he came to face his questioners.

According to Fowler's petition, one of these men entered the prison in civilian clothes, sat down in front of Fowler and told him that he was going to give him one more opportunity to make a confession. As Fowler looked at him, this man unbuttoned his coat, "pulled it open and placed his hand on a gun he was wearing."

The officials deny the truth of many allegations in the petition filed on behalf of Fowler, but they don't deny this elaborate rigmarole over the "stolen car." Some of Fowler's statements sound incredible to us, but nothing sounded more utterly incredible than this automobile setup—and the truth of this story so far as the main essentials are concerned now seems fairly well established.

It appears that the officer of the Highway Patrol who made the arrest understood that Fowler was actually being arrested on "the investigation of murder." Was this officer told anything else?

We keep coming back to the questions. What was the *purpose* of all this rigmarole? What was anyone trying to accomplish by it? What did they hope to accomplish? Someone had thought out this elaborate scheme. What was behind it? What was the idea that person had in mind?

Now then, according to newspaper reports, when reporters called on the various officers and asked them about the allegations made in Fowler's petition concerning the weird, bizarre circumstances in connection with this arrest, the persons readily admitted that Fowler's release was engineered so Fowler could be rearrested in the car that had been furnished for this purpose.

It would certainly seem that justice has no right to resort to all of this cat-and-mouse type of thing. Justice should have dignity. Justice should use every scientific skill at its command to carry out its investigative work, but justice should never obtain the release of a suspect through the intervention of a detective impersonating a lawyer nor arrange to have the suspect drive a car with an out-of-state license to a predetermined point where he is to be stopped and then rearrested on a charge that is a fabrication.

If those officers of the State of Oklahoma had wanted to arrest Fowler for murder and take him to Duncan, all they had to do was to serve a warrant while Fowler was in jail and say, "We're sorry, Fowler, but you're now being arrested for the murder of Helen Beavers." Or they could simply have said, "We have reason to believe that you may know something about the murder of Helen Beavers and we're going to take you to Duncan, Oklahoma, and hold you for investigation.—You can, of course, apply for *habeas corpus* if you want to, in which event we'll file a murder charge against you, and let it go at that."

That is being done every day of the week in every state in the union.

Why all the run-around?

It would appear that the leading newspapers in the State of Oklahoma feel the same way about it.

The following is a quotation in part from the Tulsa *Tribune*:

> We trust the pardon and parole board will devote a special meeting, as Chairman Tom Phillips suggested yesterday, to the "Lefty" Fowler case. There seem to be several places to take hold of this subject, now that it has been reopened for a second time by *Argosy* Magazine's Court of Last Resort and three prominent Oklahoma lawyers, including the president of the state bar association.
>
> Fowler is a former Duncan policeman who confessed five years ago to the murder of a woman employed there as

a waitress. He was sentenced to life imprisonment. He has since maintained he was beaten and confessed to save further torture. Erle Stanley Gardner, the author and Court of Last Resort conductor, believes him and apparently has convinced the lawyers who are co-operating with him in the appeal for a pardon.

This would stand as a clash of opinions between Gardner and the others and the prosecutor, judge and jury at the trial if it were not for the presence of a number of other alleged facts. . . .

A fourth point can stand a lot of amplification, though the elementary facts are admitted readily by those who should know best about them. Fowler was subjected to a story-book detective experience while in jail in Waurika. A pseudo drunk was put in the cell with him by state crime bureau operators. A pseudo lawyer gained their release and then a highway patrolman stopped them between Waurika and Chickasha and charged them with car theft. Their car hadn't been stolen, but was loaned the operatives for the drama. . . .

This, we want to hear more about. If the object was to arrest Fowler so he couldn't leave the state upon his release from his short jail sentence for drunkenness, why wasn't he arrested on a new warrant while he was in the Waurika jail?. . .

Fowler made several confessions. The first confessions simply weren't usable. They didn't conform to the existing facts as the officers knew them and so they were not satisfied with them.

It is significant to note that the first confession starts out, "This statement made by me, E. L. (Lefty) Fowler, on this 25th day of March 1948, at the hour of five o'clock A.M. . . ."

Again, according to Fowler's petition, "No one, however, attempted to deny the fact that the final statement was signed *fourteen* days after Fowler's initial arrest or that during that period of time he was incarcerated in three different jails. . . ."

There are some things about the Lefty Fowler case which simply don't make sense no matter how one looks at them.

Helen Beavers disappeared on the evening of January 23rd. Her disappearance remained a complete mystery until the following February 9th when a man opened the trunk of an automobile which had been parked in his back yard. The automobile had a flat tire and the man wanted to get out a jack.

He flung open the lid of the trunk and found himself confronted by the frozen, well-preserved body of Helen Beavers. The body was lying on its back, one knee elevated so that it enabled the trunk to be closed. The clothing was pulled well up so that the lower portion of the body was bare. Helen Beavers had been clubbed to death and there had been considerable bleeding.

The physical facts show that Helen Beavers was a chunky girl, weighing around a hundred and forty pounds. She had been killed by blows on the head. There were thirteen of these blows and, according to the testimony, any one of them would have killed her. The confession that the authorities finally used showed an admission by Fowler that he had hit Helen Beavers twice, apparently with his fist. He had "no memory" of hitting her with any weapon or hitting her more than twice.

A neighbor, some time after the murder, found a twelve-inch "Giant Western" wrench under his porch. It was covered with mud and leaves so he washed it with gasoline and then observed what he thought were hairs and bloodstains on the wrench, so he turned it over to the police.

The police sent the wrench to the FBI. The FBI found there was no blood on the wrench. They found some hairs on the wrench that were similar to Helen Beavers' hair, but there was not sufficient similarity so that they could make an identification.

The police station at Duncan seems to have been operated on such a basis that the "disappearance" of evidence was not at all unusual. A number of wrenches had been seized in a burglary and placed in a drawer in the chief's office for "safekeeping." The wrenches all disappeared. It was the theory of the State that this particular "Giant Western" wrench was the murder weapon; that Lefty

Fowler, as a police officer of Duncan, had access to the wrenches in the drawer in the chief's office and had taken either this one or all of them.

This theory is full of holes.

According to Fowler's final "confession" the murder was committed around five o'clock in the morning, on the spur of the moment, in a rage, over an argument about a whisky bottle.

Had he been carrying a twelve-inch wrench with him all during the night? Was it in his hand?

One doesn't put a twelve-inch wrench casually in a pocket as one would carry a notebook or a gold pencil.

If the wrench had been used as a murder weapon and there were hairs on it, why wasn't there blood on it?

No one could identify the wrench except by saying that it "looked like" one of the wrenches that had been there in the police station. Probably a million other wrenches "looked like" it.

In other words, it was impossible to prove that the wrench was the murder weapon. It was impossible to prove that it was one of those that had been in the police station. It was impossible to prove that Lefty Fowler had taken it, and it was impossible to prove it had ever been used to hit Helen Beavers or anyone else.

However, the most significant thing, and the thing which interests us mainly about the Fowler case, is that, after the body of Helen Beavers was discovered, the police checked back to the night of her disappearance and tried to find the men who had been with her on that fatal night.

They built up a good enough case against one suspect to put him in jail.

How good a case did the authorities have against this suspect?

The facts are, of course, within the exclusive knowledge of the authorities. Quite naturally they haven't seen fit to confide in us. There are certain things, however, which we do know.

After Fowler's conviction, one of the officials turned a ring over to Helen Beavers' mother. He thought she might like it as a memento of her dead daughter. It was a ring that her daughter had been wearing, etc., etc., etc.

Quite apparently it was Helen Beavers' ring.

Our investigators found a witness who said that she had seen Helen Beavers on the night of her death. That, as it happened, they had been comparing rings; that Helen Beavers' ring was similar to her ring, and that it had been bent in a distinctive manner so as to fit Helen's finger.

She identified this ring which had been given to Helen Beavers' mother as being Helen Beavers' ring, presumably a ring which she was wearing on the night of her murder.

How did the authorities get that ring?

Apparently the story is that, after Helen Beavers' body was discovered, a young woman went to the authorities and said, in effect, "I secured this ring from a man who knew Helen Beavers. I got it from him *before* Helen Beavers' body was discovered and I have reason to believe it's Helen Beavers' ring."

According to the best information we can get, she gave the name of the person from whom she had secured this ring, and that person was the same individual the authorities were holding for investigation.

Some time after Fowler's conviction, we learned that an hysterical, frightened woman had told the authorities that she had been an eyewitness to the murder of Helen Beavers; that she had been out in the car with Helen Beavers and two men; that one of the men had clubbed. Helen Beavers to death, and that both of them had lifted her body to put it in a place where it could be concealed and that this woman had taken advantage of that opportunity to run away.

Later on we learned that apparently she had pointed out to investigating officers the exact spot where Helen Beavers had been murdered, and it was within a few feet of the place where the body had been discovered.

We found this young woman. She is, quite naturally, in fear of her life. She told her story to our investigators.

It is, of course, difficult to know exactly what evidence the authorities had, but apparently they had a suspect in jail and could have introduced evidence that he had been with Helen Beavers on the night of her murder; that a ring, which a witness would identify as being that of Helen Beavers, had been found in his possession prior to the time Helen Beavers' body was discovered; that a person who claimed to be an eyewitness had told the authorities and was presumably ready to testify that she had seen Helen Beavers clubbed by this man and the body dragged toward a place of concealment by this man and a companion.

Notwithstanding such a case, the authorities suddenly dropped the case against this man, released him from custody and concentrated on Lefty Fowler.

Why?

We don't know.

Apparently from all of the information that has been divulged publicly there were just two reasons: One, Lefty Fowler had known Helen Beavers; two, he had quit his job about a week after the murder.

Now all that, of course, is something concerning which we have to conjecture. The authorities undoubtedly had *some* reason for what they did.

But here is the point: Suppose the jury trying Lefty Fowler had known these facts? What would that jury have done?

In all human probability, that jury would have turned Lefty Fowler loose without even leaving the box.

Fowler didn't know these facts. The authorities did. After Fowler had been convicted an official delivered the ring to Helen Beavers' mother. If Fowler had been able to produce that ring at the time of his trial, if his attorney had been able to show the history of that ring and how it came into the possession of the prosecutor, the case against Fowler would have gone out of the window.

Here was a fact that was known to the authorities. It was not known to the defendant. It was, to our minds, an important fact in the case.

Those are some of the things that are disclosed by Fowler's petition before the Board of Pardon and Parole, and it will be interesting to see what happens.

According to the newspapers, one of the investigating officials said in an interview that the Court of Last Resort, after all of its investigation, had not uncovered any fact that was news to the investigating officials.

That may well be.

That's the significant thing, the tragic thing. The officials may have known all these facts, but the jury didn't, and Fowler didn't.

And there, of course, we run up against a situation that is more and more significant.

The police investigate a case. They come to the conclusion that John Doe is guilty. They marshal whatever evidence they can find against John Doe, they put it in the hands of the prosecutor, and the prosecutor goes ahead and presents that case to the jury.

But what about evidence that indicates John Doe is innocent?

The police are pretty apt to consider all of that evidence as being a "false lead." But suppose they uncover evidence directly indicating that some other person is guilty of the crime. What do they do with this evidence? Do they turn it over to John Doe's attorney and say, "This is evidence that is undoubtedly pertinent to the case. We think you should have it"?

Should the police prosecute a case when they hold evidence in their possession that strongly indicates the man is innocent?

Let us cite an interesting example from a case in our files that was partially investigated.

The scene was a dimly lit cocktail lounge. It was fairly well filled with people. Two men entered, went to the bar and suddenly announced, "This is a stick-up." One man held up the people in the cocktail lounge and ordered them to sit still. The other tried to get the money from the cash register. The bartender resisted. In the struggle, a shot was fired, and the bartender fell dead. The stick-up men fled.

The police picked up two men. These men had been in trouble before. They were tried for the crime. Two persons who had been in the cocktail lounge unhesitantly identified these two men as being the murderers.

The defense attorneys tried to find out who else had been in the cocktail lounge. They were unable to do so. The police had the names of these witnesses. They refused to divulge them. After the two men had been convicted of murder, the police belatedly filed a supplemental list of persons who had been in the cocktail lounge.

Friends of the defendants went to these persons. One by one, they took these persons up to the state prison where the men were incarcerated. Each one of these people swore positively that the convicted men were *not* the men who had perpetrated the holdup.

Friends of the convicted men secured affidavits from these witnesses, and then went to members of the jury who had convicted the defendants.

These jurors stated that if that evidence had been introduced at the time of trial they would have acquitted the defendants.

What was done about it?

Nothing.

Now quite obviously this is not right. A man who is charged with crime is thrown in a cell. He doesn't have any opportunity to investigate and quite frequently he doesn't have funds to make such an investigation.

The police represent a big, powerful organization. They have the facilities, the authority, and the numbers to make a complete investigation.

An investigation should be fair and it should be complete, otherwise innocent men will be wrongfully convicted.

We admit that the Fowler case is a puzzling one, but there are these facts to be considered: One, the authorities were in the possession of information which, if it had been disclosed to the jury, the court or the defendant, would undoubtedly have resulted in the defendant's acquittal; two, the authorities, for some reason best known to themselves, proceeded to enact a cat-and-mouse drama which is unworthy of the dignity of the law; three, one of the best polygraph examiners in the country, after a series of careful examinations, has concluded that Lefty Fowler is innocent.

This makes for a sequence of events that can well mean the perpetration of a gross injustice.

Let us concede for the sake of the argument that the authorities were acting in the greatest of good faith. In fact, for the sake of this argument, let's concede that Lefty Fowler is lying (and there is some evidence indicating he is) about any physical violence having been used in connection with obtaining his confession.

The law should act with dignity. The law should act with justice. Fowler's attorneys should have known that the authorities had this ring which had been identified as that of Helen Beavers, and they should have known under what circumstances the authorities acquired this ring.

If the authorities had wanted to arrest Lefty Fowler for the murder of Helen Beavers, they should have done so in an orderly and dignified manner. They should have advised him of the charge against him, advised him of his rights, seen that he was arraigned and given the benefit of counsel.

When the law becomes confused, then the case becomes confused, and it is very possible that the wrong man is convicted.

There is, of course, much more to this Fowler case. We can, at the present time, comment only on facts that are fairly well established. We still don't know all of the facts. We are, however, reasonably certain that we do know all of the facts that were used as evidence to bring about Fowler's conviction.

We have an affidavit from an investigative officer who stated that he talked with this young woman who claimed to be an eyewitness to the murder; that he took her to Duncan, Oklahoma, and asked her to point out the scene of the murder; that for some time she avoided doing so, and then finally, breaking down and weeping hysterically, took him to the very spot where the murder had been committed and the body discovered.

Someone had administered a terrific beating to this young woman. Her eye was black. She was bruised, frightened and almost hysterical.

While it is expecting too much of human nature to ask the police to turn over to the defendant on a silver platter any evidence they may have uncovered indicating a defendant is innocent, they certainly should report to the court any evidence they may have uncovered indicating that some other person may be guilty of the crime.

Furthermore, we believe that prosecutors who wish to be fair should use their judgment as to what facts are and what are not significant, and see that all of the significant facts are presented to the court.

In the long run, we are apt to pay a terrific price if we fail to follow these rules. Let jurors get the idea that there may be evidence in the case which the police have held back, and all testimony introduced by the prosecutor is going to be viewed with such suspicion that guilty men may well escape in even greater numbers.

And there, of course, we have the other horn of the dilemma, the greatest injustice of all, the guilty man who "beats the rap" and, having perpetrated the crime, goes free to again prey upon society.

It would certainly seem that the only way we can steer a safe course between these two reefs is to encourage a spirit of scrupulous fairness on the part of all investigating officers.

If evidence won't stand the light of day, it shouldn't send a man to prison or to the chair. If a prosecutor wants to ask for a conviction, he should be perfectly willing to see that the truth, and all of the truth, is placed before the jury.

There are, of course, rules of professional ethics designed to cover these matters, but it is difficult to draft a rule that will cover all of these situations.

Prosecutors usually adopt the position that they are called upon to present the case for the state; that the defense attorney is retained to look after the interest of the defendant. If there are any weak links in the evidentiary chain, the prosecutor believes that it is the duty of the defendant's counsel to hammer away at those weak links.

But how about positive facts?

It is as though someone, in putting a jigsaw puzzle together, found there were several pieces left over, and, at the same time, noticed there were several gaps in the jigsaw puzzle. Since the pieces won't fit, he decides they are irrelevant and have nothing to do with that particular puzzle.

It probably never occurs to him that it is his mental concept that is at fault. If it does occur to him he is, of course, strongly tempted to put that thought out of his mind.

And so in this Lefty Fowler case, as I write this, we are in the midst of a peculiar but exceedingly interesting situation. There are many things about Fowler's story I personally don't like. There are, however, many things about the Fowler conviction that need clearing up.

12

In recent years, there has been a tendency to build up a system of rating prosecutors, a sort of box score or batting average, which has served to weed out and expose a lot of lazy incompetents, but which, in turn, has brought a whole attendant train of its own evils.

In many states prosecutors are required to keep a record showing the number of cases they have prosecuted, the number that have been dismissed, the number of acquittals, the number of convictions, the number of pleas of guilty, etc.

The result is a box score or batting average by which the efficiency of the prosecutor can be measured.

It is, of course, only natural that the prosecutor should want to make a good record. That's the very purpose of keeping this type of box score. It furnishes him an incentive.

In many ways it is a dangerous incentive.

Personally I don't think we should measure the efficiency of a prosecutor in the same way we measure the efficiency of a baseball player. Justice is more subtle and illusive. You can't simplify cases into classifications of black and white. We have grays and blues, and, here and there, we have the very flaming red of the danger signal that is inherent in this system.

To be sure, until this system was inaugurated there were prosecuting attorneys who were lazy, who were inefficient, who would dismiss a case rather than engage in a hard-fought trial where some brilliant defense attorney might show them up.

Now we have hard-driving prosecutors who are intent upon establishing a good over-all average. Some of them, of course, remain immune to this type of pressure, but others do not.

Let us take the case of Mr. X, a prosecutor. He likes the job. He knows that when his term of office is up he is going to have to run again. If he is to be re-elected it will be on the strength of his record. Naturally he wants his record to be one to which he can "point with pride."

John Doe is in jail, awaiting trial on a charge of armed robbery. There is some evidence indicating John Doe is guilty. There is some evidence indicating John Doe is innocent. John Doe has refused to plead guilty.

The prosecutor considers his box score record.

If he goes to trial, if the court appoints an attorney to represent John Doe, and John Doe secures an acquittal, that acquittal will loom large on the debit side of the prosecutor's ledger.

John Doe won't plead guilty to the charge of armed robbery.

But suppose one of the officers goes to John Doe and says, "Look here, you're sticking your neck out. We have enough evidence to convict you of armed robbery. That's going to mean a long term in the penitentiary, but if you want to cooperate with us we'll meet you halfway. You plead guilty to larceny and we'll let it go at that. That will only be a misdemeanor. You'll get six months in the clink. How about it?"

So John Doe may very well decide to make the trade, particularly if he is guilty.

Even if John Doe is innocent he may feel that the cards are stacked against him, and prefer six months in jail rather than having to "take a chance," particularly if the right sort of selling argument is used.

If John Doe is guilty, this deal puts him in a position to laugh at the law.

For purposes of the record, the case of John Doe shows up as an entry on the credit side of the prosecutor's box score instead of one on the debit side.

Don't think these things are farfetched. Only a few months ago I was investigating a case where there had been an armed robbery. The defendant had a previous record. He was incarcerated, awaiting trial. He made a "deal." He pled guilty to larceny and received a sentence of six months in the county jail. (If he had been convicted of armed robbery his sentence would have been ten years to life.)

It happened that owing to other circumstances it became the duty of some of my associates and myself to examine this man, and to try and find out the true facts about this case.

Quite obviously the crime was either armed robbery or it was nothing.

We examined into the facts, secured what information we could, and finally went into session with the individual, pointing out to him the information that we had.

He admitted to us that he had committed the armed robbery.

Prosecuting attorneys should not have to guide their actions by a paper record, and voters must learn to measure the efficiency of a prosecutor by some other yardstick than a "percentage of convictions."

As a nation we are prone to think altogether too much in terms of results.

I remember, several years ago, when I was an archery enthusiast, studying a manual of Japanese archery which I picked up in Yokohama and had translated. Under the Japanese system of marking, an arrow in the bull's-eye was good for only fifty percent on the score board. The *manner* in which the archer conformed to the traditional legends of the sport, the form with which he released the arrow, counted for the other fifty percent.

In American archery, a man could lie on his back, pull the bow with his feet, release the arrow with his teeth, get the arrow in the bull's-eye, and still the shot would count for a hundred percent.

We worship results.

Now that can be dangerous when it comes to legal matters, particularly matters involving the detection, apprehension and conviction of persons who have perpetrated crimes.

A criminal commits a particularly atrocious crime which receives a lot of newspaper publicity. The chief of police is immediately put on the spot by the mayor. The chief passes the word down to the officers under him, and virtually all other work is dropped while the entire force concentrates on getting the man responsible for the crime.

We investigated one case where it was rumored that the grand jury had said to the district attorney, with whom it had been having trouble, "Either apprehend the man who committed this crime within forty-eight hours or hand in your resignation."

That sounds apocryphal because presumably the grand jury had no way of forcing the district attorney to resign, and it wasn't up to the district attorney to do the police work but only to present the case after the police had rounded up the criminal. It is, however, presumed to be a true story, and, in any event, is indicative of the pressure that is brought to bear on persons who are engaged in enforcing the law.

In the case above referred to, a person was arrested within the forty-eight hour period.

One thing is certain. The careful deliberation, the sifting of facts, the impartial weighing of evidence, can hardly be accomplished when newspapers are bringing pressure to bear on the police for an immediate arrest, hinting at incompetency and inefficiency, and the mayor is putting the chief of police on the carpet because his men can't turn up *the* culprit.

Under such circumstances it is only human nature for the police to take the heat off themselves by turning in *a* culprit.

The case of Silas Rogers was one where the police were working under pressure. A popular police officer had been ruthlessly shot down. The murderer had literally slipped through the fingers of the police.

The police knew that the murderer was a Negro; that when last seen he was probably wearing a white cap. Silas Rogers was a Negro. He was on his way out of town. He was wearing a white cap. That was all the police had to go on.

For a while the police apparently held Silas Rogers simply because there might be a possibility he had been connected with the murder. He "matched the description." In other words, he was a Negro in a state where there are thousands and thousands of Negroes, and he was wearing a white cap.

Later on, when other suspects had slipped through the fingers of the police and made good their escape, and only Silas Rogers was left, Silas Rogers became the fall guy. He was it.

The police had arrested Silas Rogers as a suspect. He was being held for investigation in connection with a murder. There was no other likely candidate who hadn't eluded the police and escaped. Silas Rogers was there. There was widespread public interest in the case. There was a wave of public indignation. The newspapers were going to press.

All of that was an unhappy combination of events for Silas Rogers, who had been picked up simply because, in a very vague, general way, he matched the description of the man the police were looking for.

Perhaps the greatest weakness inherent in the whole police system is that once the police have made an arrest, once a man has been accused of crime, our vaunted freedom of the press, which gives newspaper reporters the right to know what is going on, crucifies further investigation on a cross of public prejudice and newspaper publicity.

There is every indication that, without waiting to develop any additional evidence, the police "worked Silas Rogers over," leaving scars which remain to this day.

That, however, was more or less to have been expected under the circumstances. A popular police officer had been murdered, presumably by a Negro. Rogers was brought in as a suspect. Police officers were suffering from an emotional shock and frayed nerves, so they went to work on Silas Rogers.

By the time the afternoon papers had gone to press, Silas Rogers was the official suspect held in custody by the police. After that he became the defendant. The prosecutor had to try this defendant in front of a jury. Naturally he wanted to have evidence that would bolster his case. Naturally the police wanted to get this evidence, so gradually the police found themselves drawn into a net where they had to get evidence against Silas Rogers rather than investigate the murder.

This happens in case after case. The police pick up a suspect. They don't have too much on him. He may or may not be guilty.

It looks a lot better for the police, however, to have a suspect actually in custody, and so the combined forces of publicity soon make the suspect the defendant, and then the prosecuting attorney quite naturally says to the police, "Well, where's *your* evidence? You expect *me* to prosecute this man. You want him charged. Where's the evidence?"

Under those circumstances it is inevitable that evidence tending to prove the suspect is the right man is put forward by the police, while evidence tending to show that he is not the right man is ignored, pushed to one side, covered up and forgotten.

That is all very well when the suspect happens to be the right man, but not when he happens to be the wrong man.

That is what happened in the Rogers case.

Looking back on it, it is very easy to say that the police bungled the investigation. However, that is to discount the slow process by which a suspect tends to be forced into the position of a defendant.

Briefly, the facts in the Rogers case go back to the early morning of July 18th, 1943, when two police officers of the city of Petersburg, Virginia, were making a routine automobile patrol.

They noticed a red Studebaker automobile driven by a Negro wearing a white cap, and containing two white soldiers.

On that July morning officers W. M. Jolly and R. B. Hatchell saw something about that Studebaker automobile which immediately impressed them as being out of key. Perhaps it was the way the Studebaker was being driven. Perhaps it was the incongruity of the two white soldiers being driven by a Negro.

Whatever it was, the officers whipped their car into a U-turn and caught up with the Studebaker, flagging it down.

There were some cars parked at the side of the road, however, and the driver of the red Studebaker couldn't pull in to the curb until he had rolled along some little distance, so the police car, riding on the tail of the red Studebaker, loafed along behind.

Suddenly there was a break in the traffic ahead. The driver of the red Studebaker gunned the car into high speed. The police car promptly followed suit.

The red Studebaker shot through a red light at better than sixty miles an hour, made a screaming turn, and the driver suddenly found he was on a dead-end street. A barrier had been erected at the end of this street on the edge of a drop into a stream bed covered with brush and dense foliage.

The Negro did some remarkably expert driving. There was not room to stop the car. He swung it into a skidding turn up a narrow walk-way between the Petersburg Hospital building and the barrier on the edge of the steep drop.

At this point the car crashed into a hedge. The front wheels were actually dangling over a perpendicular cliff. The Negro driver jumped out, darted behind the hospital, and then, presumably, down into the brush-covered stream bed.

The officers put handcuffs on the two white soldiers, who remained in the car, and then started cruising around the edges of the stream bed trying to find the Negro.

It will serve no useful purpose to detail the step-by-step incidents of the search. Suffice it to say that Officer Hatchell eventually went down into the stream bed and disappeared.

A short time later a nurse in the hospital heard two shots. Going to the window she saw Officer Hatchell lying on the ground less than thirty feet from the place where the Studebaker had been wrecked a half hour before. Hatchell was carried into the hospital and died.

The shots had been fired at about seven forty-five A.M.

Approximately two hours later two police officers cruising the roads saw a Negro wearing a white sailor's cap and a tan shirt, on the north end of a bridge leading out of town. He carried a small bundle of clothing.

That man was Silas Rogers, a twenty-one-year-old Negro, who was headed for New York to report to his draft board in response to a summons he had received in Miami, Florida, where he had been working for some little time.

Silas Rogers told the officers that he had decided to hobo his way up to New York in order to save transportation money. He had done it before and so knew the ropes. He said he had traveled by freight train from Florida to Hamlet, North Carolina, and there had secreted himself aboard the Seaboard Airlines northbound train, the "Silver Meteor." He claimed that he had been discovered by a railway employee who had ordered him to get off the train at Petersburg.

Tired from his experiences in bumming rides, he had gone into the Negro washroom at the railroad depot. There he had taken off a shirt and green pin-striped pants which he had worn over another shirt and blue trousers in order to protect these inner clothes from the grime of train travel. He had wrapped the discarded garments into a small package, and had decided to try hitchhiking.

It transpired that the two white soldiers were AWOL, that the red car had been stolen. The story of the soldiers was that they knew nothing about the car having been stolen, that they were hitchhiking to be near their pregnant wives at the time of delivery when they were picked up by the Negro driver who had offered them a ride.

There were, of course, certain defects in the police reasoning which made Silas Rogers a suspect.

In the first place, the stories of two AWOL soldiers riding in a stolen car, trying to save themselves as much as possible, should certainly have been open to suspicion.

Both soldiers, both having pregnant wives, both wives expecting to be confined at the same time, both AWOL. It was a touching story.

A subsequent check indicated that neither of them had pregnant wives, and that one of them was not even married at the time. Moreover there is evidence to contradict their statement that they had been picked up by the driver of the stolen car "outside of Raleigh."

Secondly, even conceding that Rogers was the driver of the stolen car, there was absolutely no real evidence to indicate that it was the driver of the stolen car who had shot Officer. Hatchell. It was, of course, possible that the driver of the car had jumped out and concealed himself in the brush and had waited nearby within a distance of some thirty feet, but the probabilities are against it.

There was very considerable evidence that at that very time there were two men in the stream bed who had entered there a short time earlier after having escaped from prison the night before. These men had been seen entering the stream bed by a reputable witness. It was possible to find their tracks.

That statement about the tracks needs a little explanation. There had been a very heavy dew the night before. The stream bed was choked with a thick growth of vegetation, and people walking through the vegetation in the early morning hours brushed moisture from the leaves and grass, leaving a trail which in places was quite plain. Such a person also would have become soaking wet at least from his knees down if he had traveled any distance at all through that wet vegetation.

There is confusion about what happened next. There is evidence to the effect that the two soldiers promptly identified Silas Rogers as the driver of the car. There is also evidence that they stated he was *not* the driver of the car and maintained that position until it became apparent that as far as the police were concerned it was Silas Rogers or no one. At that point it became apparent that, unless Rogers was the guilty party, the murderer of Officer Hatchell had slipped through the fingers of the police.

Some of the evidence indicating that the police did not really believe Silas Rogers was the guilty person until some time after he had been picked up is most persuasive. For instance, the police search for the murderer continued. Officers trailed one giant Negro who certainly seemed to have been trying to make his escape. He was accosted by the officers at a distance of some two hundred feet. At first it appeared that he intended to shoot it out with the officers, but then he thought better of it, turned and took to his heels. Two officers fired twelve shots at him and missed each shot.

That left the police with two empty guns, a record of twelve clean misses, and Silas Rogers. It had to be Silas Rogers. If the murderer had been the big Negro, twelve consecutive misses in a running "battle" would have made poor copy.

But here again there seems to be a contradiction. There was some evidence that the two soldiers made a prompt identification of Silas Rogers, and that Officer Jolly did the same.

However, there were certain things about Silas Rogers that simply didn't fit into the picture.

In the first place, his trousers and his shoes were completely dry. They showed no evidences of having been wet that morning. The driver of the stolen Studebaker had been expert. Rogers had never driven a car in his life and didn't know how to drive a car. He had never held a driver's license or even a learner's license. Whenever it was that the soldiers made their identification, one of them mentioned studying Rogers' face while it was illuminated by matches the soldier was lighting and holding to cigarettes in the driver's mouth.

Rogers never had smoked.

Yet the unmistakable fact remained that a police officer had been killed. The assumption was he had been killed by the Negro who had been driving the car. The two soldiers said Rogers was the man, and that was enough for the jury.

Rogers was found guilty and sentenced to death.

That sentence would, in all probability, have been carried out if it hadn't been for Jack Kilpatrick, editor of the *News Leader* of Richmond. He started checking into some of the discrepancies in the Rogers case, and the more he saw of the case the less he liked it. Discrepancy after discrepancy began to pile up. Much of the evidence was contradicted by indisputable physical facts.

As a result of Kilpatrick's investigation and the disquieting things he turned up, Rogers' sentence was commuted from death to life imprisonment.

That, however, was small solace for a man who had been improperly convicted. It was, of course, a relief to be taken from the death row. Having a death sentence hanging over one, watching time trickle down through the squares of the calendar, is a harrowing experience. There is always a surge of relief when such a sentence is commuted.

However, that surge of relief soon gives way to a dull despondency at the contemplation of a lifetime that must be spent at hard labor within the walls of a penal institution.

Many attempts were made to check on the story told by Silas Rogers. Had he been bumming his way on the "Silver Meteor"?

Undoubtedly some Negro had been on the train, but was that Negro Silas Rogers?

Rogers was able to produce a witness who said he had seen him hide himself aboard the "Silver Meteor." He found the conductor who had ordered him off the train, but in the darkness was unable to identify him. A station porter knew of a hobo being aboard the "Silver Meteor" that night but was unable to identify Rogers as being the man. Rogers' attorneys located a colored man at a gas station who was able to identify Rogers and remembered his tight little bundle of clothes.

However, the key witness in the case could not be located, which, of course, led to the suspicion that this key witness might be only a figment of Silas Rogers' imagination. He insisted that he had talked with a "mechanic" on the train and that this "mechanic" would be able to identify him.

No matter how they searched they couldn't get any clue to this mechanic. He seemed to have no existence in reality.

Then, more than a year after Silas Rogers had been convicted, a chance conversation among train men disclosed that a diesel supervisor, who lived in North Carolina, and whose work rotated him from one train to another, remembered a conversation with a Negro hobo on the "Silver Meteor."

A quick check of dates showed that this supervisor had been on the "Silver Meteor" on the date of July 17th, so this man was rushed to the penitentiary to see if he could identify Silas Rogers.

He gave Silas Rogers a long, searching look, then nodded his head. "That's the boy," he said.

This Rogers case is interesting because it shows what can happen when we relax our rules of evidence, or when we let down our guards. It is to be noted that there was absolutely no evidence indicating that Rogers had killed Officer Hatchell.

There was evidence of a sort that Rogers had been driving the stolen car, that he had tried to conceal himself by running down into the barranca. There was an *inference* that this driver of the stolen car might well have had a *motive* for killing Officer Hatchell.—Two links in the chain of evidence, but absolutely nothing connecting those two links. Along toward the last, when so much doubt was cast upon the testimony of the two soldiers, the authorities countered by adopting the position that Rogers might not have been the driver of the car, but that in any event, no matter how he came to Petersburg, he was the one who had killed Officer Hatchell.

Jack Kilpatrick put in untold hours of work trying to find some positive proof in the case. He examined voluminous records to show that Rogers had never had a driving license or a learner's license. That, of course, was trying to prove a negative.

We made a search which supplemented Kilpatrick's search. There once more, of course, we were trying to prove a negative, a recognized, legal impossibility.

However, it is almost certain that Rogers didn't know the first thing about driving an automobile. It is very certain that the Negro who was driving that red Studebaker was an expert driver, a quick thinker, and had that deft touch in an emergency, that instantaneous reaction to changing circumstances which comes only with years of driving.

Joining forces with Kilpatrick and the Richmond *News Leader*, we campaigned for a full pardon for Silas Rogers.

Months dragged by. It seemed no new evidence could possibly be uncovered. Yet it became more and more apparent that Silas Rogers had been improperly convicted.

Careful search of the stolen Studebaker, developing all latent fingerprints, failed to disclose any of Rogers' prints. Police who had later claimed they had never doubted Rogers' guilt from the moment they had apprehended him, were shown to have spent hours with bloodhounds chasing a more likely suspect—AFTER the arrest of Rogers.

Yet the Governor hesitated over the case. It received much executive deliberation. An officer had been murdered. There must be no mistake. Rogers could not be pardoned if there was any chance he was the guilty party.

It was no longer a case of proving Silas Rogers guilty beyond all reasonable doubt. He had already been convicted. He couldn't expect clemency under the circumstances until every shred of evidence had been reconsidered.

At length Governor John S. Battle told us that there was only one feature in the case which remained uncleared and which stood between Silas Rogers and a pardon. That had to do with the identification of an article of wearing apparel, and *Argosy* investigators, getting on the job, trailed witnesses around the southeastern United States until finally they had clarified that one point which had stood in the way of clemency. On December 22nd, 1952, Governor Battle issued a pardon to Silas Rogers.

Rogers was released from prison a free man but with his life completely and utterly disorganized. Harry Steeger gave him a job with *Argosy* Magazine, giving him work so that Rogers could "find himself" and build up a little cash reserve. He is now a clothing worker.

That Rogers case indicates what can happen when there is a lack of proof and a jury is forced to resort to inference.

But what about society?

Remember that if Rogers is the *wrong* man then the *right* man escaped. That man, who deliberately killed a police officer, walked out of Petersburg and vanished. He is somewhere in our midst today, a dangerous killer.

Could improved investigative methods have resulted in the apprehension of that killer, and the release of Rogers, while there was still time to do something about it and while there was an opportunity to get proof instead of surmise?

Looking back at it, it is quite apparent that the investigation of the case was inept. There should have been more men on the job. Officer Hatchell shouldn't have gone down in the stream bed by himself.

Yet the police were presented with a problem and apparently with inadequate equipment. If the police, who fired twelve shots at the running fugitive, had had a rifle, the story might have been different. If there had been a helicopter that could have been made available on reasonably short notice, that stream bed might have been sealed off and carefully combed. There was evidence that no less than three desperate men were concealed there. Any one of these men might have killed Hatchell.

One of these men might have been apprehended with the weapon which had discharged the fatal shot still in his possession. Then there would have been some *proof* instead of mere conjecture.

We desperately need to pay more attention to our police problems, to give the officers every facility, and to arrange for added equipment for emergency use *before* the emergencies arise.

13

When we started our Court of Last Resort we did not foresee that appraising the cases of innocent men who had been wrongfully convicted would inevitably lead us to consider wider problems— police organization, the administration of penitentiaries, the extent to which science can come to the aid of investigative officers in furnishing proof, and a dozen others.

But these subjects are all inter-related and have necessarily led us into a broader field. We feel that perhaps the most important thing we can do is to act as a spark plug, to arouse public interest to the true meaning of crime and to the necessity of finding answers to at least some of the problems, to help society recognize the necessity for a fair, impartial administration of justice everywhere.

To make a beginning, the investigators who comprise The Court of Last Resort worked out a program of ten points covering the areas which they feel will most immediately respond to efforts to improve the administration of justice in this country. The last chapter of this book will be devoted to a listing of these ten points in full. But since much of the material in the balance of this book will concern those same problems, I am listing here a condensed version.

1. Preventing the conviction of innocent men and the escape of guilty men by better standards of proof so that jurors are not

asked to rely upon inference and conjecture where proof should be available.

2. Bringing about a better understanding of police problems by the taxpayer so that police can be given more technical education and more economic security, relieving officers of both economic and political pressure; providing ample insurance for death in the line of duty, and seeing that officers are not called on to face 1953 living expenses on 1943 salaries. Only in this way can we attract competent personnel.

3. Letting competent medical examiners have the sole responsibility of determining cause of death in homicide cases.

4. Establishing boards which have the power to review *facts* in proper cases just as appellate courts review errors of *law*. These boards should have powers equivalent to those exercised by the British Home Office.

5. Putting power in the hands of the courts to see that the defense of each person accused of crime is adequately and competently conducted. This means furnishing impartial, competent experts for both sides, and seeing that competent, experienced legal counsel represent the penniless defendant.

6. Adopting procedural changes which will eliminate technicalities by which the guilty escape, without at the same time weakening Constitutional safeguards.

7. Educating the public to a realization that the *professional* criminal is an avowed enemy of organized society, while the amateur criminal who errs because of weakness or environment is primarily a rehabilitative problem. Giving our professional penologists more co-operation, and paying more attention to their recommendations.

8. Promoting greater respect for our courts and American institutions. The contemptuous conduct of those attorneys who seek to belittle and disparage our courts is a breach of professional ethics and should be regarded as such. Every defendant is entitled to a vigorous, fearless defense, but attorneys supporting foreign ideology, who deliberately seek to undermine respect in our courts in order to try the courts instead of the defendants, should be subject to prompt, vigorous disciplinary action.

9. Bringing about greater respect for the organized legal profession. In addition to trying individual lawsuits, which are naturally sharply controversial, attorneys maintain organizations to safeguard the Constitutional rights of the people. This branch of legal activity is not properly appreciated. The organized bar is entitled to greater public respect. Failure to respect the leadership of the bar in matters in which it is expert is a dangerous tendency.

10. Bringing about a closer co-operation between the legal and medical professions so that attorneys can become more familiar with the function legal medicine can play in establishing proof, and so the medical profession can establish and enforce higher standards for the expert medical witness.

14

At about the time we first became interested in the possibilities of *Argosy's* Court of Last Resort, I received an invitation from Captain Frances G. Lee, an honorary captain of the New Hampshire State Police, to attend a seminar on Homicide Investigation at Harvard University.

Invitations to these seminars are highly prized by investigative officers. The class is limited. Eighteen or nineteen represent about the highest number who can receive the intensive training given at one of these seminars, although on special occasions one or two additional pupils have been taken in. Because the instruction is so highly individualized, Captain Lee refuses to weaken the impact of the lectures and examples by overcrowding.

For the most part those selected are picked officers from the various state police organizations. The head of the state police selects two men who he feels are worthy of training. The names are submitted to the governors of the respective states for approval. From time to time there has been a sprinkling of distinguished foreigners.—A superintendent of Scotland Yard, representatives of the British Home Office, persons high up in the investigative world in Canada.

I felt very diffident about accepting this invitation. I knew that the attendance was so strictly limited that my presence in the class would preclude the attendance of some professional investigator who was certainly more entitled to take the course than I. Nevertheless I didn't hesitate very long about wiring an acceptance.

Captain Frances G. Lee is a fabulous character, a woman of around seventy who has donated a fortune to establish a school of legal medicine at Harvard University. In addition to this she has taken a keen interest in police work, and in her position of honorary Captain of the New Hampshire State Police has some duties and a very considerable responsibility.

There is not space available here to describe that seminar on Homicide Investigation, and it probably would be entirely extraneous so far as the subject of this work is concerned. Suffice it to say that the training is intensive and unique. In addition to a course of lectures and demonstrations covering the latest wrinkles in scientific investigation, each student is assigned two practical problems. These problems have to do with miniature reproductions of crimes that have actually occurred and have at one time or another puzzled the police.

The detailed execution of these miniature crimes is a result of painstaking work by a perfectionist.

It is, of course, necessary that this should be true, since not only are the visible clues of importance, but any missing clue may, because of its absence, be a factor of considerable importance. This accounts for the careful attention to detail.

If, for instance, a magazine appears in one of those models, a magnifying glass will disclose nothing wrong. Despite the fact that the magazine conforms to the over-all scale of the models, which is exactly one inch to the foot, that magazine will be a true copy. The magazine has been carefully photographed, and then reduced to size. If a notebook is shown in one of the models bearing annotations made in pencil, and the pencil is also visible (as happens in one of the models), despite the fact that it is hardly bigger in diameter than a toothpick, it is actually a real pencil, it contains lead, and the entries which were purported to have been made in the notebook by that pencil were actually made by it.

These models require careful study and keen observation. It must be remembered that these are not merely abstractions, but as above mentioned they represent actual problems which have puzzled the police in historic cases. The models show the scene of the crime as it was found by the police. The students are supposed to second-guess the police, to guess right—and then give their reasons.

It was while I was attending this seminar that I learned for the first time that trained investigators much preferred to deal with circumstantial evidence, considering it far more reliable than the evidence of an eyewitness.

As a lawyer this came as a shock to me. I had from time to time stood up in front of juries and made sneering comments about circumstantial evidence.

Before I had finished the seminar I came to a realization of what circumstantial evidence actually is and something about what can be done with it.

Circumstances don't lie.

The reason circumstantial evidence has become the target for so many disparaging remarks is that untrained observers fail to see all of the significant circumstances. In other words, they fail to collect all of the evidence.

The second place where circumstantial evidence may lead the investigator into a trap is that facts may be capable of more than one interpretation.

Actually it is a rule of criminal law that if there is any reasonable hypothesis other than that of guilt which will explain the circumstances in a chain of circumstantial evidence, the defendant is entitled to an acquittal.

The first thing that is necessary in the investigation of any case is to find *all* of the circumstances, collect *all* of the evidence, and then consider *every* reasonable hypothesis. A trained observer can do this. An untrained observer may come up with the wrong facts and the wrong conclusion.

A newspaper once consulted me in a case which was bothering the police. They had found a body inside of a locked garage. Quite obviously the man had been killed by a contact wound made with a firearm. (When the muzzle of a firearm is pressed directly against human tissue the exploding gases inflict damage in addition to that of the bullet. This type of "contact wound" damage is distinctive and it is almost impossible for the trained investigator to overlook the cause.)

However, despite the fact that this man was found in a locked garage, despite the fact that he had evidently been killed by a gun held in contact with his head, despite the fact that he had left a suicide note, the police were unable to find the gun which had discharged the fatal bullet, nor, search as they would, could they find the bullet. The bullet had gone clean through the man's head. The police literally took the garage to pieces. They never found the bullet.

Now quite obviously that was a case where there must have been a failure to discover *all* of the significant circumstances connected with the death. Fortunately good pictures had been taken, pictures showing the body from every angle, and those pictures were clear enough so that they could be enlarged. As it happened, an examination of those pictures furnished certain additional evidence, which had been overlooked by the police, proving certain things happened after death.

I am not at liberty to tell the complete story here, but a study of those photographs showed clearly that the dead man's body had been searched for a money belt, after death. Whoever did that probably removed the missing gun. More expert medical examination of the corpse showed that the bullet had just barely broken through the skin at the back of the head. It probably had dropped into the clothes at the back of the neck as the body fell backward and was lost at some point after the corpse was carried away.

The trained investigator can learn an astonishing amount from circumstantial evidence. I remember being greatly interested in a case in New Hampshire where a hunter stumbled on some bones in the woods. He thought they were those of a human being.

It happened that the New Hampshire State Police (because of training in Captain Lee's seminars and because of Captain Lee's influence) had a working arrangement with scientific investigators at Harvard University, and therefore knew what was to be done and how it was to be done.

A small trench was dug to a depth below where any evidence could be expected. Glass was then inserted under the remains and they were actually transported in a glass cage so that careful microscopic examination could be made of the bones just as they had been found by the hunter.

This extreme care furnished a most significant clue. It appeared that there were the remains of a rotted garment on which a small plant had taken root, pushing its roots down through the decaying garment.

Scientists were able to tell how long it took for falling pine needles and leaves to form a humus which would support plant life. They discovered the exact age of the small plant, and, putting two and two together, were able to determine almost exactly how many years it had been since the person's death.

Carefully investigating the scattered remains which indicated animal molestation, the investigators found a tooth which had certain significant aspects. From that tooth they were able to learn something of the shape of the jaw of the dead person. An examination of some of the bones which remained intact gave the investigators the sex and approximate age of the dead person. Then, by investigating disappearances which had taken place just about so many years earlier, they came up with a complete answer.

Contrast that with what would have happened under ordinary circumstances if human bones had been reported.

Some untrained deputy would have gone out, found a few bones scattered around, with evidence of animal molestation. He would have picked up the bones, looked at them, probably he would have failed to discover the rotted garment. If he had, he'd have pulled it away from the surrounding vegetation, and once he had done that the chances of the case ever having been solved would have been virtually nil.

In another case, a body was found after months of exposure. Skilled investigators, working on their hands and knees, found underneath the body a bit of dead vegetation that had been broken in two.

Botanists were able to tell that that was a piece of vegetation which flowered in May, that the break in the vegetation had been made approximately two weeks before the period of flowering, and so were able to determine almost to the day when the man's body had crashed to the earth.

A careful examination of the bones disclosed an arthritic condition which indicated the man must have walked in a certain distinctive manner. Further examination of the bones in the head disclosed the approximate age of the individual. The time of disappearance, the age, sex, and distinctive physical characteristics being known, resulted in an identification of a body that had been so badly decomposed it ordinarily would have been considered impossible to make an identification.

I think most scientific investigators agree that circumstantial evidence, if it is carefully gathered and skillfully interpreted, is far more reliable than eyewitness evidence.

Circumstantial evidence that is not carefully gathered may be very misleading.

Circumstantial evidence that is not skillfully interpreted is downright dangerous.

The strides made by science during the last few years offer a wonderful opportunity to improve the administration of justice.

This means that we must have trained investigators, men who are familiar with scientific developments. These men do not need to be scientists. They don't necessarily need to be able to perform the scientific tests themselves, but they should know enough about what science can do to know how to look for evidence and how to preserve that evidence so that science can help.

Quite obviously the more jurors are forced to rely upon inference, the more opportunity there is for mistake. Those mistakes are twofold. The wrongful conviction of innocent persons, and the wrongful release of the guilty.

Our way of life, our type of civilization, our brand of liberty here in the United States is founded upon the administration of justice. If we're going to keep our heritage bright we're going to have to keep the administration of justice abreast of the times.

15

Some people criticize the police, pointing out that in many of our larger cities the municipal police forces are corrupt.

Whose fault is that?

The smug citizen likes to think it's the fault of the police.

Perhaps the smug citizen had better take a second look and a longer look.

Let's take prohibition, for instance.

In how many communities did shrewd politicians try to keep the votes of both the wets and the drys?

The formula was rather simple. Let the law against liquor be "enforced," promise strict enforcement, make a certain number of raids, a reasonable number of arrests, and do all these things to the fanfare of trumpets and with much newspaper publicity.

That would keep the "drys" happy.

As for the "wets," be sure that there were enough high-class speak-easies so the sophisticated man who "knew his way around" could knock at a certain door and shortly afterwards he and his date would be seated at a table in a dimly lit room enjoying good food and liquor that wasn't too poisonous.

This was a fine formula for the politician, but what did it do to the police force? What did it do to officer morale? What did it do to our respect for the law?

That's past.

But now we have gambling. How many communities are controlled by politicians who have adopted the old formula of "enforcing" the law just enough to satisfy one type of citizen, yet leave enough gambling to satisfy the class that wants "a little action."

These things put the honest police officer in an impossible position. They make for graft just as inevitably as stagnant pools make for mosquitoes.

If we are going to have laws we should abide by them. Actually we shouldn't try to control the actions of large numbers of protesting individuals on controversial matters by prohibitory statutes. In the long run it can only make for police corruption and "underworld influence."

Let's be honest with our cops if we expect them to be honest with us.

A short time ago it was announced in the press that a well-known chief of police had been offered the job of chief in one of the largest cities in the country. He turned it down because he didn't think the attitude of the citizens in that community would make it possible for him to do a good job. He felt that the community itself had become too tolerant toward crime.

Suppose we quit kidding ourselves and look at basic facts. You can't expect a man to do a good job unless you give him adequate remuneration, a fairly free hand, depending on his merit, and proper appreciation. Moreover, once he has done a good job he has to have security of position, otherwise you take away the inspiration for him to do a good job.

Just so long as the job of chief of police is a political plum, to be passed out on the basis of political patronage rather than merit and record of achievement, you need not expect the police captains to work their heads off trying to become police chiefs. Just so long as police captains can be juggled around for political reasons, you need not expect lieutenants to work their heads off trying to become captains. Just so long as sergeants and lieutenants are ruled in matters of major policy by the strangling hand of political chicanery, you need not expect up-and-coming young men to choose police science as a career.

At present there's an iron screen which tends to prevent the best class of young men from choosing police science as a career. I say that it *tends* to prevent them. It doesn't actually prevent all of them. I have addressed a class on police science in one of the universities that gives this as a course. The students of that class were high-grade young men, exceptionally high-grade. They were clear-thinking, they were determined, and they went into that branch of study because they had a natural inclination, an inherent aptitude, and were willing to face the obstacles with the idea they could be overcome.

But how many of these young men will actually go into police work?

A young man *who is entering college*, who has the choice of a profession, is more apt to take up law, medicine, dentistry, oil geology, or a dozen other different courses than police science.

The men who do volunteer as rookies are pretty high-class, all things considered. They have to be. Fortunately, as we are getting better standards, better working conditions and better pay, that class of men is constantly improving. But the fact remains that police work is not now, as it should be, enough of a profession to inspire men to take college training in police science so they can fit into the highest echelons of investigative personnel.

What about the police officer himself?

For some years now I have had a sporadic association with police in investigative work on certain cases. I have from time to time ridden in cars on radio patrol, talked with officers who are out on the firing line, and I have been interested in learning some of their duties and finding out something about how they feel.

In the first place, the police officer is a human being. He is an individual. He is usually married. He has kids. He is attached to his home and his family life.

Just put yourself, for the moment, in the position of a police officer. You are working on night shift. You have slept during the day. You kiss the wife and say good-by to the kiddies at about the time other men are coming home from their work.

You don't know whether you're ever going to see your wife and kids again. Don't think that's being unduly dramatic. The chances, of course, are only one in umpty hundred you won't be back right on time for your early breakfast. But there's always that one chance hanging over you and the knowledge that it is there exerts a steady nerve strain on both your wife and on you.

During the course of your night's work you are going to stop and investigate several automobile drivers. You're going to ask to check their driving licenses. You're going to ask them what they are doing in that particular neighborhood. You'll stop those cars because there is something about them that looks suspicious to you.

During the course of your work you are going to check on a few pedestrians, making certain that they are all right.

During the course of the evening's work you are going to answer quite a number of calls. These calls will vary all the way from a disturbance of the peace in some apartment to a prowler, a peeping Tom or an assault with a deadly weapon.

Some one of these people whom you stop may be a killer. He knows that if you once take him to the police station and start to book him, his death warrant is engraved on the tips of his fingers.

You don't know that. You don't even dare to act on the assumption that it *may* be true. You have a job of public relations to consider. An officer can't go around jabbing his gun in the ribs of every person he is questioning about a car registration. If he tried to do that the citizens would rise up against him in a wave of indignation. Therefore you have to take chances.

Naturally you try to cut those chances down as much as possible, but the fact remains that you're taking them.

You see a car being driven along the road. Perhaps it's going too fast. Perhaps it's going too slow. Perhaps there's something in the attitude of the man at the wheel that makes you realize he's crouched and tense as the police car eases up alongside of him, whereas if he were an ordinary citizen he would be relaxed and perhaps just a little curious.

You flag that man down. You just want to check his driving license and make sure that the car he's driving isn't stolen.

You get out of your car and walk up to him, realizing that he is a citizen and a taxpayer, and therefore potentially your boss; that you represent the dignity of the law; that you may be firm but that you must be polite.

You say, "I beg your pardon. May I check your driving license, please?"

A hand comes up from behind the concealment of the car door. For a split second you get the glint of the street light reflected from blued steel. Then, before you can even make a motion toward your own gun, you see a stabbing streak of vivid flame, and feel a searing pain.

There are more stabs of pain. Your knees buckle. Your groping hand can't find your gun. You see the taillight of a car speeding away, and then everything goes black.

You come to in a hospital. You've just had a blood transfusion and the doctors are giving you a fifty-fifty chance, or perhaps one chance in ten.—Or perhaps you don't come to at all.

An officer faces that risk every time he goes on duty. That's part of the job. You may figure percentages and reassure yourself. But the point is that you face that risk every single time you stop a driver and ask to check his driving license.

It is somewhat as if you were called on to put a revolver at your head and snap the trigger a dozen times a night. Only one in five thousand of those guns would be loaded. But you would always be aware there was that one.

You can't figure mathematical chances of that sort because the nerve strain is cumulative. You may keep your conscious mind under control, but the subconscious winces just a little bit every time you pick up a gun.

Now let's look at what you, as a police officer, get in return.

You get a salary that enables you barely to get by. In some cities it's even less than they pay the garbage collectors.

You get by all right because your wife is a good manager. You keep the kids clothed. You have a radio. You aren't able as yet to afford a television. You have a family car that you picked up secondhand. You drive it on your days off, and your wife uses it for shopping. You don't have money enough to live in the close-in districts, so you're out quite a ways from town. You have a few more debts than you'd like to have, and there's always the feeling that if one of the kids gets really sick, or some emergency comes along, you'll have to scrape pretty deep to get by.

You probably don't budget with such deadly accuracy that you realize just how thin the margin is, but statisticians, who do, estimate that by the time routine expenses are paid there's just twelve dollars and a half per month left for pleasures or medical expense emergencies.

And always you have that realization that tomorrow your two kids may be without a father, that tomorrow your wife will have to assume the payments on the house and start supporting the kids. How's she going to do it? She gets by all right running the house. She gets pretty tired at times. She doesn't complain but she has to do a lot of washing, a lot of mending, a lot of sewing, a lot of cooking.

Suppose she had to go out and start doing general housework at so much per hour in order to keep the kids going?

You don't like the thought. Your wife doesn't say anything about it but you know darn well it's something that she faces all the time.

Now let's look at another end of the picture. If you're working in a city where you have a chief of police who's trying to give the taxpayers a good service, if he's promoting men strictly according to merit, if he's scrupulously trying to maintain high standards of performance, you're relatively free from danger as long as you do your duty.

There are lots of cities where the chief of police would like to do that but where he simply can't.

You are coming to an intersection. You see a car ahead that stops for the red light but beats the signal a little when it changes. The car crowds dangerously close to another driver at the next intersection. It picks up speed. It weaves over to the left side of the road, then cuts back to the right.

You drive alongside and take a look.

There's a young chap at the wheel trying to be a big shot and impress the cutie who's alongside of him. You can tell that they've been drinking. You don't know how much. You decide to find out.

You stop the fellow and he's the son of a businessman who is the client of a lawyer who is the adviser of an alderman.

The kid has had just enough drink so that he feels a little arrogant. He wants to show off in front of the doll. Unfortunately he isn't drunk enough so you dare to take a chance on running him in for intoxicated driving. Yet he has been drinking and he's going to drink some more. Perhaps his last two drinks haven't quite caught up with him yet, but he certainly rates a warning.

You try to caution him in a polite way. You try to point out the danger of the situation to him and to the attractive young woman whom you don't want to see disfigured in a smashup.

You get insulted. Next day the kid gives his own version of what happened to his father, who, in turn, rings up the lawyer, who, in turn, etc., etc., etc.

Then perhaps a new mayor is elected. The mayor has made a lot of smug promises to the taxpayers, who believe him. He throws out the chief of police and puts in a new one, a buddy of his. The citizens may not know, but you know, and you know it mighty quick, that you aren't going to get any advancement because of efficiency in enforcing the law. The best way you can get along under the new regime is to fail to see certain things.

All over the city representatives of the new regime are making nice speeches to luncheon clubs. There is a lot of reassuring publicity being released, but all over the city little hole-in-the-wall places spring up.

You know that you're not supposed to see those places. Not if you know what's good for you.

Now that's not a very attractive picture.

The trouble is that it gets worse before it gets better. We have a steady trend toward inflation. The dollar keeps getting cheaper. The cost of living keeps going up. You try to make last year's dollars pay this year's bills. You were stretched enough financially a year ago. As it is right now, you're cutting down on a lot more things than you want to.

Most trades are organized. They perform a standardized work. There's a yardstick for measuring the wages for that work. When pay goes up ten cents an hour in adjoining communities it's a standard for comparison.

There isn't any such standard in police work because salaries always lag behind the increasing costs. When police finally get a pay boost it's because the economic pressure has been building up until it has reached such a point something has to be done.

That economic pressure has been retroactive, but a pay raise isn't retroactive.

The pay raise barely lets you get even with the board again, and then, before you can draw a deep breath, the steady increase in the cost of living starts melting away your pay raise.

Then perhaps some new-found friend offers you a television set. A man with a big diamond, a high-powered automobile and fine cigars wants to do you little favors. Those favors cost money. No one wants anything much in return—not at first.

There's a man in the cigar store down the street. You know he's making book. Virtually everyone who is in the know in the neighborhood knows that he is making book. He doesn't even bother to be nice to you. He ignores you. That's because his pay-off is higher up. He has a political green light. Nothing is said. No one tells you so in so many words, but you know that if you bother him you're headed for a prompt transfer. But people think this guy is paying *you* off, and treat you accordingly.

Is it any wonder that in some communities police have become tolerant of crime, have formed an alliance with organized gamblers?

In the long run, and, mind, this is in the long run, the police department reflects the attitude of the citizen. Not the individual citizen but the aggregate citizenry in the community.

Nothing is quite so potent as the force of an aroused public opinion.

But let's go back for the moment to being a cop.

Remember you're on nights.

You know there's gambling going on in the city. You're smart enough to know that under the new regime you're not supposed to see too much of that gambling. The man in the cigar store on the corner is strictly out of your territory. There's a place down the block where you see quite a few people going and coming, a modest little apartment house where normally you'd expect to see a person entering or leaving at relatively rare intervals. You see quite a few people going and coming. You know that you should leave that place alone.

But a man comes out of the gambling house. He has money. He's been drinking. He starts to walk down to where he's left his car parked. A figure jumps out of the alley, throws a stranglehold on him, puts a knee in his back, wrestles the man down to the sidewalk, grabs the roll and runs.

That's where you come in.

Someone runs to a telephone. A call flashes in. You're near the scene. You pile on the gas and start weaving through traffic.

You see a man who looks back over his shoulder. He sees the police car and ducks down an alley.

You slam the police car to a stop, draw your gun, jump out and race down the alley after him.

The light is behind your back. You can't see him, but you're silhouetted, a perfect target. Yet you have to go on. You don't dare to shoot unless someone shoots first. The way you're situated you couldn't even see a threatening motion.

There may be a lot of talk about the city being "wide open," but there's no talk about cowardly cops. There never is. Make no mistake about it, as long as you're a cop there's no turning back from that shadowy figure at the end of the dark alley. You keep going on. You don't even hesitate. You don't slacken your pace.

Finally you see him, dodging ahead of you, a vague shadowy figure. You call to him. He doesn't shoot. He stops. You breathe a sigh of relief as his hands come up.

You get up to him and give him a quick frisk. You don't find any weapon. You don't find anything. You ask him what he's doing down the alley and he clams up on you, the unmistakable mark of the professional criminal.

You handcuff the prisoner, go back to your car, get a flashlight and start investigating. Halfway down the alley you find a gun and a wallet.

The victim identifies the wallet as his. Okay, you've made an arrest. You take your man up and book him.

What happens?

You have to be up in the morning in order to appear. You have to identify the man. By that time a lawyer has shown up. The lawyer gets a continuance.

Because you're living within your salary, and can't afford a close-in house, it's a thirty-minute ride out to where you live and you have to take your own car to make the trip. By the time you get back out to the house you've lost most of your day's sleep. You grab some rest during the afternoon and then start out again on your beat.

Other people get time and a half or double time for any overtime they put in. As a cop you only get straight time and in some cities all court appearance time doesn't count as duty time. It comes out of your time off.

You go up to court half a dozen times. Each time the case is continued on one excuse or another. Finally, it turns out that the victim doesn't really want to prosecute. He's afraid someone will ask him how he happened to be in that particular section of the city at that particular time, and where the money in the wallet came from. It's "policy" to "hush it up," "let it blow over."

Or perhaps the citizen stands by his guns. He can't make an identification because the holdup man grabbed him from behind, but he has identified his wallet and he's resisted all pressure to make him "let the matter drop." He's going to go through with it.

The case comes to trial. You get on the witness stand. You tell your story.

The lawyer for the defense starts in on you. He has a field day.

"How do you know that's the same exact wallet you picked up there in the alley?—How do you know that someone else wasn't in that alley? You couldn't see down that alley, could you?—Oh, you saw the defendant?—Yes, yes, you saw him as a 'shadowy figure.'—Oh, you couldn't see him distinctly? Then how do you know some-one else wasn't in the alley? How do you know someone else didn't go in there just ahead of the defendant? How do you know someone else wasn't hiding in that alley, someone who remained hidden while you bunglingly arrested an innocent man?—There were boxes and barrels in that alley, weren't there? There were garbage cans. How do you know someone wasn't hiding in one of the boxes? How do you know someone wasn't crouched behind the barrels? You didn't look in those barrels?"

The lawyer sneers at you. He begins to interrogate you about every detail of that alley, how many boxes? How many barrels? How many doorways? How many fire escapes?

Naturally your memory is a little hazy about all those details. You went in there in the dark to get a man. You got him.

Now, under this cross-examination you begin to sweat a little. You don't have the faintest idea how many packing cases were stacked in that alley, how many garbage pails, how many doorways.

The lawyer is going good. "Were there a dozen? Two dozen? Four dozen? A hundred?"

You tell him there were less than a hundred. How do you know? You say it stands to reason. That opens up a new line of attack. Are you testifying to what you *know* or what you think stands to reason?

Quite obviously after you had apprehended the defendant and taken him back to the car, after you had secured a flashlight and had found the wallet and the gun, you weren't in a position to leave your prisoner, go back and prowl around behind every box and lift the lid on every garbage can, count every packing case, every garbage can.

The lawyer has had sixty days to think up verbal traps for you, to think of the things you should have done. You had two-fifths of a second to make up your mind and get into action.

Finally the attorney gets done with you. He has created the impression that you are a dumb, blundering ignoramus.

You did a courageous act in going down that dark alley after an armed man. The twelve jurors, who are grinning at your discomfiture, don't look at it that way. To them you committed a whole series of blunders. You didn't use your head. You left yourself wide open. It never occurs to them that no matter what you did or didn't do, a good lawyer, given sixty days in which to think, could have found something wrong.

If you'd spent an hour looking in all the garbage cans, he'd have claimed the real culprit had slipped out of the alley while you were looking for a holdup man mixed in with the garbage of a restaurant.

He'd show you hadn't seen the gun and the purse on your way into the alley the first time, which showed conclusively they hadn't been there then—(otherwise "even a dumb cop" would have stumbled over them).

So the lawyer sneeringly says, "That's all," in the tone of voice usually reserved for mangy cur dogs.

You'd give a month's salary if you had a chance to cross-examine that lawyer, and could only have one half of his gift for sarcasm.

Instead you get off the witness stand, trying to keep your shoulders back, your chin up.

People smile tolerantly.

The defendant takes the stand. He tells a simple, straightforward story. He should be able to. He's rehearsed it for sixty days. He's thought about that almost constantly since he's been in jail.

He is, he admits, a man who had previously been "in trouble." For that reason he had a fear of being picked up because police always "pushed him around." Whenever they picked him up on suspicion they'd try to beat a confession out of him.

He was walking along the street in a decent, law-abiding, orderly manner. A man walking very rapidly was just ahead of him. He heard the siren of a police car, and the man ahead of him dashed into the mouth of the dark alley. The defendant, without thinking, decided that that alley would be the best place for him, too. He didn't know what the police were after. He had a perfectly clear conscience but he was worried about his past record. So he ducked into the alley, too, standing just inside the alley, waiting for the police car to drive on past.

But the police car didn't drive on past. The car came to a screaming stop and a big, burly officer jumped out.

Quite naturally the defendant ran down the alley looking for a way out. He could see the other man in the alley ahead of him. That man was also running. Then it occurred to the defendant that the cop might be chasing that man ahead of him. So he turned to face the cop, ceased to run and raised his hands high above his head.

But the dumb cop didn't go after the man who was running. He pounced on the hapless defendant who was only trying to surrender, slapped on handcuffs and dragged the defendant back to the mouth of the alley.

All the time the defendant was trying to tell this dumb cop that the man the cop really wanted was down at the extreme end of the alley, hiding behind a packing case, or in one of the doorways.

Every time the defendant tried to say anything, however, the officer jerked on the handcuffs, telling him to "save it for the judge."

The officer picked up a gun and a wallet halfway down the alley. The defendant knew nothing whatsoever about them. He had never seen them before in his life. He had been beaten up so much by the cops he had a horror of police brutality.

He made three attempts to tell the arresting officer that the man he wanted was there in the alley. The arrogant officer had refused to listen, had told the defendant to "save it for the judge," so the defendant had kept quiet.

The defendant, having finished his well-rehearsed story, stands up pretty well on cross-examination.

Then the attorneys start arguing. The attorney for the defense doesn't talk about the case. He talks about the dumb cop, the police brutality, the arrogant attitude, the unpardonable failure on the part of the arresting officer to make certain that the man he wanted wasn't down at the far end of the alley.

The attorney says to the jury, "This officer saw *a* man run into the alley. He doesn't know whether that man was the defendant or someone else. It was a vague, shadowy figure. So what does he do, ladies and gentlemen of the jury? He plunges into the alley and finds the defendant standing meekly and unarmed, with his hands up trying to surrender, trying to tell his story. The officer slams handcuffs on him. Then he goes and gets a flashlight and searches the alley until he finds a gun and a wallet. But does he continue his search to make certain that only the defendant was in the alley? No, he won't listen and he can't think. There, ladies and gentlemen of the jury, was where the cop made an unpardonable blunder.

"Has anyone said they saw my client committing the holdup? Has anyone said they saw my client in the possession of a gun, in the possession of the stolen wallet? Did anyone find my client's finger-prints on either of them? No, a thousand times No! Can any one of you jurors truthfully say in your own conscience that the real culprit was not in hiding at the far end of that alley all the time this arrogant cop was manhandling my client? Is there anyone who can truthfully say that at least he doesn't have a reasonable doubt that the real cul-prit was hiding in that alley?

"It was up to the officer to make sure, ladies and gentlemen. It isn't up to a defendant to prove himself innocent. My client tried and tried to tell the officer, but each time he tried to speak the officer jerked the handcuffs so there was a cruel pressure on the defendant's wrists, and said, 'Save it. Tell it to the judge.'"

The way the lawyer tells the story, it would seem that a failure to search the rest of that alley was absolute criminal negligence on the part of the arresting officer. There the officer was, with a flashlight in his hand, the defendant safely apprehended and handcuffed. The officer doesn't *know* whether the defendant was the man he saw turn into the alley or not. He doesn't know anything. He's just a dumb, blundering, brutal cop, who acted on an assumption. He acted on the assumption that the defendant was guilty because he found him in an alley.

"However," the lawyer goes on, "you jurors can't act on assump-tions. You must have proof. It's the duty of an officer to get proof. Here's a cop who went to a police school to find out what evidence was. He knew that he was supposed to get evidence, but what did he do? He simply picked up the first man he came to in the alley and carted him off to jail without searching the alley. It isn't a crime to stand in an alley."

And then the lawyer gets tears in his voice. "The defendant has told you under oath, ladies and gentlemen, that he saw another man run into that alley, a man whose every motion, whose every telltale gesture indicated that he was fleeing from the police. The defendant tried desperately to tell the arresting officer about that other man in the alley. Each time he was cut off.—Each time the handcuffs were jerked so the steel bit cruelly into the bone of the wrist. Just try it on yourselves, ladies and gentlemen of the jury. Place a piece of metal against the bone of your own wrist and then press, press as hard as you can. Feel the pain. And yet you can't exert the pressure that an officer can exert on handcuffs just by twisting his wrist. That's because there's leverage exerted when one twists handcuffs. They're built that way—to police specifications.

"Of course the officer now denies the defendant's story. He has to. His job's at stake. He has to save his reputation. He's in a position where he doesn't dare admit the truth, but there are some things he's forced to admit. He's forced to admit that he didn't go on searching that alley. Why? Why in the name of common sense, didn't he? You would think even a cop would have sense enough for that. And the cop has made another damaging admission. He has admitted that he didn't talk things over with the defendant. He was in a hurry. As soon as he handcuffed the man he dashed back to the automobile for a flashlight. As soon as he found the flashlight he located the gun and the wallet, and then he was busily engaged trying to get the victim to identify the wallet.

"Figure it out for yourself, ladies and gentlemen. The cop was too busy to listen. He dashed back for his flashlight. As soon as he found the wallet, he was trying to get it identified. By that time a crowd had collected, and the officer telephoned in for the wagon. The patrol wagon came up and the defendant was bustled into the wagon."

The lawyer for the defense sits down.

A couple of people on the jury nod their heads imperceptibly. The young deputy district attorney makes a perfunctory argument. The jury goes out. Word comes back that it's a hung jury. That might mean another trial. The jurors are taxpayers. There's no use subjecting the state to the expense of another trial. The ones who are holding out for acquittal aren't going to change. The ones who want a verdict of guilty shrug their shoulders, and, after four or five hours of debate, say, "What the heck, the case isn't that important."

The jury file into court. They've agreed on a verdict. They find the defendant not guilty.

The deputy district attorney feels that you lost the case for him. The jurors feel that you committed an unpardonable blunder in not searching the alley the way the defendant was trying to tell you to.

You go on home with a bad taste in your mouth. You are too tired and too disgusted even to tell your wife about it and get her sympathy. You drag yourself into bed for a couple of hours' sleep before you have to go out on night patrol again.

You did a brave thing in going down that dark alley. You didn't get any credit for it. You were tagged as a dumb cop because you didn't think of the things in two-fifths of a second that a smart lawyer thought up after sixty days.

You can't win. Until the public understands more about police work you're bound to be behind the eight ball every time some shrewd lawyer starts off on the "dumb cop" gambit.

Let's consider another type of case.

You're cruising quietly along the streets, your headlights dimmed, looking things over. A block or so ahead of you, you see a pedestrian. Even while you're watching, a powerful, thick-chested man jumps out of a dark doorway, grabs this pedestrian and wrestles him down to the sidewalk.

You give the car the gun, get to the place, skid to a stop and dash out to apprehend the man.

You tell him he's under arrest and he grapples with you. He's a powerful, thick-necked, heavy-chested adversary. He outweighs you by thirty pounds.

However, you're a cop. You're supposed to know your way around. The man may be unarmed. For all you know, he is. If you should draw your gun and shoot him, you'd be charged with killing an unarmed citizen. If you let the man wrestle himself free, or knock you out and get away from you, you're incompetent. You've arrested this man and you're supposed to make the arrest stick. As a cop you have to dominate the situation.

This fellow knows something about wrestling. He tries to use his superior weight and strength and skill. You have to think fast. You bring your heel down on his instep. Then you punch him in the stomach and grab his wrist. Before he quite knows what has happened you've managed to get the grip you want, one that holds him powerless.

By this time the citizen has regained his feet. You get handcuffs on the man and call for the wagon.

When this character has been booked you find out that he's "Bill the Mug." He's been arrested thirty-five times. He's been convicted twenty times. He has a police record studded with all sorts of sentences, probation, a couple of terms in the pen, parole and then a series of dismissals after arrest.

They keep turning him loose for you to pick up.

The point I'm trying to make is that the job of a police officer under the present setup is not so attractive that a person who has a choice of professions is apt to pick out a career in police work and start studying for it.

It wouldn't take too much understanding on the part of citizens to change many of these conditions.

Fortunately the number of officers who actually are killed in the line of duty is not so high that on a percentage basis it would bring about prohibitive insurance rates.

Officers themselves try to carry some group insurance. It is inadequate.

No one wants to be killed, but if an officer knew that in the event he happened to stop a fatal bullet there was an insurance policy which would place twenty-thousand dollars in his wife's hands, either on an annuity basis or in a lump sum, depending upon the circumstances, so that she could pay off the mortgage on the house and put the kids through school without working harder than her health would stand, he'd feel a lot better about going out on the job. One very big cause of worry would have been eliminated.

The cost of such insurance would not be prohibitive. In fact, it would be a very fine investment purely from a standpoint of good business.

16

How about these youngsters who get in trouble? How about the ones who go through a period of probation, get in trouble again, and finally are sent to the penitentiary? What about our penitentiaries themselves?

Here is where the average citizen entertains the most alarmingly erroneous concept of crime.

The average citizen thinks that the penitentiary is the place that criminals go to.

Actually the penitentiary is the place that criminals come from.

Another error in public thinking is that prison inmates are all classed as a unit.

Men who go to prison are of many sorts. Some of them are viciously depraved. Some of them are killers. Some of them are psychopathic misfits. Some of them are weaklings. Some of them are all right when they are sober, but get into trouble when they start drinking. Some of them are just plain habitual criminals.

Yet when these men come out, so far as the public is concerned, they are all the same. "Ex-convicts."

It is to be borne in mind that nearly all of these men do come out. Some of them are in there two years, some five, some ten, some only for one year, some are in there for twenty years and up. Some of them, of course, die in prison. But far better than ninety percent of the inmates of almost any penal institution are discharged back into society.

Quite obviously society should be greatly concerned with the attitude, the aptitude and the capabilities of the man when he emerges from the front door of a penitentiary to become once more a member of society.

Actually nothing could be farther from the truth. Society wants to dismiss the whole problem of crime and particularly the problem of prisons.

Because a prison is a high-security unit, with guards at the towers, walls surrounding the yards, an elaborate system of locks, guards and turnkeys, the average citizen thinks that the prison inmate has been "put out of the way."

It happens that I'm quite friendly with the warden of a certain penitentiary. That penitentiary is now being occupied by approximately thirty percent more inmates than the number for which it was designed. That represents the capacity of that prison to its point of complete saturation.

Yet every year the courts of the state send to that prison *as much as seventy percent of the total maximum prison population!*

What does that mean?

It means that something has to be done with the men who are already in that prison.

This state, in common with most other states, is having its own financial problems. An attempt is being made to provide facilities to a constantly increasing population. As every citizen knows, taxation has reached a point where it can only go higher at the expense of diminishing returns. All bills to increase facilities at the prison so as to provide additional prison space have been pigeonholed by the state legislature.

"This is no time to add to prison costs," the backers are told. "The state has no money to 'waste' on prisoners."

That is in keeping with the thinking of the average citizen. He doesn't know anything about penitentiaries in the first place, and he wants to forget them in the second place. The criminals are "out of the way." Let them stay there.

"Rehabilitation?

"Oh, I guess so. It's all right if you can do it, but why waste time with those guys?. . . Oh, sure, go ahead. Rehabilitate them if you want to, but don't bother me with it."

Rehabilitation costs money. Any type of constructive prison work costs money. Taxpayers' money. Taxpayers don't want to put out that money. Taxpayers don't want to be reminded of the penitentiaries. They know the penitentiaries are there and they want the problems kept shut away behind those same walls.

The governor appoints a warden. He hopes he is getting a good man, but his definition of a good man is one who can keep the penitentiary out of the newspapers for the governor's term of office. Just let him and his administration forget there is a penitentiary and that warden has done a swell job. Let something happen that puts the penitentiary in the headlines, a riot, an escape, a plea for improved facilities, for more funds, for better pay for prison guards, and the administration is "embarrassed."

Every day from every prison in the country, there is a trickle of ex-convicts which must be absorbed by society. Society knows nothing about it. It wants to know nothing about it. It knows nothing about the attitude of the men who come out to join society, and it cares less.

That trickle shouldn't be a muddy stream of contaminated human beings. It should be an influx of men who have made mistakes, have paid for those mistakes, are ready to "begin over" and have the facilities for a new start.

Of course that's an idealistic, Utopian, impractical view. But with a little money, a little change in thinking, a little human consideration, that muddy stream could be segregated. Some of it could become good, clear water. The rest of it, hopelessly muddy, would need to be put into settling tanks.

Some day we won't have such a horribly large percent of hopelessly muddy water. We must learn how to keep the mud out of the water so far as possible, how to handle the polluted stream once it does become contaminated.

But if we are going to keep mud from the stream we must start with the young man who has become too "tough" for the juvenile authorities, who has passed the statutory age limit during which some form of consideration is mandatory and keeps getting into trouble. The exasperated judge, who has found this boy a recurrent problem, decides to "teach him a lesson." He sends the young man to the penitentiary.

What happens?

All too frequently he has taught the young man a lesson, but it's the wrong lesson.

The young man has been callow, surly, defiant, impudent. He goes to the penitentiary and he starts to get vicious, hard and bitter.

In too many instances penitentiaries, particularly when they are run under an old-time regime, are nothing but the finishing schools of the underworld.

He comes out with ten or twenty dollars, a prison-made suit of clothes, a prison haircut, and prison shoes.

He is called on to find a job and re-establish himself in a society which sent him to a penitentiary to "teach him a lesson" and which utterly ignored him while he was there.

He is a young man with all the surcharged energy of youth. For a period of years now he has been deprived of women—not of sex—you can't deprive a man of sex. You can deprive him of women. That's a "punishment."

That's all very fine as a punishment. It's a grim punishment. What does it do to the individual?

Ask authorities on penology what it does.

It's a subject they don't like to discuss. They avoid it wherever possible. They close their eyes to it as much as they can. It's a problem of penology that even the penologists try to "forget" and solve by ignoring it.

Yet that is one of the factors that must be taken into consideration in determining what has happened to our surly, defiant, uncooperative juvenile, who was "taught a lesson" by society.

Let any average individual who is capable of adjusting himself to a normal society put on a prison suit of clothes, a prison pair of shoes, and, with a prison haircut, go out and try to get a job.

Suppose *you* should try it. Just put yourself in the shoes of a discharged inmate—prison shoes.

You don't dare tell where you have been for the past three years. If you tell the truth the police will suggest you had "better leave town." If you try to lie, you have to make a good job of lying otherwise someone is going to catch up with you.

Suppose you got out with twenty dollars in your pocket. Your tendency is to get rather far away from the penitentiary, and as a rule the penitentiary is located rather far away from the principal cities in the state.

You get to a strange town. You want to look for employment. You have to eat. You have to have a place to sleep. You need a razor, a shaving kit, numerous personal belongings.

How long is your twenty dollars going to last?

So you try to get a job. It certainly won't be a very choice job. It's a job that the average worker doesn't want, therefore the employer can't afford to be too discriminating.

And you have to be lucky to get this job. Suppose you do get it within two or three days of the time you leave the penitentiary. How are you going to finance yourself until payday?

And you're going to be very, very lucky indeed if you can find such a job before your money runs out.

What are you going to do then?

Now remember that this problem involves *you*. A man who has always been able to integrate himself in society, a man who has been living a normal life for the past few years. But suppose you were not a normal individual. Suppose you hadn't been able to integrate yourself in society. Suppose for the past few years you had been living a life where you had been completely deprived of women. Suppose you had been living a regimented life, where what you did and the time you did it, what you ate and the time you ate it, and everything about that life was worked out and regimented.

You suddenly find yourself in the midst of a society that is strange, and which you regard as hostile. Your own friends have turned their backs on you. In place of those friends you have picked up a whole new circle of friends at the penitentiary. You probably know a few hundred men who have "gone out" since you made their acquaintance. You know some who are located in the city.

What are you going to do for friendship? What are you going to do for companionship? You're naturally going to look up some of those friends.

There are other aspects of the situation. You get a job. In some places if you have been convicted of a certain type of crime the law requires that you register with the chief of police. In any event, the police are pretty apt to know where you are.

You get the job. You try to work. You're making good. It's not much of a job but you're doing all right.

A crime is committed somewhere in the locality.

The police have no clues but there is a public demand that they do something, that they get busy and track down the culprit.

So what do the police do?

They "round up" all of the questionable characters in the neighborhood.

You're a questionable character. You're an "ex-convict." You've served a prison sentence. You really don't have any rights any more. The police come down and "pick you up." It's "only for questioning," but you go up to the jail and into the tank, and when you don't show up for work the next morning your employer knows why you didn't show up and all about your past record.

By the time the police have finished their questioning and released you, you find you don't have any job to go back to.

Moreover, the heat is on and you don't dare to be hanging around the neighborhood where the crime has been committed. You'd better go some place else.

How?

Once more the question arises, What are you going to use for money?

So that's what happened when an irate judge decided that it was time to "teach the young man a lesson."

The only change in that callow youth is that he's become hard, bitter, and stir-smart. He's been exposed to years of perversion and degeneracy. He's lost the perspective of a man who has been permitted to make his own decisions and stand or fall on the consequences.

Now society doesn't have a surly, defiant youth. It has a shrewd "ex-con."

But what could the judge have done? All the juvenile controls had produced no effect. Lectures, probation and restrictions had rolled off this young man like water off a duck's back.

There isn't any easy answer, but undoubtedly there is an answer somewhere. To find it will take thought, planning, sympathy, understanding and work.

In this connection I have recently enjoyed a very interesting experience.

I was invited to spend a day at a "ranch" in Southern California where an attempt is being made to solve the problems of tough juveniles.

It's an interesting experiment, and the significant thing is that it is paying tremendous dividends in the realm of character rehabilitation.

The young men who go there are fellows who have been too tough for the ordinary juvenile procedure. Probation doesn't work with them. They're on the road to becoming vicious, depraved criminals.

They are sent to this "ranch," not for any fixed term. They are simply sent there.

Now there's a good deal of corn and showmanship in the operation of that ranch, but apparently that's what is needed. Every youngster has a certain amount of make-believe in his system, a certain something that can be reached by showmanship, or, if you want to so label it, just plain corn.

You see a reflection of this in the heroes who are popular in the comic strips, in a certain type of motion picture, in some of the Western fiction that is devoured by the teen-ager.

The juvenile delinquent who is a candidate for this ranch is loaded into an automobile. He's taken over mountain roads until he comes to a wild, secluded section of Western country where sagebrush and pine trees are mingled on the edge of a mountain slope. He's a tough kid, hard, surly, defiant. He's fighting the law. The law and the officers are enemies.

Then the car in which he is riding comes to a stop. He sees a gate, and over the gate is the legend *"Howdy, Pardner."*

A big man in a Western sombrero, driving a buckboard, to which are hitched two pinto ponies, comes jogging along a winding mountain road. Behind the buckboard are two outriders, young men sitting in graceful ease on spirited Western horses.

There's an element of dust and sweat, the outdoors, the creak of saddle leather, the big hats of Westerners, and there's something in the easy carriage of those two young men, who sit so expertly on their spirited horses, that makes the young delinquent subconsciously want to be like that himself.

The big man shakes hands, says, "Get in, pardner."

The automobile with the law enforcement officer drives off. The juvenile finds himself seated in the buckboard, which is turned expertly and starts up a mountain road—narrow, hairpin turns, steep grades, a scenic road which runs through wild Western scenery.

The man introduces himself. He's Ralph Johnson who runs the "ranch." He casually explains to the juvenile during the ride to the ranch headquarters that he can escape any time he wants to. There aren't any restrictions. All he has to do is walk off. But if he walks off he forfeits the privilege of ever coming back.

That's the keynote of the conversation. It's subtly suggested that it's a privilege to be there—and it really is.

Johnson points out to this boy that he'll have his own horse and saddle, that he'll have an opportunity to become a part of the camp, that that's going to be his home, that before he graduates he'll be like these outriders who are jogging along behind the buckboard, in fact, he may even have the job of being one of those outriders.

Johnson goes on to tell him there aren't even any rules in the place.—That's right, not a single rule.—"But we do have traditions and we try to live up to those traditions."

It isn't as though the young man were ushered into an office and had someone lay down a lot of rules that he had to observe—or else. He's given a ride in a buckboard over an exciting road that makes him hang on to the side of the seat. He is given an entirely new outlook on life, an entirely new set of goals. There aren't any rules for him to memorize and abide by—only traditions.

And those traditions really exist.

They exist because Johnson has that rare gift that enables him to get the confidence of young men and to hold and maintain that confidence. That means that ninety percent, or perhaps a hundred percent of the boys who are there are for Johnson and for the traditions.

It's mighty hard to cram rules down the throat of a defiant young man. It's mighty hard to think up any form of punishment that will force him to abide by those rules. But when he becomes one of a gang, and the gang has traditions, it's very easy for him to fall in with those traditions.

Johnson and his wife try to see that the traditions are wholesome, that they appeal to the imagination of a boy, that they are the type that will build character.

The young man has left all of his outside life behind him. He's there in ranch surroundings, where everything is of the outdoors and of the West. He starts work. That's one of the "traditions" of the place.

There is a certain amount of schooling (the place is an accredited high school and furnishes a high grade of education). There's a certain amount of manual labor. Johnson keeps that manual labor interesting. Whenever a task threatens to become a chore, he alternates it with something that is interesting. He keeps his boys interested in what they are doing. They can see a purpose in it.

The boys live clean lives and they lead active lives. They're so busy every minute of the time with something that keeps them interested they don't have any time to think of any deviltry.

And when finally Johnson feels that the camp has done its job and that it is time for the boy to go out, there's no such crude thing as announcing that a "sentence has expired."—The boy is "ready to graduate."

Those graduation exercises are impressive.

When it comes time for a boy to graduate, he starts out on his favorite horse and rides alone over the mountain trails that he has learned to love. To the accompaniment of creaking saddle leather, the boy has an opportunity to think about the past and to contemplate the future.

Then he returns to camp after a couple of hours of solitude and the graduation exercises are under way.

They're inspirational. They're filled with pageantry and showmanship. At last the boy has achieved recognition. It's his big day. He's achieved a great honor. He's going to the outside world to "carry on the traditions" of the camp.

Does he do it?

He does.

The statistics show that. The camp hasn't been in operation long enough to show all that it can do, but it has been in operation long enough to show that it is highly successful. Boys with a new education, with a new concept of life, with a new quota of traditions, go out into a friendly world.

We need more camps of this sort for the juveniles, and we need something of the sort for men. Personally I don't think you can take anyone, except a weakling, and club him into such submission that he is going to be worth a damn when the club is removed. I think you have to give him a set of traditions to live up to, and in order to do that you have to have *bona fide* traditions. You can't have purely synthetic "rules."

The only persons who can really make traditions are one's companions. You have to sell them on the idea before you can sell anyone else. That means that traditions have to be good, they have to be wholesome, and they have to appeal to the imagination. They have to be really inspirational.

Mind you, I'm talking now about trying to keep the mud out of the stream in the first place.

After a man has served one or two terms in a penitentiary I think there is only one force on earth that can rehabilitate him and that is something within himself, and altogether too few of those people feel the urge for rehabilitation.

We can, I think, improve the administration of our penitentiaries enormously, but the penitentiary itself is an archaic, outmoded, unsuccessful method of coping with a crime problem that continues to get bigger and bigger. The penitentiary is not a cure. It's a punishment.

Personally, I don't think you can mix punishment and rehabilitation any more than you can mix oil and water. Punishment makes a person bitter or else it breaks his spirit. Theoretically it's a deterrent. Actually it's proving otherwise.

I'm not a penologist. I'm just an observer. But I've seen a lot, and the more I see the more I wonder.

This much I do know. I know there aren't any easy answers. I know that you can't just pass a law or advocate a theory and solve the crime problem.

The crime problem is just as tough, just as vicious, and just as hard-boiled as the men who make up our professional criminal population, and there are a lot more of these men than the average citizen realizes.

Then there are men of unstable emotions subject to psychic storms, who had virtually no control over what they did until after the law had been violated. There are men who became involved in the complexities of our civilization and made mistakes. There are, in fact, all sorts of men.

What are we going to do with them?

What are they going to do with us?

It's high time society woke up to a realization and an intelligent consideration of this problem. You can't evolve a solution just by ignoring the problem any more than you can cure a malignant sore by covering it up with a piece of adhesive tape and pretending it doesn't exist.

Here again society needs quick, alert minds—men who have imagination, vision and daring, who are willing to try and find the causes and to experiment with solutions.

Here again society erects an automatic screen. The men who could do this work and who should be doing it, are virtually forced to turn to something else, some more dignified and remunerative profession. They don't want to get into a work where political control and inadequate compensation represent the rewards for original thought, faithful service and painstaking research.

It's an interesting problem. It's a challenging problem. It's one that society may well solve some day, but it's going to take work to solve it, and it will never be solved until society wakes up to the problem and is willing to face it intelligently.

17

No people need fairness and justice more than those who have been segregated in prisons for violating the laws. If these men are to be rehabilitated they must learn to respect law and justice. And much of this work must be done within prison walls. So it is important for all of us to know more about prisons, their personnel, their inmates, and the peculiar problems in human behavior which are produced by confinement.

Penitentiaries are, for the most part, a strange conglomerate of human beings who are thrown together in overcrowded conditions and in the closest possible physical association.

When you build a house you consider the basic costs of construction. Any good contractor will tell you that no matter how you figure, no matter how you skimp, how ingenious you try to make your construction, any really first-class construction is going to cost you a minimum of so much per square foot of floor space.

The same is true of any jail, penitentiary or other high-security unit, except that there the costs mount astronomically as plans call for the installation of concrete and steel, locks and corridors, safety devices and cells.

The result is that virtually nowhere has any state said, "We are up against overcrowding in our penitentiaries. We're going to have to do something about it. The history of penology shows that prisons are habitually overcrowded. Also that crime is on the increase. So let's look ahead and build a penitentiary that will be adequate for the needs of the community for ten, fifteen or twenty years to come."

Rather, the position seems to be that since it is finally, absolutely necessary to spend some money on new construction, the money spent should be limited to the lowest possible amount, and the construction only sufficient to relieve the congestion. That means within a few months there is again the problem of congestion and overcrowding, but nothing will be done for years because, "We've just finished digging down into our pockets to modernize the prisons. What do these convicts want—a clubhouse?"

In many of the larger states an attempt is made to segregate the inmates in different types of prisons. There will be one high-security prison for repeaters. One for first offenders. One for men who do not need the restrictions of the high-security unit.

This works out very well in theory, and would work out in practice were it not for the constant problem of overcrowding.

Quite obviously when a man who is sent up for the first time comes in contact with hardened criminals, close association is going to bring about a deterioration of the new inmate's moral fiber far, far more rapidly than the unsophisticated outlook of the new inmate will rehabilitate the character of the "four-time loser."

In short, where prisons are crowded there is a tendency for new offenders to come out just that much worse than when they went in.

Quite obviously that is a suicidal mistake on the part of society.

If society couldn't afford to have that man in its midst when he went into the penitentiary, it certainly cannot afford to have him in its midst when he comes out more hardened, more embittered, more desperate, and with less opportunity to get legitimate work.

The picture would be hopelessly discouraging were it not for one fact. That is the inherent desire on the part of most men to better themselves and to build their own characters.

Sometimes it seems almost impossible that any man could be subjected to the environment of some of these prisons, be released with his prison clothes and his conventional ten or twenty dollars in his pocket, manage to find employment, and then go straight.

The surprising thing, the encouraging thing, is that so many of them do just this. A big percentage of the men who leave prison are determined to go straight. They want no more of disciplinary institutions. They want to be self-respecting citizens. They try, but the cards are stacked against them. The system is against them. The percentages are against them. Society itself is against them.

There is, of course, the minority, the hard-bitten men who make their livings by stick-ups and murder. They have underworld connections, and within a matter of hours after they get out they're planning some new job, desperate to get a stake and determined this time to avoid the mistakes which resulted in their previous arrest and conviction.

What are we going to do with those men?

The easy answer is, shut them up and keep them shut up for the rest of their lives.

That's another thing that simply doesn't work out in practice.

I have always been opposed to capital punishment. I used to talk about giving a man a life term and having it mean life.

Those were in the days when I thought I knew what should be done, when I thought I knew the answers, and before I knew anything about prisons. Now I don't know what the answer is except that I do feel pretty certain that life imprisonment isn't the answer.

There are several reasons against it.

One of them is that when you take hope away from a man you make that man unbelievably desperate. The other is that when a criminal knows he has a life sentence to look forward to in the event he is arrested, he'll kill rather than surrender.

Take away hope of release and you can count on building up a surly, defiant, desperate class of potential murderers.

The uninformed man says, "Well, that's all right. Let them be desperate. Let them be tough. Just keep them shut up."

How?

As things are right now, a term of life imprisonment means different things in different states. In some states it means a minimum of twenty years. In some states it means virtually life imprisonment. In some states it means about seven and a half to ten years.

The man in the penitentiary is a human being. He is a thinking human being. When he has leisure time which he can spend in brooding, thinking and planning, he becomes diabolically ingenious.

Up in the Washington State Penitentiary at Walla Walla, there was a hard-bitten core of desperate criminals serving life sentences, who had little hope of getting out by any legitimate means because life imprisonment meant just that. A man sentenced to life for rape or first-degree murder was not eligible for parole.

The institution had a prison library. From time to time a Catholic organization loaned books to this library. A shipment of books would be sent in, kept for a certain time and then taken back.

One of the priests who was very much interested in the reading habits of convicts took occasion to examine a shipment of books which had just been returned.

To his surprise he found that a certain book on African travel gave evidence of having been exceedingly popular. He wondered what in the world the inmates of a state prison at Walla Walla, Washington, would find in a book of African travel that was so absorbingly interesting that they had all but worn the book out.

He balanced the book in his hand and then gently released his fingers so that the book would open at the place where the binding had been the most worn. Invariably the book opened to a certain page. That page dealt with travels in the Pygmy country.

The priest couldn't understand it.

A day or so later he happened to see the warden and mentioned the peculiar phenomenon to him.

The warden said, "There's my car. Jump in it. Go get that book just as fast as you can and bring it back to me."

The puzzled priest did so.

The warden studied the chapter on the Pygmies. It told about the telepathic means of communication by which they were able to anticipate the arrival of travelers. It told about their uncanny skill as woodsmen, their ability to hide in trees and make themselves invisible. It told about how they could drift into the forest and become a part of the shadow, entirely disappearing from sight. And it told about their blowguns.

After a moment the warden decided that the blowguns represented the source of prisoner interest.

He sewed up the prison. All men were confined to quarters. All unnecessary movement of prisoners was restricted. They tore the prison apart.

Eventually they found two blowguns.

At one time I was friendly with a man who had been a champion archer. Then he had his right elbow severely injured in an automobile accident. For months he couldn't use his right arm. He couldn't pull a bow. He liked to hunt small game with primitive silent weapons, so he started experimenting with blowguns, using the best of modern equipment. He'd prepare feathered, well-balanced darts which he placed in a blowgun and aimed with his left arm.

The man became startlingly accurate and I was amazed to learn the power that there was in a blowgun.

For instance, he would take a magazine such as *The Saturday Evening Post*. He would have me hold it up and he would take a *blunt* dart—a blunt-nosed dart, mind you—and he would shoot it through the magazine. It would hit the paper with an explosive crack, go clean through and come out the other side. I have seen him do this time and time again.

You can imagine therefore something of the power of a modern blowgun activated not by human breath but by compressed air.

That was what the inmates had done at the Washington State Penitentiary. They had manufactured the blowguns and then they had disconnected the air tanks from the sprayguns which were used to spray paint in the institution. They had connected these air tanks to tubes by means of a unique trigger device, and they were able to shoot ten-penny nails through thin sheet steel.

I have seen those blowguns. One of the inmates told me that the whole thing was grossly exaggerated, that the inmates had made them only for the purpose of shooting birds and monkeying around. But the warden found "proving grounds" where they had tested the penetrating powers of the missiles, and he was quite confident that these guns were intended to blast the guards out of one of the towers some night as efficiently as could have been done with gunfire, but without any noise and without any flash.

Perhaps the warden was wrong. I don't know. I only know that those blowguns existed and that they were capable of sending a ten-penny nail through thin sheet steel.

That was only a mild case of desperation. Here's another.

One day the warden, looking through the books, found an order for cyanide of potassium, one of the quickest and most deadly poisons known. It was used in the prison blacksmith shop for hardening metal.

He started checking, and found some of the powder had already been used.

He confiscated what was left and weighed it. Some was missing.

Again the prison was sewed up. Again there was a search. Eventually they found the missing powder and learned the whole story.

Guards in the prison towers had a midnight lunch of sandwiches and coffee made in the prison kitchen and delivered by other guards to the men in the towers.

Some of the inmates had planned a party for the guards. One night they were all to be served cyanide sandwiches. The whole prison would fall apart. Fifteen hundred desperate men could go over the walls without any alarm.

Those are some of the things that happen when you take hope away from men and try to make life imprisonment mean life imprisonment.

That's the type of thing which inevitably follows an attempt to get tough with prisoners and make then do "hard time."

Washington found that the answer wasn't to get tough with prisoners. That was really the cause of the trouble.

So Washington listened to some of the men who knew their way around and who understood professional penology. The laws were changed so that after twenty years of confinement even a life termer sent up for murder would be eligible for parole if his record over the twenty years was such as to indicate reform.

The things that men can do when they have plenty of time to think are such as to challenge human imagination.

There is, of course, an enormous amount of surreptitious cooperation on the part of prison inmates. There is a prison grapevine and a co-ordination of effort that would be remarkable if it could be used for better purpose.

For instance, I have among my souvenirs a letter which was received by the warden of one of the state prisons. That letter came through the mail and purportedly was from the California Adult Authority (a board which is somewhat the equivalent of the Board of Pardon and Parole in many states), stating that California held a detainer on a prisoner who was shortly to be released from that institution.

A detainer is a hold order which one state places on a prisoner in another state. For instance, if John Doe is wanted for robbery in California but is arrested in Idaho, convicted on another charge of robbery and sentenced to a five-year term, California will file a detainer with Idaho. The effect of this detainer is that as soon as John Doe is released from Idaho he will find a representative of the State of California waiting to take him back to California where he will be tried on the California offense.

The letter the warden received was on high-grade stationery. It was engraved with the great seal of the State of California. It bore the title of the California Adult Authority. It seemed official in every respect, and it advised the warden to vacate the California detainer against the particular prisoner and release him, warning the prisoner, however, that he must keep out of the State of California, otherwise he would be prosecuted under the old charge.

There was something peculiar about that letter. For the moment the warden didn't realize what it was. It just didn't look right. So he went to the files and picked out some other letters he had received from the office of the California Adult Authority. Then the incongruity became apparent.

The printing on the letterhead he had just received was in a type entirely different from the lettering on all of the other letterheads of the California Adult Authority.

That started an investigation. It turned out that the letter was a forgery.

The surprising part of it is that that forgery had been made in the prison.

Here was an inmate who was not supposed to have access to certain types of tools, who was not supposed to be able to do any printing, particularly any printing that would be in the nature of a forgery of an official letterhead. Yet with a patience and ingenuity that can only be surmised, and a surreptitious co-operation which must have existed between this inmate and other inmates, that letterhead had been forged. The great seal of the State of California, which required an intricate amount of engraving, had been forged so carefully and so perfectly that it was impossible to detect the forgery. In fact, the whole thing had been done so neatly that had it not been for this different style of type the warden would have been fooled.

Those are some of the things a warden has to contend with. He must be on guard against surprise. He must carefully plan his every bit of prison routine so that there are no weak points.

His first responsibility is that of security.

Men are sent to his institution because they are supposed to remain there until they are released. That's his primary responsibility—to see that they do remain.

He is usually appointed by the governor. The governor nearly always has political adversaries who worked against him at the time of his election, who are now waiting for the next election, intent upon making capital out of anything that will disparage the administration.

A prison break or a prison riot is duck soup. Those things are always newsworthy and can be counted upon to cause the administration embarrassment. The governor knows that. The warden knows that. Therefore, one of the warden's duties is to prevent escapes and riots, to keep his prison off the front pages.

But the warden also knows that there is nearly always digging going on.

One of the more interesting cases of escape by digging occurred in the Eastern State Penitentiary in Pennsylvania. It illustrates the almost incredible ingenuity, resourcefulness and patience of convicts intent on escape.

This prison is an old, old prison, going back for Lord knows how many years. The cells are cement lined and grimly efficient, but convicts are persistent and resourceful. Some of them started poking and experimenting, and finally decided, probably by means of sounding, that back of one of the areas of cement in the side of the cell was a weak point in the structure. (Actually, as I remember it, there had at one time been a fireplace at that point.)

Anyway, these men carefully worked along the seams of this cement until they had loosened the connecting bond and were able to lift out an entire section. Sure enough, they found behind a hollow and some good old Pennsylvania dirt.

That was all they needed.

They snitched spoons from the prison table and right away were in business.

That tunnel took considerably more than a year to construct. It ran for more than ninety-seven feet underground. There were two convicts in the cell. They would take turns. One of them would rig up a dummy, the other one would stay there to keep watch and allay the suspicions of any guard who happened to glance in.

The other inmate would descend into the tunnel, scratch away with his teaspoon, fill up his pockets with dirt, come back to the cell, sift the gravel out from the dirt, flush the dirt down the toilet, stash the small pebbles in the pockets of his prison suit. That operation would keep up at intervals all night.

The next day, during exercise periods, these convicts would walk out in the yard, put their hands in their pockets, lounge against the wall, squat down on the gravel while they talked. Surreptitiously they'd deposit the contents of their pockets, a few pebbles at a time, on the gravel of the exercise yard.

That's the way a long tunnel was built, week in, week out, month in, month out, with the aid of two spoons and the dirt that could be carried out in a man's pocket.

The cement slab that covered the opening to the tunnel had to be lifted carefully back into position so that the seam wouldn't be disclosed by a jail inspection. In all probability it was put back into place after one of the convicts had gone to work in the tunnel. The other convict was on the alert to allay the suspicions of any guard who might stop by to look in and make sure both men were in the cell and sleeping. That meant a dummy had to be rigged up every time one of the men went into the tunnel.

When it came time to screen the pebbles from the dirt and flush it down the toilet, both men must have worked feverishly.

When, after many months, the tunnel was completed, these convicts did escape. But their engineering had been bad. Their exit outside the prison walls came up at a point almost directly under a guard tower. So they were caught immediately and returned to prison.

One of the most famous escape artists among modern criminals is Willie Sutton. Sutton, it will be remembered, escaped from a good many institutions, including New York's Sing Sing. He enjoys the distinction of being the only inmate ever to escape from Holmesburg, which is considered the Alcatraz of Pennsylvania.

When he was transferred to Holmesburg, they called him into the office and explained to him that he was his own worst enemy. In place of trying to cooperate, he had been trying to escape. Now he had been transferred to a prison from which there was no possible hope of escape. He'd brought it on himself.

The prison is at present conducted by Dr. Frederick S. Baldi, an M.D. who, on a board of health, found that he had a penchant for organization and executive control, and eventually became Superintendent of Pennsylvania's escape-proof prison.

That prison is *really* escape proof.

In the first place, there is a big wall, some thirty feet in height, surrounding an enclosure.

Within this enclosure, but at no place coming anywhere near the wall, are structures laid out around a central hub, very much like the spokes of a wheel. Each one of these corridors is lined with cells. The hub is an office, which is separated from the corridors by barred steel doors. Two guards, sitting in this hub, can see everything that goes on down the long corridors. Even if prisoners could get out of their cells, through their individual cell doors, and into the corridors, they couldn't get to the hub because the guards in the hub are isolated behind locked doors with bars of steel. The guards can see through them but no inmate could get through them.

Any inmates in the corridors would instantly be seen and reported. They couldn't even get to the corridors unless they could open the individual steel-barred doors which lock them in their cells. Even if they could find some way of getting into the hub, they still couldn't get to the yard because the corridor doors leading to the yard are locked and barred behind the guards who are in the hub. Even if they got into the yard, they couldn't escape because there they would then be confronted with a sheer thirty-foot wall, which is kept perpetually illuminated, surmounted by towers in which guards with rifles are waiting to shoot any prisoner who appears in the yard except during carefully restricted periods of exercise.

Dr. Baldi told me about his interview with Willie Sutton. He said, "Now I'll tell you, Mr. Gardner, Willie was sitting in that chair, right where you're sitting. I was standing here. I said to him, 'Willie, you were sent here because you were always trying to escape. Now you can forget it because you can't escape from here. No one ever has and no one ever will. I'm not going to hold your past record against you. All you have to do is conform to the rules of the institution and I'll treat you just like any other inmate. I'm not going to make it tough for you.'

"And Willie looked up at me and grinned and said nothing.

"I said, 'Now, Willie, I'm going to tell you about the rules of this institution so you can conform to them.'

"And Willie, keeping that grin, said, 'Never mind the rules, Doc, I won't be here long enough to bother with them.'"

Dr. Baldi's hands are powerful, thick-fingered hands. As he told me about that interview the fingers doubled over, the hands clenched into fists. The skin was tight over the knuckles.

Dr. Baldi doesn't like to think about Willie (The Actor) Sutton.

Willie Sutton escaped from that prison. He's the only man in history who ever escaped from it, and probably no one else will ever have the temerity, the daring, the resourcefulness, the shrewd knowledge of human nature that will enable him to puzzle out all of the different combinations and work them into a winning gambit.

The reason I cite the case of Willie Sutton is because it illustrates the responsibilities of a warden, and the ingenuity of prison inmates. Per thousand prisoners a warden will have a few who want to become Willie Suttons. He'll have some incipient Dillingers. He'll have some green kids. He'll have a few who shouldn't be there at all, but were sent up because some irascible judge happened to be out of patience that morning, or through some blunder in penal administration.

He'll have some psychopathic personalities who should be confined in hospitals for the criminally insane. He'll have some weak chaps who committed a crime under stress of circumstances, or as the result of some emotional storm which shook their stability to its foundations. Those people probably shouldn't be there either.

A warden, who doesn't want his name mentioned, told me at one time, "Imprisonment shouldn't be for any fixed term. It varies entirely with the individual.

"In almost every instance there comes a time when the inmate feels truly repentant for what he's done, and feels that if he can have another chance he's going to make good. That's not just a period of wishful thinking. It's a period when the punishment has taken hold just enough and remorse has taken hold just enough, and when there's been just enough meditation over what has happened to convince him that crime doesn't pay and that what he wants to do primarily for the rest of his life is to keep out of prison.

"That's the time to turn that man loose on parole. That's the time to take a chance on him.

"It seldom happens that you can catch things that way. The parole boards make careful studies. They rotate the inmates so they come up at intervals which are rather far apart.

"You leave that man there too long and the punishment begins to sink in. A certain amount of bitterness begins to develop. You let him out too soon and he thinks he got away with something, that doing time isn't so bad after all. Or perhaps you let him out when he just thinks he's repentant, but really hasn't had an opportunity to let the experience germinate, ferment and sink into his soul."

That, of course, brings up the whole problem of parole.

It is better to parole a man out of a penitentiary before his term is served than to wait until he has served the full time. That is true no matter how bad a moral risk that man may be.

The reason for this is obvious.

No matter how vicious a man is, no matter how much trouble you expect you're going to have with him, it's better to release him on parole while you can have some supervision over his activities at the cost of chopping a year or two off his sentence. Once his sentence has expired, and he can move out of the place a free man, society has lost its control.

That's where the newspapers and, above all, the newspaper-reading public don't give parole boards a fair break.

Parole boards understand the necessity of releasing even the tough ones so that they can try to rehabilitate them into society. Penologists understand it. Probably newspaper reporters do. But the newspaper readers don't.

So when a crook murders someone in a stick-up, and the newspaper reporters find the man had been released on parole, the headlines almost invariably scream:

"PAROLEE MURDERS LIQUOR STORE DEALER IN HOLDUP"

No one says very much about the benefits that our parole system is accomplishing day in and day out. There's nothing dramatic about it. It isn't news.

No one bothers to point out that the parolee who commits a crime would have been released because his sentence had expired if he hadn't been placed on parole. The insinuation is that some dumb parole board turned a murderer loose on the community.

That gives the parole system a bad name, a black eye, and causes it to miss out on a whole lot of co-operation from the citizen.

Not that our parole boards are perfect.

Here again we have all sorts of conditions to contend with. There are some parole boards who bitterly resent a person making an application for pardon, on the theory that that person is "trying to go over our heads." There are some members of parole boards whose sole qualification for the job was the fact that they were able to pick the right gubernatorial candidate prior to the time of election and render valuable political service. They have no desire to improve penal institutions. Their sole desire is to pick a political plum.

Prison inmates who are without recourse, who have no means of arousing public attention, or even reaching the public, bear the brunt of these mens' prejudices, ignorance, arrogance and self-importance. The public, of course, isn't the least bit interested. The governor has paid off a political debt.

Fortunately, these appointments are a lot less common nowadays than they used to be. It's getting so most governors try to make a good job of prison administration.

If the public would only take a little more interest, if we could have a few more men of the right caliber embarking upon a career of professional penology, we'd have an enormous improvement in conditions.

Society should extend a helping hand *before* the man walks down the front steps. That's the best time to condition men's thinking.

There again we run into a snag.

Someone invented the phrase "coddling criminals." It has become a very popular catch phrase.

Time after time prison officials are reminded that men are sent to prison as a "punishment." The idea is that inmates must first be punished and then perhaps they can be rehabilitated.

It's difficult to mix punishment and rehabilitation. Wardens are ready to do what the public wants them to. The trouble is that society wants to send men to prison to be "punished" and then have the inmates turn to model citizens the moment they walk out the front door.

That's like telling a man to stand on his head to eat dinner and then it won't make him fat.

Lots of men in prison could be rehabilitated if we were in a position to devote more attention to rehabilitation and less to security.

My friend Art Bernard, Warden of the Nevada State Penitentiary at Carson City, has a rather unique system.

I don't know whether he is working under a particularly under-standing governor, or whether he is just enough of a two-fisted fighter to stand by his principles without giving a hoot as to what happens.— Of course, he is in an exceedingly fortunate position because Nevada is a state of large area but small population, and Bernard only has a few hundred prisoners to supervise. That gives him an opportunity to get pretty well acquainted with each man.

But when the court sends up some young fellow who has been in trouble yet who isn't a vicious enemy of society, Art Bernard throws security to the winds. The boy doesn't ever get thrown into the yard with the tough men who look on organized society as their enemy.

That boy starts almost immediately on one of the prison farms.

Art Bernard talks to him. He gives him one chance and that's all. Bernard says, "I'm going to give you a chance to make good. Don't muff it. I don't like alibis. I don't like excuses. I like results. They hold me responsible for results, and that's what I'm holding you respon-sible for. If you're man enough to go out there and make good, that's fine. If you double-cross me that means you're going behind the walls, and, so help me, you're going to stay behind the walls."

Bernard is a peculiar combination of a gentle man and a tough man.

He isn't a career penologist. He was appointed to the job with-out any previous experience, except some experience in handling men—quite a bit of experience, and Bernard is a fighter. Few men can stand up to him. Few men want to.

He's not only a physical fighter, he's a mental fighter.

Shortly after he entered the prison, the convicts decided they were going to riot. They'd take Bernard hostage if they could. If they couldn't, they'd take some of the guards. They'd smash up the tables and the chairs and burn them. They'd smash all the dishes. The prison kitchen and dining room are on an upper floor and they decided they'd take the kitchen range to pieces and throw the pieces out in the warden's front yard.

It wasn't one of those spontaneous riots. It was a deliberately planned affair. They were going to put the prison on the front page. They were going to take the measure of the new warden.

One of the anxious guards found out about the plot. He came to Bernard and told him about it, told him that those riots had happened before, that the prison was tough, that the only thing to do was to keep out of the way until the riot subsided, not let the men get hold of any guard as a hostage, and, above all, not to let them get the warden.

Bernard thought things over a bit and said, "Tell me if you can find out exactly when this riot is going to take place."

The guard, who had, of course, an informer who was keeping him posted, learned that the riot was to take place on a certain night immediately after supper. The prisoners would get their bellies full and then go on a tear.

The guards were conspicuous by their absence.

Bernard walked unarmed to the dining room, putting himself at the mercy of the rioters. He made them a nice little speech.

He said, "I'm trying to run this prison on a decent basis. I'm trying to give you men a break. You weren't sent here as a tourist being sent to a resort. You aren't here because you want to be here. You were sent here as inmates because you violated the laws.

"Now, I'm going to tell you sons-of-bitches something. While you're here, you're going to conform to the rules. They tell me you're planning a riot. They tell me you intend to take hostages. You intend to smash up the tables. You intend to break the dishes. You intend to take the stove to pieces and throw it out in the warden's front yard.

"I don't know as there's anything I can do to stop you. I don't know as I intend to try. I'm just going to tell you this. You can smash up all the dishes you want to. You can burn up all the tables you want to. Those are things that are furnished by the taxpayers for your convenience. If you don't want them you don't have to use them.

"We have a cement floor here. I don't think you can smash that, and I know damn well you can't burn it. Now then, if you don't want to eat off dishes, sitting at tables, you just show me that you don't by smashing them up. I'll put you fellows to work cleaning up the mess, and after we get it cleaned up you'll scrub these cement floors until they shine. We'll have them just as clean as you can get them, and we'll serve the food right on the cement floor. If you boys don't want tables you can eat on your hands and knees. Nobody's going to starve to death. The food will be there. It'll be the same type of food you're getting now.

"But don't think for one minute that I'm going to let you fellows smash up all the dishes and tables and then go to the taxpayers and ask them to replace the stuff that you've smashed up. They've furnished the tables. They've furnished the benches. They've furnished the plates. They've furnished the knives and forks. It's good stuff, but I'm not going to force you to use them. There's the floor. If you want to eat off the floor, you go right ahead.

"Now then, I'm just going to tell you something else. I'm new here, and probably some of you fellows would like to find out just how far you can go. You'd like to find just how tough I am. I'm putting myself on record. If anyone backs up it won't be me. Now then, all you fellows have got to do is start something. I'm going to be here to finish it. Just help yourselves, boys."

And Bernard turned and walked out.

There hasn't been a riot in that prison from that day on.

That, of course, is one advantage a good, two-fisted man has over a career penologist. The career penologist doesn't dare to make a bad mistake. He's making his living out of penology and he has to consider the temperament of the taxpayers.

Bernard simply doesn't give a damn. He's in there to do a job and he's going to do the best job he can while he's in there. Any time they want him out, that's okay by him. He made a living without knuckling down to any man before he became warden and he can make a living without knuckling down to any man after he ceases to be warden. While he's warden he's going to call the turns.

Some political appointees make pretty sorry wardens. Some of them don't. I've known some good ones. After all, it depends on the man.

Within the limits of what he can do, Art Bernard is fighting for the prison inmates. He's trying to get them the best food he can, the best conditions, the best treatment. He expects co-operation in return. If he gets it, everything's fine. If he doesn't get it, he can be just about the roughest, toughest, two-fisted fighter in the country.

The interesting thing is that his personality is colorful enough and his ideas are fresh enough so that the citizens, in place of getting shocked, have begun to take an interest.

That's probably one of the things we need most in penology today. If we had the real interest of an enlightened group of citizens who would take the trouble to study the problem, the strides that could be made in the work of rehabilitation would be enormous.

Of course, one of the black blotches on prison administration is the rioting that took place in the State Prison of Southern Michigan at Jackson.

The history of those riots was written up in *The Saturday Evening Post*, and anyone who is interested in the problem of prison administration should read the history of what happened.

When it came to a showdown, in order to save the lives of guards who were hostages to a crowd of prisoners, the leaders of whom were felt to be completely insane, one of the deputies waved an olive branch all over the place, and even went so far as to give the rioters a verbal pat on the back, following which they were ushered into the prison dining room for a banquet of beefsteak and ice cream.

That may have saved the lives of some guards—just what it accomplished is controversial, but one thing it certainly did accomplish was to instill prison inmates everywhere with the idea that they might—just might—get the upper hand and win sweeping reforms and a change in administrative personnel if they became desperate enough.

As it happened, I had been in that prison several times and had talked with some of the men. It had the unenviable distinction of being the country's largest prison from the standpoint of population, and anyone who knew anything at all about prisons knew that putting so many thousand men of all types together, in such a small space, under such crowded conditions, was like playing Russian roulette. You can win so many times and then the time comes when your luck runs out.

I haven't had a chance to talk with Warden Frisbie since the riots took place, but he is reported to have blurted out at about the time of the riots, "This is what comes of trying to run a prison without any money."

Society has tried just about everything as far as crime punishment is concerned. We've gone through a period when stealing a loaf of bread was punishable by hanging. We've had enough capital punishment so we certainly should be beginning to realize that it doesn't work, at least not in the way its proponents hope and intend.

Regardless of whether the severity of the punishment acts as a deterrent (and most penologists feel that it is the certainty rather than the severity of punishment that is the only deterrent), capital punishment has probably resulted in releasing more murderers on society than any other single factor.

When a man charged with a capital crime comes into the courtroom he's making a last-ditch fight for life. That's always dramatic, and because it's dramatic it attracts public attention. The attorney for the defense is able to dangle the death penalty in front of the jury, and even after the man is convicted the fact that he is facing death does a lot to arouse public sympathy.

On the other hand, I am among the first to admit that where capital punishment has been abolished *without at the same time making sweeping reforms in penal administration*, it hasn't been so good.

I am in the peculiar position of opposing capital punishment, and, at the same time, opposing the abolition of capital punishment without at the same time making sweeping reforms.

I think if we'd study the problem, I think if we could give our professional penologists the right kind of public interest, co-operation and support, we could abolish capital punishment, and, by *investing* a few million dollars in prison administration, could save a good many million dollars and quite a few lives, including the lives of children, of holdup victims, and of conscientious cops who are trying to do their duty.— And always remember this, regardless of how you may feel when you read about police corruption and the fact that gamblers and prostitutes have taken over and are running wide open, you don't often read about a cop who sticks his hands up during a holdup.

That's a tradition of the force. It's a splendid thing, and by the same token it's a dangerous thing. When a mobster in a stick-up, "going it blind," finds that there's a cop or an ex-cop in the place, he knows he's up against a showdown. Words aren't going to count. He either has to kill the cop, or the cop's going to kill him.

Strangely enough, injustice is one of the greatest factors in perpetuating crime in this country and molding the habitual criminal.

We have, for instance, known some men whom we were convinced were innocent of the crime for which they had been convicted. Our polygraph tests have completely convinced Alex Gregory of the innocence of these men; our investigations have confirmed Gregory's findings. For one reason or other, the circumstances surrounding these cases are such that there's nothing we can get hold of, no way that we can reopen the case.

It is, of course, instantly apparent that we can't go into a state and say, in effect, "We've examined the evidence in this case, the same evidence that the jury had before it. We don't agree with the verdict of the jury. We think this man is innocent. We've given him a lie detector test, and that indicates he's innocent. Therefore we want him released."

Even as it is, we have all too frequently run up against newspaper editorials somewhat along these lines:

> John Doe was fairly convicted in this state by our esteemed contemporary, the able District Attorney of Whosis County. His guilt was passed upon by a jury of twelve reputable citizens of this community, men of judgment and integrity.
>
> Who are these outsiders to come stalking into our community and tell us how to run our business, to set aside the verdicts of our jurors, to insinuate that our courts were incompetent or corrupt, and, above all, to try to smirch the splendid record of our popular District Attorney?

As one newspaper put it, in quoting an irate prosecutor, after Tom Smith and I had been investigating a case, "What right have two men, one an ex-superintendent of a small penitentiary, and the other an author of cheap, twenty-five cent mystery fiction, to set themselves up as a court of last resort in our sovereign state?"

So what about these men who are innocent yet for whom we can do nothing, at least at this time, without jeopardizing our whole work and sacrificing the advantages we have so far gained.

In at least one instance I can recall offhand, one of these men went up before a parole board. According to the story we have, and we have it on pretty good authority; the board was all set to release the man on parole. One of the board asked him if he was now properly repentant. The man told him that he was sorry, but he couldn't be repentant for something he hadn't done, that he had been wrongfully convicted.

According to our story, which came from the grapevine but from sources which we consider thoroughly reliable, the board promptly tore up the man's parole papers and sent him back to prison on the ground that his attitude was "still antisocial."

Just let us assume, for the sake of the argument, that those facts are all true. One can well imagine how such a man would feel at being sent back to prison, knowing that he could have been released if he had told a lie.

Then, of course, there is the question of varying sentences.

Some men can commit a crime in one state, or even in one county of one state, and the judge, who is noted for his intolerance, will "throw the book at him."

Another person can commit exactly the same crime even under conditions that make it many times more flagrant, but simply by being in another political subdivision, and coming up before another judge, receive a rather short sentence.

These men rub elbows in a penitentiary. One of them surrendered to impulse and committed a crime. He's up for a long period of years. The other one is an habitual criminal who intends to return to a career of crime as soon as he can get out, and he was sent up for a short term.

The Indeterminate Sentence Act is supposed to take care of situations of this sort, and to some extent it does.

But here again we're up against a problem.

A lot was expected of the Habitual Criminal Act. We were going to take the men who had previously been convicted of three major felonies and put them out of circulation. They were going up for life.

What happened?

It all depends on the temperament of the district attorney and on the political expediencies of the situation.

There are some men in prison today who have criminal records as long as your arm, and they're going to get out within a few months. There are other men in the same institution who have committed three crimes, none of which is any more serious than the long list of crimes committed by the other men, and they're branded as habitual criminals and sent up for life.

How does this happen?

It can be as simple as the case of the overworked district attorney. He's trying to get away on a vacation. His office is crowded. He has a weak case against a desperate individual. The police have tried to get the evidence that is necessary to convict. They've only managed to amass enough evidence so that the district attorney doesn't dare dismiss the case. He realizes, however, there's a fatal weakness in it. The attorney for the defense is going to give him a bad time with one of his witnesses.

The district attorney passes the word down to the man in prison. "All right, my friend, if you want to go ahead and fight this case I'll amend the information and plead your prior convictions. Then, in case you're sent up, you'll be sent up for life as a habitual criminal. But if you want to cooperate with me, if you're willing to come in and plead guilty, I'll not plead your prior offenses. In fact, I'll even reduce the charge."

That's done every day.

In a good many states the prosecutors deliberately use this Habitual Criminal Act as a lever or a club, depending upon how you happen to want to look at it.

I am reminded of a case in Washington not long ago. A man pleaded guilty to the charge of forging a check. He was sent to prison for a term of years.

The forgery was not isolated. It was part of a string of forgeries carried on with a certain well-defined *modus operandi*. The forgeries continued after the supposed culprit had pleaded guilty, been sentenced, and incarcerated in prison.

Eventually the right man was apprehended. There could be no question but what he was the one who had perpetrated the string of forgeries.

The prison board sent for the man who had pleaded guilty and said, "What on earth ever possessed you to plead guilty to a charge of which you were so manifestly innocent?"

He twisted his face in a cynical grin. "Because I was smart," he said.

They asked him to explain.

"The D.A. came to me and said, 'I've got you dead to rights. If I put you on trial you're going to be convicted. If you stand trial I'll plead your priors and you'll go up for life as a habitual criminal.' That way I never would have stood any chance of getting out. This way I stood a chance after five years of getting out on parole. What would you have done?"

18

There is one other point which should be considered in connection with this subject of prisons and prison inmates.

I have mentioned the advantage a good, two-fisted, appointed warden has if he enjoys the confidence of the governor and if he also happens to be fearless and willing to fight for his convictions.

It is, of course, a temporary advantage. Sooner or later the governor, who is his friend, is going to be out of office, and a new governor coming in will say, "So-and-so is the political appointee of my vanquished opponent and I see no reason for continuing him in the job."

But what if that warden is a career penologist?

Some of these men have acquired a great deal of scientific and empirical knowledge about prisons and prison administration. Some of these men are employed as wardens of penal institutions. Some of them are on parole boards. They are respected everywhere in the country by their fellow workers. If anybody ever comes up with the correct answers to our crime problem it will probably be these men.

But these men are laboring under enormous handicaps.

They suffer from lack of operating funds, lack of adequate personnel, overcrowding of prison space. But their greatest handicap is the attitude of the public.

The public simply doesn't know anything about the problems of handling prisons. The public doesn't want to learn. It doesn't want to be bothered. Yet—and this is a paradoxical condition—whenever the public does become aroused it promptly proceeds to undermine the efficiency of the career penologist by interfering with his work.

Because the public has little knowledge of what goes on in prisons, because it has a very limited knowledge of the thoughts, the problems and the psychology of prison inmates, it clings to the old vindictive attitude that the sure way to cure crime is by punishment. If crime is on the increase, according to the reasoning of the general public, it stands to reason that our laws are too lax. We need to put teeth in them. We need to increase the punishment, to make penalties more severe. That will teach these men a lesson.

So what does the public do?

Let us suppose there have been an unusual number of service station holdups. The citizens don't like that. They are angry. They are resentful. They want to "do something about it."

So some legislator, who is going to be a candidate for reelection and is looking for a popular issue which he can champion, comes out with a bill providing that any person caught robbing or attempting to rob a service station shall be sentenced for a minimum period of ten years in the state penitentiary, that there shall be no probation and no parole for the minimum of ten years; that any person who has previously robbed a service station and then been caught robbing another service station must serve a minimum of fifteen years without parole, etc., etc., etc.

That looks good to the citizen. The candidate for legislative office comes out and announces that this is his platform. He reads the statistics on service station holdups. He cites the number of citizens who have been killed in such holdups.

His audience bursts into enthusiastic applause. "Attaboy! That's the spirit! Show 'em who's running this country. Put those crooks where they belong and keep them there."

Unfortunately the answer isn't that simple. The penologist knows it, but he is hardly in a position to risk public disapproval by saying so in a very loud tone of voice. He's willing to give his opinion if he's asked, but his opinion isn't asked. The public *tells* him what to do. It doesn't *ask* him what he thinks should be done. After all, the public is the boss. The penologist is the servant of the public.

Suppose we had an epidemic of polio in a community. People who are shocked by the twisted, deformed bodies of children, by the pain and suffering, want to do something about it. That's perfectly natural and very commendable. However, the public wouldn't think of passing a law telling the physician what type of treatment he should use, what drugs he should rely upon, or how many days he should keep the patient in bed.

Yet that's what the public does in effect when it starts telling the penologists how to do their job.

Penology isn't an *exact* science, but it is an *exacting* science. The career penologists are groping their way toward a solution. If they had more public understanding and more public co-operation they might be able to do a good deal, but from time to time the public steps in and ties the hands of the penologists.

By this time, crime being on the increase the way it is, it should be pretty apparent that the old-fashioned concept of curing criminals by punishment isn't particularly effective. Yet whenever the public becomes angered and embittered over an outbreak of crime it immediately resorts to the old formula. It acts upon the assumption that parole boards have too been lenient, that punishment has been too light, and so it starts "putting teeth in the laws."

In a way it's like the story that a Western guide told me about a big bear who was running around a tree. The tree was smaller in diameter than the bear thought it was, and as he saw his own tail ahead of him he thought it was another bear. So he bit at what he thought was the other bear. He immediately felt the stab of pain and assumed the other bear had bitten him, so he really went to work on the other bear, running around and around the tree.

The Western guide looked at me with mournful solemnity and shook his head. "You know," he said, "that goldanged bear ate himself up as far as the shoulders before he found out who he was."

In many ways that's what the public is doing when it interferes with career penologists and starts "putting teeth" in the laws.

Right now citizens are shocked at disclosures of dope sales to school children. There is much talk of passing a law providing life imprisonment without possibility of parole for dope peddlers.

How much good will that do?

A little later on I want to discuss some of the facts concerning this dope problem, but at the moment I want to point out that people aren't asking the professional penologists what to do about dope. They are listening to legislators who are advocating the age-old remedy of punishment. That remedy has been in effect for hundreds of years and all it has done is increase the number of criminals to a point where our prisons are bulging.

Quite obviously it would seem that some day the public would say to itself, "We've been trying this particular form of remedy for a couple of hundred years and we aren't getting anywhere. We aren't even holding our own. How about trying something else?"

Once a career penologist loses his job because of public repudiation he has lost his entire profession. Therefore he doesn't dare to experiment the way he would like to. He doesn't dare to try out new ideas, at least to the extent that he would like to try them. He doesn't dare to institute reforms until he is sure the public is willing to ride along.

I have talked with many career penologists who have had good sound ideas that certainly seem logical. I have wanted to publish these ideas, but in every instance the penologist has thrown up his hands in horror. "No, no!" he exclaims. "Don't quote me."

During the past two decades we have taken great strides in almost every branch of science. The automobile of today, for instance, is a far cry from the machine of twenty years ago. In fact, I can remember when the goal of the industry was to have an automobile that was capable of a sustained speed of thirty-five miles an hour. How far would the automobile industry have progressed if there hadn't been research work, experimentation and the exploration of new ideas?

If the public would only co-operate by getting the best penologists it could possibly find, giving them a relatively free hand and letting the penologists tell the public what should be done to cope with the crime problem instead of insisting on telling the penologists what they must do, the public could reasonably hope for some improvement.

The probabilities are that the conventional type of penitentiary is hopelessly obsolete. The greatest disservice that society can do itself is to confine the ordinary law violator in the present conventional type of penitentiary.

What would take its place? I don't know. I am not a penologist. But I know that there are penologists who are giving the subject very careful attention. Some of their ideas are revolutionary. They hesitate to advocate them for fear that the public is not yet ready to accept new concepts.

Gradually, however, bit by bit, quietly and unostentatiously, professional penologists are exploring the possibility of a new type of prison wherein the average, non-vicious offender can be given more space, more latitude, more freedom.

Take the men's prison at Chino, California, for instance. There inmates' families may come for informal visits. There the men enjoy relative freedom. That experiment is paying off in a big way.

One warden told me he was convinced that the big percentage of his inmates didn't even need a wall or a cell. If they knew that they could escape at any time, but that if they escaped they would be brought back with added time on their sentence and less privileges, closer confinement and closer surveillance, the men could be confined in relatively inexpensive, light, airy barracks, and the results, so far as inmate rehabilitation was concerned, would be correspondingly improved.

However, these prisoners have been branded as felons. The conventional concept requires that they be housed in buildings of concrete with barred windows and steel doors, that the prison be surrounded by a wall with guards, rifles and machine guns. This means added costs. Added costs mean less space. The whole program means overcrowding,' with all of the vicious problems of perversion and mass regulations.

It is to be remembered that prison inmates have been taken out of society because they couldn't exercise their own free will without endangering society. After they are sentenced, in place of being taught how to exercise free will and independent judgment so that they can be released without endangering society, they are deprived of all opportunities to exercise any free will or any judgment. Their lives are completely regimented.

Then they are released.

What happens?

Take, for instance, the cases of innocent men who have been released, men who had committed no crime at all. We have watched some of these men gropingly trying to readjust themselves to society after being released, trying to get so they dared to cross the street of their own volition without being afraid.

If character deterioration can happen to *innocent* men who are confined in prison, what is the effect upon *guilty* men who were sent there for some actual crime?

Penology is a profession. It would be a better profession if the public would give it greater encouragement, greater recognition and more respect. If the men who are recognized in the profession itself as outstanding penologists were given greater opportunity to study and to experiment, I think we would be on our way to a big decrease in crime.

The first move is to unshackle the hands of penologists and let them try to do the job and report to the public.

That's only a first step but it's a constructive step.

Right now the biggest obstacle in the way of solving the crime problem is the attitude of the public.

19

One of the big troubles today is that the citizen doesn't know the cost of crime. And since he doesn't have any idea of the cost, he can't tell what he can profitably spend to curb crime and still make a good business investment.

Let us look briefly at certain factors which enter into the cost of crime.

A jewelry store carries burglary insurance. An item in the cost of that burglary insurance is the amount the insurance companies are called upon to pay out in the aggregate for crimes in the aggregate. The cost of the burglary insurance goes on the jeweler's books and becomes a part of the cost price of the merchandise.

Similarly anyone who thinks his own automobile insurance rate is not affected by the number of crimes involving automobiles, the number of drunk drivers who habitually use the roads, the number of gangs who make a business of hijacking new spare tires or stealing the entire automobile, is simply being naïve.

We read of a payroll stick-up during which twenty-thousand dollars was lifted, of a bank being held up for fifteen-thousand dollars.—Who pays for all this?

In one form or another these losses are passed on to you, the citizen.

There are other costs that enter into this crime picture, and they are not the obvious costs of how much it takes of the taxpayer's money to support the prisoners in the city jail, the prisoners in the county jail, the inhabitants of the various state penitentiaries, but they are nevertheless costs that should be taken into consideration.

I was called on at one time to assist in the investigation of a rape killing.

This girl had just finished high school and had moved away from home to start attending college. To say that she had been a good girl would be a masterpiece of understatement. She was one of those children who develop a sense of responsibility, who have a goal and an ambition in life. She was a strong, husky, wholesome country girl. Her ideas of sex were clean, normal and wholesome. She was very much attached to her parents, and they to her.

This girl's dead body with the clothes stripped off was found in the bottom of a snow-covered stream bed. She had been callously dumped from the place where the automobile road crossed a bridge above the stream, during the height of a blizzard. She had put up a terrific fight. Her hands had been scratched on the frozen ground during her struggles where her assailant tried to pin her hands beneath her body until skin and flesh had been scraped from her fingers. She had been clubbed unmercifully about the head. She had been choked. She had lost so much blood that she was almost exsanguinated. Evidently she had been struggling for a long time. Her struggles had been in vain. Her courageous fight terminated in death.

That represents one item, and only one item, of the cost of crime.

There is yet another entry on the debit side of the crime ledger that should be taken into consideration.

I can well remember the harsh, inarticulate sobs of a big, grown man echoing through a solemn courtroom as the judge sentenced his son to a term in state prison.

That boy was not a particularly bad boy in the ordinary sense of the word. He was a normal, attractive young man who didn't have quite enough responsibilities, who had a "drive" for excitement, for experiencing new thrills.

What normal boy hasn't?

His father was a leader in the community, a man who had saved a small amount of money by hard work and careful planning. The main asset which he had was his reputation in the small city where he lived. He was looked up to, a solid, substantial citizen, people respected him, sought his advice.

The boy naturally went out with other boys. Some of these boys had automobiles. They had an eager curiosity about life. They wanted to live. They wanted variety. They wanted excitement.

They had heard about marijuana. Someone introduced a marijuana cigarette. The boy took a few puffs just to see what it was like.

One thing led to another. Then came the night when two of the wilder members of the gang suddenly decided on impulse to "stick up" a service station.

This boy "went along." He didn't participate in the stick-up but he did remain in the car and made no protest. Something went wrong with the stick-up and there the boy was, jointly accused of felony with the others.

The other boys didn't have quite as good backgrounds. They had been in a little juvenile trouble. No one had known just how to straighten them out.

And so the judge sentenced all the boys to the penitentiary, and the father, who had sat dry-eyed and tight-lipped through the court proceedings, trying to control his emotions, suddenly found that he was facing something too big for him.

The clerk of the court called on his son to stand up, his only son, the pride of his life. The boy who was to have carried an honored and respected name on through life. The judge pronounced the words that made this boy a felon, branded him for life.

The father's head suddenly sank down on his arms and he began to sob, harsh sobs that filled the courtroom, sobs that threatened to tear this big man's heart in two.

That is part of the cost of crime.

Of course the boy was to blame. Of course he should have known better. Of course he'd betrayed the training, the sacrifices his parents had made and the love they'd given him. But how much was he *really* to blame? He was to blame for some of it, but not all of it.

Somewhere along the line there was someone among his associates who introduced him to marijuana, someone who introduced him to a rapid, heady whirl of life which took more money than was presently available. There was a craving for excitement that overcame his training and his basic principles.

Where did that come from? Who furnished the marijuana? Never mind trying to fix an individual blame. Let's simply remember that it was someone and that this is a part of the cost of crime.

The father had done the best *he* could. He hadn't known where his boy was every minute of the time, but he didn't want to seem to be tying the boy to his parents' apron strings. The father had worked and sacrified. His good name in the community was his big asset.

Now he was no longer John Doe, the substantial businessman, the solid citizen whose words were listened to with friendly respect. He was John Doe, the father of a stick-up man who was serving a term in state prison.

That's a cost of crime.

And don't think that these cases we read about every day in the newspaper can't happen to us.

Judges and police tell me that it is surprising the number of parents who really don't know just what their kids are doing.

There comes a time when boys and girls have to be turned loose on their own, when they have to learn to stand on their own two feet. Hardly a one of them but what makes mistakes somewhere along the line. Sometimes those mistakes don't catch up with them. Sometimes they are minor mistakes.

Sometimes a hideous combination of circumstances puts the youngster behind the eight-ball.

Officers have told me a lot about the looks of utter, incredulous dismay on the faces of parents when the news is brought to them that their son is in jail. Perhaps it's drunken driving. Perhaps it's manslaughter as the result of reckless driving. Perhaps it's being picked up on a wild party with marijuana cigarettes. But for the first time a parent who has been smugly certain that crime can never touch *him*, finds that it has.

Nowadays we are learning a great deal more about how to handle juveniles. It is hoped that some of the constructive procedures can be put into operation before it is too late. One of the alarming things that face us today is the graph showing the lowering age of the vicious criminal.

A generation ago it was only after a mature man had been exposed to viciousness for a good many years that he became the tough, hardened, killing type of criminal.

Nowadays the average age of vicious depravity has dropped alarmingly.

A friend of mine who has made quite a study of juvenile delinquency, and who has attracted a good deal of national attention because of the manner in which some of his more or less revolutionary ideas have been working out, made it a point to lecture before clubs and various civic organizations, telling about the work he was doing and what he was finding out.

He was invited to speak before one of the exclusive women's clubs, and to their surprise, chose as the subject of his talk a phase of juvenile delinquency and parental responsibility, which at least some of the members thought was definitely out of place.

One of the women came to him after his talk and voiced a protest. Why in the world would he take up *their* time by commenting about such things? His remarks didn't apply to them and didn't apply to their children.

Within seven days of the time she made her public denunciation, her own son had become involved in exactly the situation that the lecturer had been discussing and she found herself as one of the parents tearfully occupying a chair in the juvenile courtroom, trying to adjust herself to a brand new concept of life.

All of these things represent the cost of crime. The broken hearts, the blighted lives, the kids who have been sucked into a vortex before they have fully realized the grim possibilities of the situation.

It is only human nature for youngsters to have lots of drive, to crave action and excitement. They want to find out about life for themselves. They want to break away from parental habits and traditions.—That's the way we make progress. The most defective reasoning on earth is that which begins, "If it was good enough for your father, it's good enough for you. . . ."

But nowadays a vicious something has been added.

A couple of generations ago children were raised against a background of discipline. Parental control was taken for granted. It never occurred to children to doubt the rights of parents to administer discipline.

For some time now psychoanalysts have been warning against disciplining children. Children should be permitted to grow up in their own way.

That's all very fine as far as it goes, but there must always be discipline. If we remove outside discipline we must emphasize the necessity of self-discipline.

The trouble is our educational system doesn't do that.

So the younger generation suddenly finds itself in a position to question parental discipline, with no attempt made to emphasize the importance of self-discipline. The result is that too many kids grow up without any discipline whatever. They have no reason to fear outside discipline, and they haven't developed the habit of judging consequences, of looking at an act from all angles, and, above all, they haven't learned that civilized life consists of subordinating primitive desires to an over-all ethical concept.

Add to this the presence of dope.

Whether we like the picture or not, a good many teen-age kids start playing around with marijuana and some of them get "hooked" with heroin.

How many? No one knows the exact figures. The percentage, we hope, is small, but there are too many.

This gets back to the fact that everything we do along the line of legislative tinkering seems to have a habit of backfiring. For some reason man is incapable of thinking legislative action through to its logical conclusion. He starts out with the grim determination to "put teeth in the law," to bring about this reform and that reform. He passes the necessary statutes. Then he dusts off his hands, smiles a contented smile which comes with the knowledge of having done a good deed, and starts thinking about something else.

I heard an old druggist talking about dope a few weeks ago. He made quite an impression on me because I can remember exactly the conditions that he described.

In those days people could buy narcotics. A druggist could give them away if he wanted. He could sell them. He had lots of narcotics. Because there were no restrictions worthy of note, opium and morphine were dirt cheap.

Many people acquired the dope habit. There were quite a few of these unfortunates, perhaps more than now, but some say a whole lot less. But those addicts were for the most part the derelicts of skid row. And when they were hopheads, that was all there was to it. They weren't criminals, they were hopheads. They'd get the shakes at night and wait at the door of a drugstore for it to open up. The sympathetic druggist would look them over and give them a shot, just enough to get by. It was part of the druggist's daily routine.

That was a terrible situation.

So they began to pass narcotics laws, and they began to make them stiffer and stiffer.

What was the result?

Are there any less persons addicted to narcotics?

That's a question that is debatable. Some say yes. Some answer it with a loud and emphatic no.

But this much *has* happened. The law which prohibits narcotics has been enforced to such an extent that the retail price of narcotics has gone up, up, up and up.

Nowadays you read about some person being arrested, and the officers find "in his possession" uncut heroin worth fifty-thousand dollars on the retail market.

Fifty years ago, fifty-thousand dollars' worth of dope would have required a team of horses to drag it around.

Fifty years ago, when a person became a dope addict, it was an unfortunate experience. He was a dope addict and that was that. But that was about all he was.

Nowadays when a person becomes a dope addict the price of dope is such that he can't hope to engage in any legitimate occupation that will bring him in enough money to buy the dope his system craves, so he starts embezzling, burglarizing houses, and committing stick-ups. When something goes wrong with a stick-up he is jittery, nervous and desperate. He tries to smoke his way out.

So nowadays the young dope addict is almost automatically a young desperate criminal.

All the time we are spending more and more money trying to enforce the narcotics law which drives the retail price of narcotics on the black market higher and higher, which makes the trade more and more profitable, which attracts more and more people to it, which, in turn, requires they have more and more outlets, which, in turn, means that they start peddling dope to kids in high school and college, and that these kids, driven to desperation, start holding up more and more service stations and liquor stores.

Of course, that's an oversimplification, but it points up something that we must take into consideration. WE CAN'T LET THE CRIMINAL DETERMINE THE EXTENT OF OUR LAW ENFORCEMENT.

The trouble is that society always lags behind the criminal. It lets the criminal set the pace. As narcotics become more prevalent we reluctantly appropriate more money for more police, which, in turn, boosts the price of black market narcotics so that the trade becomes more profitable, etc., etc., etc.

That is all a part of the cost of crime. People won't wake up. They won't face the issues honestly and fairly. The reason is that they like to feel crime doesn't concern them and can't affect them.

It concerns every one of us, and directly and indirectly it affects every one of us.

If we pass a law we should see that it is enforced. If we don't intend to enforce it we shouldn't pass it. If we pass it we should see that it is enforced *before the forces of opposition get a head start.*

If there is a forest fire the fire fighters concentrate on trying to put the fire out while it is small. If they started putting in a small force to fight a small fire, and then, as the fire got bigger, gradually adding to the force, always keeping one jump behind the fire and letting the size of the fire determine the number of fire fighters in the interests of "economy," it wouldn't be long before our forests would all be gone.

That's the way with crime.

Citizens don't want to give the police the facilities they need until it can be determined they are "necessary."

By that time the fire has become altogether too big.

But even then we don't make a survey of what is required to cut it down, but only what is needed to "cope with it."

Our whole reasoning on the problem of crime and criminals, of law enforcement, of police and even of penitentiaries, is completely cockeyed.

We can discuss the matter in terms of dollars and cents, but primarily crime isn't an economic problem. It's a problem that strikes at the character of the nation. The more we permit crime the more we are letting character become corrupted, the more we are encouraging dangerous thinking, and the more we are sacrificing potential future good citizens to the forces of contamination and degradation which turn them from potential assets into moral and economic liabilities.

It is time we woke up.

20

The initial objective of The Court of Last Resort was to espouse the causes of innocent men who had been wrongfully convicted of serious crimes. That, in our opinion, was the most dramatic way to arouse public interest in an improved administration of justice.

It was inevitable that our activities would go beyond that first objective and point up broader problem areas. The time has now arrived, we believe, to supplement the original approach by calling attention to these important ultimate objectives.

1. Better standards of proof so that fewer innocent persons are accused, arrested, or convicted, and more guilty persons are apprehended and punished. Too many times jurors are asked to rely upon inference or conjecture where proof might have been available.

2. A better understanding between the taxpayer and the police so that investigative work can be continually upgraded. In order to accomplish this, the conscientious police officer should feel secure against political pressures on the one hand and economic pressures on the other. He should realize that adequate advancement will follow meritorious achievement. Taxpayers should recognize the importance of having higher echelon investigative officers attend conventions, seminars, and panels where they can improve

their techniques and acquire knowledge which, in turn, can be passed on to their police associates. Police officers should receive adequate salaries commensurate with increased living costs, and should have the assurance that in the event of death in the line of duty dependents will be protected by an insurance policy of at least $20,000 furnished as a part of their compensation, and in addition to any group insurance they may carry at their own expense. Only by giving police officers adequate financial compensation in keeping with the responsibilities and dangers of their work can we immunize the rank and file against the ever present temptations of organized under-world rackets. An officer who may have sufficient moral fiber to resist temptation for himself may well break down if he feels his dependents are or will be inadequately provided for. In the long run society will get just what it pays for. If it economizes to such an extent that police work fails to offer an honorable career, it is inevitable that police work will then offer a dishonorable career at far greater ultimate cost to society. Letting racketeers pay the police in whole or in part is the most expensive blunder society can make. An individual and an organization work for the ones who deliver the pay check.

3. Better investigative technique in the case of homicides, which means a system of competent medical examiners to investigate all suspicious deaths. In every case of homicide, adequate, trained, competent medical examiners should be available, with sufficient authority to discharge their duties properly.

4. The creation of boards in each state with power to review the facts in cases where it appears there is a reasonable possibility an error has been committed, just as appellate courts now have the power to review errors of law.

5. Power in the hands of the courts to see that the defense of each person accused of crime is adequately and competently conducted. This includes the power—in fact, the duty—of courts to appoint impartial, competent experts to furnish court and counsel for both

sides with pertinent technical information both before and during trial.

6. Procedural changes so that technicalities are subordinated, to the end that logical, substantive proof may be presented, without at the same time weakening constitutional safeguards.

7. Educating the public to a realization that a professional criminal is an enemy of organized society and must be regarded as such, while the man who violates laws because of weakness of character or the pressure of environment is capable of rehabilitation and must not be so punished that he is almost automatically turned into a professional criminal. This means far greater emphasis on the work of rehabilitation in our penal institutions and an abandonment of the old-fashioned idea of sadistic punishment, just as it means more adequate safeguards to protect society against its organized enemies. This may well cost the taxpayers more money for penal administration but will effect great savings in the money society is now paying as the cost of crime.

8. Promoting an increased public recognition of the merits of our judicial system and eliminating the exponents of that propaganda which seeks to expose our courts and our judicial institutions generally to ridicule and contempt. An attorney at law, in the true sense of the word, should be an officer of the court, and where it appears that attorneys, under the guise of upholding the rights of clients, are actually attempting to undermine public confidence in our judicial institutions, the action of such attorneys should be fearlessly exposed for what it is. There is a subtle but nonetheless sharp line of demarcation between vigorously and fearlessly representing clients on the one hand and seeking to undermine public confidence in our institutions on the other hand. Attorneys have a duty to leave no legal stone unturned so that the legal rights of clients are protected. This duty is even intensified in unpopular cases. But we are encountering an increasing number of instances where it would seem that the ultimate objective of some attorneys is to attack the institutions

before which their clients are being tried and to undermine public confidence in our system of jurisprudence. We recognize the necessity of a better public understanding of our judicial system and we believe in keeping the public well informed; but we deplore the fact that in many communities we have encountered instances where attorneys, seeking to arouse public interest on behalf of an accused client, have quite apparently released garbled, distorted or false information to the press. We believe that any reputable attorney must be conscious not only of his duty to his client, but of his duty to his profession, and the release of deliberately distorted information is a serious breach of professional ethics, just as appearing before a tribunal and exhibiting a contemptuous attitude for that tribunal becomes more than a mere contempt of court and constitutes a most serious breach of professional ethics. The seriousness of this situation and the sinister purpose back of it, is, unfortunately, not now fully recognized in its true light by the legal profession and the public.

9. Bring about a better understanding between the ordinary citizen and members of the legal profession. If we are to have a proper respect for and understanding of our judicial processes the citizen must obtain a clearer vision of the organized Bar. Surveys show a deterioration in public relations of the Bar. This is due in large measure to a failure on the part of the citizen to appreciate what lawyers generally are accomplishing and the high standards of the profession. Because one of the elements of humor is to ridicule dignity it quite frequently happens that cartoonists, gag writers, etc., find they can secure laughs by lampooning the legal profession. Our widespread contacts in investigations have disclosed numerous cases where lawyers have sacrificed their own interests in the cause of justice, where lawyers who believed in the innocence of their clients have carried on the fight over a period of years without compensation. It is high time that the public generally recognizes the over-all competency, ability and integrity of the Bar, and restores it to its rightful position. The legal profession is a bulwark protecting the public. In virtually every instance where we have addressed State

Bar Associations, prominent attorneys, whose time is exceedingly valuable, have come forward and volunteered to co-operate with us without compensation in any matter arising within their own states. We feel the public should know more of this side of the legal profession.

10. Bring the legal profession and the medical profession to a better understanding of each other's problems; to familiarize attorneys with the importance of legal medicine in the problem of proof, and to eliminate, through shrewd cross-examination, the medical expert witness whose qualifications are only as an expert witness, not as an expert practitioner.

This is, of course, an ambitious program and we are not by any means the only agency participating in it. It is surprising the rapidity with which progress is being made now that the public is taking an interest in the over-all problems connected with the administration of justice. The function of the organized Bar and of the legal medicine branch of the medical profession is constantly to bear in mind the ever present necessity of keeping the administration of justice abreast of new scientific achievements and the growing complexities of an expanding civilization.

ABOUT THE AUTHOR

Erle Stanley Gardner (1889–1970) was an author and lawyer who wrote nearly 150 detective and mystery novels. Awarded the honor of Grand Master by the Mystery Writers of America in 1962 and hailed by Evelyn Waugh as "the best American writer," he ranks as one of the most prolific specialists of crime fiction due to his popular alter ego, lawyer-detective Perry Mason.

A self-taught lawyer, Gardner was admitted to the California bar in 1911 and began defending poor Chinese and Mexicans as well as other clients. Eventually his writing, which began with the pulps, pushed his law career aside, but as proven in his Edgar Award–winning *The Court of Last Resort*, Gardner never gave up on the cases of wrongly accused individuals or unjustly convicted defendants.

INTEGRATED MEDIA

Find a full list of our authors and titles at www.openroadmedia.com

FOLLOW US
@OpenRoadMedia

CPSIA information can be obtained
at www.ICGtesting.com
Printed in the USA
LVOW08s0539250717
542513LV00001B/25/P